The Rhetoric
of
REVOLT

Paul D. Brandes
University of North Carolina
at Chapel Hill

Prentice-Hall, Inc.
Englewood Cliffs, New Jersey

This book is respectfully dedicated to Alice and Russell Anderson who first introduced me to the rhetoric of revolt by taking me to a meeting of the Farmer-Labor Party at the Hotel Metropole in Cincinnati, Ohio, in 1936, and whose thought-provoking teaching showed me the powers of oral communication while Mr. Anderson was mathematics teacher and the coach of debate for me and for my good friend Charles Royce Patton at Highlands High School in Fort Thomas, Kentucky, from 1934 to 1938.

C-13-780817-8
P-13-780809-7
Library of Congress Catalog Card No: 77-129818

Current printing (last digit)
10 9 8 7 6 5 4 3 2 1

Printed in the United States of America

Prentice-Hall International, Inc., *London*
Prentice-Hall of Australia, Pty. Ltd., *Sydney*
Prentice-Hall of Canada, Ltd., *Toronto*
Prentice-Hall of India Private Limited, *New Delhi*
Prentice-Hall of Japan, Inc., *Tokyo*

Preface

Dynamic concepts like "revolt" and "revolution" are difficult to define, but the rhetoric of revolt cannot be understood without a frame of reference. In this discussion a revolution will be considered (a) as an attempt through violence (b) to achieve economic, social, and political freedom (c) by the overthrow of an Old Regime (1) that has prevented change through nonviolent evolution on the focal point of dysfunction and (2) that is suffering from a multiple dysfunction of its institutions.[1] In France, when Louis XVI continued to prevent progress toward economic reform and when French social and political institutions so deteriorated that the church, the schools, the courts, and the political system in general had ceased to function effectively for the general welfare, an attempt was made through violence to achieve economic reform accompanied by social and political freedom. As defined here, revolution needs only to aim at freedom, so that the definition includes the Russian and Cuban revolutions that aspired to liberation, even though to a great measure they failed to do so.

The five revolutions for which rhetorical case histories are included here were chosen first because they meet the above definition. Second, they embrace revolutionary activity on four of the five continents,[2] and therefore transcend cultural lines. Common denominators about the rhetoric of revolt established on the basis of these case histories are to some measure independent of a given culture. An effort was also made to divorce observations from the personality traits of the five revolutionaries themselves. The degree to which this effort has been successful will have to be determined by the reader.

The American Revolution conveniently formed the basis for the dis-

---

[1] This definition has been developed from the philosophies of Chalmers Johnson, Hannah Arendt, Crane Brinton, and others whose works are cited in the bibliography to the first chapter.

[2] Access to source materials and severe language barriers prevented the inclusion of a case history from an African revolt.

cussion; it not only came first in chronology, but also the writer hoped that other revolutions would be more easily comprehended by Americans if their strengths and weaknesses could be compared with our own revolt. The strong parallels between the American Revolution by "the good guys" and subsequent revolutions by the "not-so-good guys" and even the "bad guys" were a source of continual surprise to the author and reminded him of how impossible it is to understand our own culture unless we are aware of the developments of other cultures.

Many of the important speeches of past revolutions have been lost, and the language of crucial meetings was often not recorded. "We hear of wild and inflammatory speeches, of violent harangues to raise a mob, of inspiring appeals for resistance against the encroachment of British tyranny," said Philip Davidson in speaking of the American Revolution, "but of these impromptu efforts only fragments remain" (6, 194). Little or nothing has been preserved of the speeches before the Continental Congress, for, out of political necessity, its *Journal* reported even less than did the terse *Procès-Verbal* of the French Revolution. Trotsky said of the famous but unrecorded debates in the Central Committee: "It is utterly impossible to picture the united spirit of these intense and impassioned improvisations by Lenin which were filled with the struggle to impress upon the opponents, the hesitating, and the doubting, the course of his thoughts, his will, his conviction, and his courage" (21, 96). The official edition of Gandhi's works has done much to make his formal speeches available, but his earnest conversations with the leaders of the British government and his spontaneous talks with the untouchables were not recorded. Modern facilities have improved our record of *fidelismo*, but there is little likelihood that what Castro said in 1958 in his rebel radio broadcasts or in his 1959 triumphant tour of Cuba has been preserved.

The student of the rhetoric of revolt must also be aware that what is extant is often imperfect. The reconstruction of Patrick Henry's speech of 1775 only causes us to wonder what he really did say. Castro's "History Will Absolve Me" was written in retrospect and was intended as a propaganda pamphlet, not a speech. We have only a few phonograph records and silent films of Lenin and a limited amount of sound film and radio transcriptions by Gandhi, but these are not of the more crucial aspects of their oratory.

The five speeches reported here have some aspiration to authenticity. John Hancock read his oration, and it appeared in print so soon after its delivery that there was ample opportunity for him to deny the accuracy of the published version. The Danton speech is the result of a collation of five contemporary newspaper accounts and has been compared with other Danton speeches to establish the flavor of Danton's oratory. The Lenin speech is also a collation, but, until freer access to Russian documents is permitted, it is impossible to say whether the best sources have been used to establish the latest official Russian version. The Gandhi address received some measure of approval from Gandhi himself, since the speech first appeared in *Young India*, an organ of the Gandhi movement. Fortunately, for reasons not yet known, there were two Spanish versions of the Castro speech published by the Cuban government, and a collation of these Spanish versions with the official Cuban government English version allowed a methodology to be established in constituting what Castro may have actually said.

The author is indebted to the cooperation of the Library of Congress, the Bibliothèque Nationale in Paris, the Massachusetts Historical Society, the Pierpont Morgan Library, the Boston Public Library, the libraries of Duke and Harvard universities and the universities of Florida and North Carolina (Chapel Hill). He wishes to express his particular thanks to Demetrius Koubourlis and to Leonid Milhalap for assistance with the Russian speech; to Frederick DeArmas and to J. M. Bohigas and his wife for help with the speech in Spanish; and to Don W. Schneider, Chief of the Business Administration and Social Sciences Division of the Louis Round Wilson Library at Chapel Hill and his staff for invaluable aid in checking sources. Finally he would like to thank his many students at Ohio University and at the University of North Carolina at Chapel Hill for their cooperation and criticism, specifically to Robert T. Bean Jr., Mrs. Sandra Nixon Boyce, Jill Sue Bumgarner, Joseph B. Cheshire, Ted Culler, Ricky Hedrick, Hansford Leake, Thomas Lane Mallonee Jr., Greg Riggs, Barbara Anne Stevens, Guilford T. Waddell, William H. Waterstadt, Doreen Williams, and in particular to James F. Morton for his helpful comments on the essays on Castro's rhetoric.

Paul D. Brandes
Chapel Hill, North Carolina

Table of Contents

Mohandas Karamchand Gandhi

Fidel Castro Ruz

The Intrinsic Characteristics
of the Rhetoric of Revolt

Revolutions occur during periods of intense change so traumatic that a prosperous, enterprising nation cannot afford many revolutions. Yet what transpires during a revolution is so important to the subsequent tenor of a nation that a country never ceases to extol the glory of its revolution(s). The French are still profoundly influenced by what happened between 1789 and 1795; the Russians still look to the years 1917-1918 for guidance, even to the extent of invading Hungary and Czechoslovakia to prevent a resurgence of the forces that Lenin defeated over 60 years ago; the Indians cling to their 1947 constitution and have encouraged to remain in office as many of its perpetrators as are available to serve; the Cubans, in spite of propaganda to the contrary, are intrigued with the events of 1959, and there appears but little chance that Castro will be other than a national hero for years to come.

Certainly our American Revolution has profoundly influenced the United States. It provided us with a Constitution which, with relatively minor changes, has lasted over 175 years. It contributed the national symbols of our country—the flag, the national anthem, the image of the Yankee. It supplied many of our national heroes. And it set forth the contrapuntal philosophies of stability and change, so that the United States has long looked upon itself as solidly mobile, or statically dynamic, or progressively fixed.

Even when a nation moves so far from its own revolution that it reacts against change, so that the sons and daughters of revolutionary movements become highly conservative and call loudly for the law and order that their ancestors violated (e.g., the sons of Lenin suppressing the Hungarian and Czech versions of communism and the grandsons of the Old West watching lawless Westerns on television as they write reactionary letters to the Los Angeles *Times*), even then each nation excuses its own revolution, so conscious is it of the profound influence of its own period of turmoil.

If periods of lawlessness have such powerful effects upon societies, certainly the rhetoric which that lawlessness produced (or which produced that lawlessness) is worthy of study. This introduction presents, therefore, the intrinsic characteristics that give individuality to revolt rhetoric. It is important to gain a comprehension of the rhetoric of agitation, not only so that we can comprehend our own past, but also so that we can deal more realistically with the present and the future. We are experiencing what will undoubtedly be called a century of revolution, and if we are to prevent ourselves from overreacting to the pressures around us, we must understand how cyclical the arguments of the agitator are. Such an understanding will assist us in distinguishing between constructive and destructive revolt. Furthermore, many of us experience at one time or another quasi-revolutionary movements—the formation of a labor union, the elimination of grades or required courses at a university, the introduction of minority groups into a neighborhood formerly reserved for the majority group, the legalization of abortion, the progression toward world government, the organized efforts to eliminate war, the control of illegitimate births by distributing contraceptives to unmarried females—all of which have possible phases of lawlessness and all of which can be more peacefully handled given an understanding of the rhetoric of revolt. Last, if we are not properly informed about how the rhetoric of agitation develops, we may see beauty, strength, and hope only in conservative rhetoric and not in the rhetoric of agitation; we may evaluate the calls for lawlessness by Patrick Henry and Sam Adams as glorious and patriotic in retrospect, but lack the criteria to seek similar inspiration from those current events that, after judicial consideration, we conclude are in keeping with the principles so ably upheld by Henry and Adams.

This chapter on the intrinsic characteristics of the rhetoric of revolt will be followed by five speeches from five revolutions. Each speech will be preceded by a condensed biography of the speaker and followed by an analysis of the speech.

Chronology and Crisis:
The Influence of Time on Revolutionary Rhetoric

The rhetoric of all movements passes through stages, but the stages through which revolt rhetoric passes have unique characteristics.

In revolutionary rhetoric, a prolonged rumble of discontent develops into what Heinz Lubasz terms "a period of increasingly sharp and widespread opposition to the existing system" (15). The Old Regime, having failed to respond to the rumble, must be deliberately discredited by what Eric Hoffer has termed "men of words with a grievance" (11, 129). The acceleration of the protest is generally triggered by a specific event, e.g., the taxes on the

American colonies, the financial bungling of the French court, the disastrous defeat of the Russian troops on the eastern front. What distinguishes this initial stage of revolt rhetoric asking for change? Revolt rhetoric openly advocates lawlessness. The Old Regime is not to be modified peacefully. It is to be amended by force. Not until there is an open call for lawlessness can the rhetoric of revolt be said to have begun.

For example, in the colonies, the assault on the Old Regime began quietly as the American planters and merchants evaded British regulations restricting trade and manufacturing. But the rhetoric did not assume the properties of revolt until after 1764. By 1774 Hancock was able to say in public that the people of Boston had determined to escape from the control of their governor, that the colonial judges were sufficiently in rebellion to decline the salaries proffered them by the Crown, and that the citizenry had decided to circumvent the tax on tea in one way or another.

Who was the man who offered such seditious sentiments? A revolutionist? A rabble-rouser? A radical? No, as is often the case, it was a man of stature who emerged from what should have been a conservative background to assume the position of reformer. Revolutionary leaders are generally men of some means who find themselves in a society that has achieved a certain prosperity. The climate of revolution does not develop until a society, on its way toward social and economic progress, has that progress threatened by a recalcitrant Old Regime. "For men to plunge headlong into an undertaking of vast change," observed Hoffer, "they must be intensely discontented yet not destitute" (*11*, 11). When a man of words unites with a cause to the extent that he openly advocates lawlessness to seek economic and social progress, we find that the rhetoric of the first stage of a revolution has developed.

Therefore two characteristics of the rhetoric of this first period in a revolution are (a) that men of words who ordinarily could be expected to uphold law and order (b) publicly advocate subversion. These are men of stature, usually with vested interests, who would normally be expected to protect those interests; but who, because they find social and economic progress impeded by an Old Regime that will not respond to milder threats, turn to advocating lawlessness.[1]

---

[1] The leadership of the American Revolution demonstrates clearly how men of stature can emerge from conservative backgrounds to sponsor lawlessness. John and Samuel Adams were important citizens of Massachusetts; Benjamin Franklin had been prominent in his state's affairs since 1737, and, as early as 1753, had been chosen deputy postmaster general for all the colonies; George Washington had been a member of the House of Burgesses in Virginia since 1758, and it was there that he established his friendship with Thomas Jefferson, who had served in that body since 1769.

James C. Davies concluded that "revolutions are most likely to occur when a pro-

One notable characteristic of the rhetoric of the first stage of a revolution stems from the revolutionary's need for identification, because, in the process of divorcing himself from the images of the past, he welcomes new symbols to restore his security. Music such as the *Marseillaise* and *Yankee Doodle* become representative of the spirit of revolution. A mode of dress becomes symbolic, e.g., long trousers replaced knee britches during the French Revolution, the homespun garment replaced British manufactured cloth in India, and the army fatigue uniform and the beard replaced the spit and polish of the Batista soldier in Cuba. Phraseology as well as music and clothing and art is instrumental in satisfying the need of the revolutionary for identification. A "costume of words" develops to separate the revolutionary from the conservative. As in most styles, there is more frill than fashion in revolutionary phraseology. Although there are certain catch phrases that do survive, such as "liberté, égalité, fraternité," "no taxation without representation," and "khleb, mir, i svoboda" (bread, peace, and freedom), most of the slogans of one revolution do not transfer well to another, and they are often repulsive to those neutral and opposed to the revolution. After Concord, General Gage is supposed to have said that he hoped he would never hear *Yankee Doodle* again, but the Americans continued to dote upon it, even to playing it after the surrender at Yorktown. "The student who comes for the first time to the literature of our American Revolution is liable to be disappointed by the dull and legalistic flavor of what he has to read," said Daniel Boorstin. "Although the American Revolution occurred in an age which throughout Europe was laden with philosophic reflection and important treatises, our Revolution," continued Boorstin, "was neither particularly rich nor particularly original in its intellectual apparatus" (3, 102). But the phraseology is *our* phraseology, and therefore still important to us for its symbolism. Therefore, however bored we may become with the costume of words of past revolutions or of present revolutions, we must not forget how important this phraseology is to the revolutionary seeking security in new ideas. Robespierre's Rousseauisms, Castro's onslaughts on *Yanqui* imperialism, and Gandhi's appeals for Indian self-sufficiency appear so frequently that we feel they must have been as banal to

---

longed period of objective economic and social development is followed by a short period of sharp reversal" (7, 6). The economies of all five nations treated in this volume had experienced a degree of prosperity that was being threatened by the Old Regime. Cuba, for example, had the third highest gross national product in Latin America, but the majority felt themselves threatened by a minority that held much of the wealth. For comment on the colonies, see Brinton (*4*, 32); for France, Stephens (*20*, I, 120-23) and Brinton (*4*, 32); for Russia, Brinton (*4*, 33 and 41), Moorehead (*16*, 15 and 63) and Davies (*7*, 11); for India, Rosen (*18*, 130). Morris pointed out how clouded the interpretations of the economic status of India in the early twentieth century were (*17*, 606).

the orator's immediate listeners as they are to us. However, anyone who has attended a sports event in which he owes no allegiance to either side can recall how many times the songs and cheers of both teams are greeted enthusiastically by partisan crowds without any signs of boredom. To the impartial observer, the excitement seems strained.

Therefore, the rhetoric of the first stage of the revolution features calls for lawlessness in language befitting the men of stature who, under normal circumstances, could be expected to uphold the Old Regime but who, because the Old Regime will not respond to gradual change and because multiple dysfunction sets in, advocate the overthrow of the old order. Experiencing a void because the symbols of the Old Regime are no longer theirs, these men of words search for symbolization for their movement, and one of these symbols is a costume of words which acts as a common denominator between them and their fellow revolutionaries.

Some revolutionary movements are aborted and never progress past this first stage, e.g., the French Commune, the German Socialist movement of 1848, and the Spanish Loyalists of 1937. For those that do achieve their objective in overthrowing the Old Regime, what developments take place in rhetoric in the second stage that were not apparent during the first stage?

The rhetoric of the second stage is influenced by the development of the revolution. It may occur during a period of relative peace, as was the case in France and Cuba. If the new government is allowed to develop without strong internal and external pressures, the man of words can, if his degree of liberalism is sufficient, make a smooth transition from the first stage into the second stage. Therefore, Danton, Robespierre, and their many well-educated colleagues spoke frequently during what Crane Brinton termed "the honeymooned stage of revolution," finding themselves caught up in a practical application of "a great intellectual movement called the Enlightenment which had prepared men's minds for a new and practical miracle" (4, 99). Even after the war broke out in 1792, the men of words continued to speak frequently, so great was the momentum they had achieved in conducting government through political debate. But, because of the exigencies of war, the main force of the revolution progressed into the hands of powerful committees, where the rhetoric of revolt was transformed into the confusion of conversation. In Cuba, even the threat of a Bay of Pigs invasion was not sufficient to prevent Castro and his colleagues from waging an intensive war of words against their enemies. Whether an elected parliament in Cuba would have followed the French pattern set in the years 1789 to 1795 will never be known, for Castro allowed no elections, perhaps because he recalled the fate of Danton and Robespierre. But the stage was set in Cuba for a parliament to enter into a similar period of intense debate on the form the government of Cuba should take.

With the jockeying for power during the honeymoon period, personal invective is highly prominent. *Argumentum ad hominem* was apparent even in the debates in the Party congresses and assemblies in Russia between the overthrow of the tsar and the overthrow of Kerensky, even though Russia was in a violent war with Germany. The tendency toward name-calling may be heightened by the suppression of debate under the Old Regime, so that people who for the first time are capable of making personal accusations in public find the opportunity too much to their pleasure. In the American Revolution, where freedom of speech had been largely uninhibited during the first stage of the revolution, personal invective is largely missing.

If the second stage of a revolution must occur during a period of armed conflict, rhetoric largely disappears, and what does remain is generally blunt and terse. The men of words of the first stage either expend their energies toward revolution in efforts other than words or they cease to be motivating factors in the revolution (a) because, although they could talk effectively about reform, they lacked ability to execute the forms they had talked about and/or (b) because they were eliminated by the New Regime as being reactionary. The energy that might have gone into rhetoric is funneled off into actions necessary to protect the new government. If words must play a part in waging war, they must be short, pithy statements designed to unify the country. Lofty rhetoric is suspect during this second stage when the country is at war, and those who use it can be accused of forwarding their own cause at the expense of the revolution. Therefore, it is not surprising that John Adams commented: "The orations, while I was in Congress, from 1774 to 1787, appeared to me to be very universally extemporaneous, and I have never heard of any committed to writing, before or after delivery" (*1*, X, 171). Adams disparaged the effectiveness of eloquence (*1*, II, 511) and of oratory (*1*, X, 279) while his correspondent Thomas McKean wrote: "I do not recollect any formal speeches, such as are made in the British Parliament and our late Congresses, to have been made in the revolutionary Congress. . . . We had no time to hear such speeches; little time for deliberation; action was the order of the day" (*1*, X, 177). The American revolutionists expended their energies in managing the war against the British; the French after 1792 more and more in combatting the Allies and their foes within; the Russians in preventing internal revolt; and the Indians in solving the complex problems of governing a divided nation. Even loquacious Castro had to divert a portion of his energies to preventing internal and external rebellion, but, since the Cuban revolution is the only one studied here where national television was a factor, it may be that the efficiency of mass media will modify the position of rhetoric during this second stage of the revolt.

Assuming that the revolution has overthrown the Old Regime and that the new government has been able to maintain itself in power for a sufficient period to secure a measure of stability, the revolution enters a third period that is largely concerned with preventing counterrevolution. The length of this phase varies widely. In the United States it extended until 1865; in France it had begun between 1792 and 1795, but the revolution failed before the third stage could achieve tenure; in Russia, India, and Cuba, the third period is still in progress. What are the intrinsic characteristics of the rhetoric of revolt during this last stage of revolution?

First, the dread of a Thermidorian reaction[2] haunts every revolutionary. When the pendulum has been forced by revolution farther and farther to one extreme, inertia forces its return. The third stage is therefore characterized by resistance to counterrevolution on the part of those in power and by sponsorship of counterrevolution by those out of power. It is very difficult for revolutionary leaders to sense that point at which vocal opposition to counterrevolution should be curtailed. In retrospect, revolutionaries dwell far too long on the theme of combatting counterrevolution. The agitator has so learned to distrust normalcy that he superimposes a vigilance against Thermidor to the extent that his aberrations become normalcy itself. Robespierre was not able to make the adjustment from the Reign of Terror to responsible government, and, because Danton and Desmoulins tried to do so, using the rhetoric of the clubs and the pamphlet as their weapons, they were guillotined. Lenin continued to tighten rather than relax his vigilance against counterrevolution and thereby prolonged indefinitely the suppression of freedom in Russia. Leonard Shapiro said of Lenin: "Few men in history can have made a greater mark on the fate of their country, and few men have thrown away a greater opportunity. . . . In 1921, when wisdom, vision, compromise, and moderation might have given Russia the beginnings of normal democratic development, he failed" (*19*, 128). The continued suppression of artists, poets, musicians, and philosophers who voice opposition to official Soviet policy underlines the difficulty that revolutionaries have in recognizing the time when attacks upon counterrevolution have lost their effectiveness. Lenin may have been justified in the glee he expressed when the duration of the Russian revolution exceeded in days that of the French Commune, but there

---

[2]Robespierre was overthrown in 1795 on 9 Thermidor Year II of the new French calendar (July 27, 1795). Thereafter, the impetus toward counterrevolution became known as Thermidor.

is a vast difference between vigilance against reactionaries for months or for a few years, and vigilance against moderation for decades.[3]

Gandhi's insistence upon his own fallibility and his willingness to reverse his position may well have been for the factors that allowed him to remain the leader of the Indian Revolution for over 20 years. His attitude of affection rather than hatred for the reactionary, demonstrated by his relationship with General Smuts of South Africa, made him avoid the usual rhetoric against Thermidor. The tone of his Round Table address shows how his conciliatory attitude toward the Old Regime gave a new look to the rhetoric against reaction.

Given Castro's experience with futile promises for free elections, it seems incredible that he should fall into similar errors himself. Yet others as intelligent as Castro have failed to know when to curtail propaganda against counterrevolution. The fear of losing power makes greedy men of saints. What will a content analysis of Castro's speeches from 1959 to 1965 show about the theme of free elections? Are there any indications in Castro's present rhetoric that he is any closer to allowing elections? If and when the time arrives that Castro is no longer dependent upon the Communists for financial support, will he attempt to restore democratic institutions?

A second characteristic of the third stage of revolution is the appearance of the theme of revolutionary export. The recurring theme that the revolutionary spirit can and will be exported is greeted by Old Regimes with horror and indignation. Nothing is more threatening to an Old Regime than to have a nation in revolution declare that it intends to aid and abet revolution abroad. Old Regimes are unable to interpret the call to export revolution as a natural trend resulting from the desire of the revolutionary to satisfy his desperate need for approval by gaining new adherents to his cause. The revolutionary is always lonely, no matter how much he protests to the contrary. Through his rhetoric he seeks companionship. Old Regimes interpret the challenge of revolutionary export as if this threat to them was the first of its kind to an Old Regime. England was shocked by France's determination to export Jacobinism, and overreacted to what was a far less threat than developed under the Napoleon that England helped to create. The Western world was

---

[3] The American Revolution escaped this overreaction for three reasons: first, the Tory had his property confiscated, so that those who had fled to England generally did not return; second, the British withdrew their forces across an ocean, which gave the colonists confidence in their independence; third, the cultural clash with the British was minimal, so that the defenders against reaction like Justice Marshall found themselves generally sympathetic with the trend of government in England. The War of 1812, however, is evidence that the American revolutionists were not exempt from the tendency to overreact against Thermidor.

traumatized by the international aspects of communism, and there are nations still suffering from this phobia. The intervention of the United States in the Dominican revolt was motivated by a desire to prove that *fidelismo* could not be exported. The degree to which revolutionary export strikes terror into Old Regimes may correlate positively with the vulnerability of the regime itself. Thus the susceptibility of Latin America to human rights revolutions makes *fidelismo* a serious threat to Latin governments.

Students of revolt rhetoric should anticipate the theme of revolutionary export rather than let it surprise them, and should evaluate it in keeping with these possibilities: (1) the internal security of a revolution can be measured by the degree to which the revolution advocates revolutionary export; for, if the revolution is going well at home, it should not need the distraction of international revolt to satisfy its followers; (2) a revolutionary will be encouraged to intensify his call for revolutionary export in proportion to the alarm it causes among the Old Regimes; (3) the revolutionary may talk much more about revolutionary export than he is prepared to act; and (4) the revolutionary spirit is generally indigenous to a given country, and its export has generally been by force rather than by contagion.[4]

A third characteristic of the third stage of a revolution is the frequent appearance of *argumentum ad misericordiam*, or the "pity-poor-me" theme. Revolutionaries delight in saying: "Feel sorry for me, friends, and for my noble revolution, because we have relentless enemies everywhere who are unjustly attacking us." Although this element can be found in all three stages of the rhetoric of revolt, it is most characteristic of the third period. The French revolutionary government overreacted to achieve sympathy; the Russians after more than 50 years still proclaim themselves as the true champion of justice attacked on every side by imperialism; Castro has made such use of the futile gestures of the United States toward invasion that he may postpone for some time any overtures by Washington toward reconciliation.

As long as Old Regimes give revolutionaries legitimate excuses for employing *argumentum ad misericordiam* in their rhetoric, the revolutionary can hardly be condemned for taking advantage of its effectiveness. The War of 1812 gave the Americans every right to feel sorry for themselves, and such sympathy did much to unify a somewhat shaky revolution. Then the United States itself made a similar mistake by offering Castro every opportunity to unify his people against Yankee imperialism. After the Dominican incident, it is relatively easy for Castro to make an invasion threat to Cuba realistic.

[4] A careful study is needed to compare the rhetoric of revolutionary export with the development of revolutionary movements to see if any cause-and-effect relationship exists.

The student of the rhetoric of revolt should first observe the degree to which he finds the appeals to pity legitimate. At that point at which the employment of *argumentum ad misericordiam* seems unjustified, the rhetorician should make an effort to determine why the revolutionary persists with what may be an effective but unnecessary appeal. The answers to his inquiry may lie in the personality of the revolution, the degree of frustration that the revolution is experiencing domestically, and/or the inability of the revolution and its adherents to progress from their revolutionary stability into the unchartered paths of progress.

The rhetorician should also inquire whether what appears vital to the average citizen of a country that is experiencing revolution will inevitably sound artificial to those not directly involved. Cries of pain are easily interpreted by those who are not afflicted as exaggerations. Is it possible for a revolutionary to so couch his appeals for pity that he has the desired effect upon all groups affected by revolution? Is the call for sympathy better stated simply or profusely? Must it be oriented for foreign sympathizers in another way than for domestic sympathizers? These are among the questions that the student of rhetoric can explore in investigating the use of *argumentum ad misericordiam* in revolutionary rhetoric.

The Focus of Dysfunction: Revolutionary Rhetoric and the Ideology

Not only do a revolution and its rhetoric pass through stages, but violence adopts an ideology or ideologies to which the rhetoric of agitation responds and which responds to the rhetoric of agitation. Modern history has seen four philosophies which have supported revolution: religion, nationalism, communism, and human rights.[5] There is a fifth that, after an eclipse, appears to be reemerging. The ideologies of religion and nationalism were the two focal points of conflict between Old and New Regimes in early modern history. The ground was set for revolution if these focal points of dysfunction were accompanied by a multiple dysfunction of other phases of social, economic, and political life. The Spanish overthrew the Muslims by combining both religious and nationalistic themes; the Roundheads beheaded King Charles I with religion and human rights as the focal points of dysfunction; the Dutch revolted against the Spanish in an effort to achieve nationalism and to pre-

---

[5] The author wishes to acknowledge his indebtedness to the article by Arthur Larson of Duke University in the *Saturday Review* (see bibliography, *14*).

serve their religion. In the latter part of the nineteenth century, when Marx and Engels exhorted the proletariat of all nations to unite in revolution, communism became an important philosophy in agitation. The Paris Commune of 1871 was the first effort in modern European history to achieve revolution using the ideology of communism. A fourth philosophy that has gained considerable momentum recently as the focal point of dysfunction is human rights. Now that the desire for autonomy among the peoples of Asia and Africa has been largely realized, and now that the international aspects of communism have been tempered by the nationalistic overtones of emerging nations, it is the struggle for human rights within each country that will dominate future revolutions. The desire for equality, for social status, or, if you like, for life, liberty, and the pursuit of happiness, is challenging societies where the Old Regimes have prevented major adjustments and where multiple dysfunction of institutions makes the Old Regimes susceptible to revolt. Communism will attempt, as it did successfully in Cuba, to use the revolution for human rights to achieve a Communistic revolt, and, if it is successful in dominating future revolutions for human rights, communism will postpone the achievement of those very human rights for which revolt took place. We are now witnessing the struggle between communism and anti-Communistic forces to become the champion of the revolts for human rights. Unfortunately, too often the anti-Communistic forces are so wedded to the Old Regimes that their ability to assist in the struggle for human rights becomes limited.

In summarizing the influence of the first four philosophies on revolution, it can be said that religion has receded as a rallying point for revolution and therefore the rhetoric of religion no longer plays a critical role in dysfunction. Nationalism reached its peak in the early part of the twentieth century, and, except for the Communist satellite countries and the Portuguese possessions in Africa, it has largely run its course. Communism may also have reached its zenith with the conversion of China in 1948, for it has largely failed to secure a hold in Africa, has experienced difficulties in Latin America, has seemingly lost its momentum in Asia, and shows signs of ripening into latent capitalism in its European strongholds. This leaves the revolution, using human rights as the focal point of dysfunction, as supreme in today's revolutions and therefore as the dominant theme in today's rhetoric of revolt.

However, there is a fifth ideology that in the past gave strength to revolution and that now promises to renew its momentum, namely, the ideology of internationalism. In the nineteenth and early twentieth centuries, internationalism offered a rallying point for revolution under the sponsorship of communism. But at present, not only has communism suffered major defeats in its efforts at internationalism, but the surges of nationalism in Asia and Africa have resulted in fragmentation rather than union. However, the dysfunctions resulting from a lack of internationalism have resulted in some notable efforts at political and economic union. Both the establishment of the United Nations and the manner in which the smaller nations have become impatient with the power politics of the large nations evidence a trend toward internationalism in politics, while the European Common Market and its prototypes show a trend toward internationalism in economics. If the dysfunctions of the remnants of nationalism, i.e., protective tariffs, armaments, inadequate distribution of the food supply, and the breakdown of cultural exchange programs, continue to impede world progress, then revolutions seeking freedom through internationalism are a possibility.

Whatever philosophy takes advantage of multiple dysfunction to achieve revolution is apparent in the rhetoric of that revolt. A notable exception was the first stage of the Cuban Revolution, for the theme of communism was not apparent in Castro's pre-1959 rhetoric. There may be several reasons for its absence: first, Castro had to confine himself to clandestine rhetoric during the first stage and, since he was seldom subject to cross-questioning, he could easily have concealed whatever portions of his philosophies he wished; second, there is disagreement as to whether Castro had embraced communism before 1959 or accepted it later, only because he found economic support from other sources unavailable; third, Castro may have experienced a void in political philosophy, having been so concerned with the overthrow of Batista that he had not made plans for what was to follow. Communism therefore found it easy to take him over.

The student of the rhetoric of revolt should seek to determine the degree to which less altruistic themes have been disguised by a rhetorical emphasis on human rights. The various phases of totalitarianism—oligarchy, dictatorship, and quasi-dictatorial "presidents"—sprinkle the human rights theme loosely throughout their rhetoric. Since communism has yet to come to power via a free general election, its efforts to succeed using the human rights theme can be included under the general heading of confounding human rights with totalitarianism. The degree to which the confounding occurs varies from revolution to revolution, and from revolutionary to revolutionary. At one extreme is Lenin, who from the beginning made clear the dictatorial nature of his philosophy and who shocked his brother socialists time and time again; at the other extreme we have Castro, whom only a few suspected of being totalitarian. An area for research lies in attempts through content analysis to isolate themes in revolutionary rhetoric and to suggest methods of distinguishing pseudo human-rights revolutionaries from genuine reformers.

The student of rhetoric should also be aware that the goals of the revolutionary are not always clear, even to him, and so the student must be prepared to find within revolt rhetoric a confusion of philosophies and ideologies. Although there may be a dominant theme, e.g., nationalism to replace the dysfunction of colonialism, the revolutionary may be so busy achieving this phase of the revolution and may involve so much of his energies in overthrowing the Old Regime that he has not given consideration to the other ideologies that concern revolution—human rights, communism, religion, and internationalism. The revolutionist can be like the alchemist who, when asked what he would do with the money he could have if he found the secret of transforming lead into gold replied: "Don't bother me with questions like that now. I have enough on my hands trying to outwit this stubborn lead. There will be plenty of time to think about that later." The rhetorician should remember that Old Regimes seem very entrenched, that revolutionaries seldom have many material resources, and that the expectation of overthrowing the Old Regime with limited strength furnishes such buoyancy to the revolutionary that he does not think about much else. Even though scholarly Lenin had over 30 years to plan the Russian Revolution, he was not at all prepared for many of the developments that occurred after he took power. The Batista regime crumbled so unexpectedly that Castro found himself with a government but no political philosophy. Therefore we must be prepared for careful content analysis to determine the position of a revolutionary on the philosophies that carry the burden against dysfunction.

The rhetorician must also consider the manner in which the theme of passive resistance supports revolutionary ideologies. Radical passivism, i.e., nonviolent resistance, is interpreted as a form of reaction by those who desire violence. Pressures are exerted on radical passivists to advocate violent action. In every revolution employing passivism, there is a point when the radical passivists consider their position indeed radical. Certainly many of the deeds of Gandhi could be termed lawless. But, as the revolutionary movement progresses and as the extremists attempt to move past the passivists, the latter find themselves labeled as reactionaries against whatever philosophy is supporting a more violent revolution. In India, Gandhi found himself accused of moderation toward religion, toward nationalism and toward human rights. Therefore, as the time came nearer and nearer for Indian independence, Gandhi found it more and more difficult to maintain his position of leadership through radical passivism when so many of his colleagues were calling for extreme tactics. Gandhi in his wisdom therefore withdrew from the politics of his revolution, finding that this very withdrawal maintained his strength as the philosopher of the revolution. That Gandhi was assassinated by a Hindu extremist, and not by a Muslim, attests to the degree to which he was attempting to maintain the true course of *satayagraha.*

When a student finds himself examining speeches in which a revolutionary is advocating passive resistance to overthrow the Old Regime, he should seek to establish (a) the degree of firmness to which the revolutionary has committed himself to radical passivism; (b) the form of the rhetoric that is attempting to divert the revolutionary away from his passive resistance; and (c) the points of cohesion and diffusion between radical passivism on the one hand and the themes of religion, nationalism, communism, human rights, and internationalism on the other hand.

Summary

This essay has surveyed the intrinsic characteristics of the rhetoric of revolt. It first pointed out that revolutions go through stages. The first stage features the advocation of lawlessness by men of stature at that point at which the Old Regime threatens the momentum toward social and economic reform by multiple dysfunction. Revolutionary rhetoric during this first stage is characterized by an endless repetition of slogans that attempt, along with music, dress, and other ritual, to restore to the revolutionary the identification that he has lost by relinquishing the Old Regime. The second stage of the revolution, which may take place during peace or war, features a degeneration of rhetoric into personal invective; for, to the leaders who are busy processing the installation of a new government, rhetoric is either a luxury that time cannot afford or it is a bid for personal aggrandizement that must be avoided. The third stage finds the rhetoric of revolt dominated by wordage against counterrevolution, an effort that often continues far past the time when the New Regime genuinely needs such vigilance. This third stage also produces the rhetoric of revolutionary export and an endless employment of *argumentum ad misericordiam.*

Revolutionary rhetoric is not only influenced by the stages through which a revolt passes, but it also interacts with the points on which the Old Regime has permitted dysfunction. Religion, nationalism, communism, human rights, and internationalism all influence and are influenced by rhetoric. The philosophy that has taken advantage of dysfunction to achieve revolution is usually, but not always, apparent in the rhetoric. Furthermore totalitarian ambitions may disguise themselves under more altruistic themes, such as human rights and internationalism. Since the goals of the revolutionary are not always clear to the revolutionary himself, the rhetoric of revolt may exhibit a confusion of ideologies making it necessary for the rhetorician to observe the words of agitation closely to see what may develop from the cross-currents apparent in the rhetoric. When passive resistance enters the rhetoric of revolt, attention must be given to the conflict between radical passivism and violence. The five case histories of revolutionaries and their revolts that follow will attempt to place these intrinsic characteristics of revolt rhetoric into context and will undoubtedly show that efforts to summarize the rhetoric of agitation result in oversimplifications, which can only be clarified by a practical application of theory to a given revolt.

Bibliography

1. Adams, John, *Works.* ed. Charles Francis Adams. Boston, 1850-1856.
   For annotation, see Hancock bibliography.
2. Arendt, Hannah, *On Revolution.* New York: The Viking Press, Inc., 1963.
   Prof. Arendt of the University of Chicago offers her definition of revolution in her first chapter, "The Meaning of Revolution," and her observations of the American, French, and Russian revolutions make this a prime source for studying revolt rhetoric. An excellent bibliography.
3. Boorstin, Daniel J., "Revolution without Dogma," in *The American Revolution, How Revolutionary Was It?* ed. G. A. Billias. New York: Holt, Rinehart & Winston, Inc., 1965, pp. 98-106.
   This short excerpt from *The Genius of American Politics* by the University of Chicago Professor D. J. Boorstin proposes that the American Revolution did not receive its impetus from the European Enlightenment of the eighteenth century, but rather that "the original creation of the United States was the work of doubly reluctant men" who, because of their loyalties to their states and to England, were unenthusiastic revolutionists.
4. Brinton, Crane, *The Anatomy of Revolution.* Englewood Cliffs, N.J.: Prentice-Hall, Inc., 1952.
   A second edition of a leading treatise uses the American, French, and Russian revolutions for historical support. Good chapters on "The Old Regime" and all three stages of a revolution. Excellent annotated bibliography.

5. Cohn, Norman, *The Pursuit of the Millennium*. Fair Lawn, N.J.: Essential Books, 1957.

   Clarifies attempts by the poor between the eleventh and sixteenth centuries to improve their condition through religion. Excellent notes and bibliography.

6. Davidson, Philip, *Propaganda and the American Revolution, 1763-1783*. Chapel Hill, N.C.: University of North Carolina Press, 1941.

   The place of propaganda in the American Revolution, with a chapter devoted to public address and pulpit oratory.

7. Davies, James C., "Toward a Theory of Revolution," *American Sociological Review*, XXVII (February, 1962), 5-19.

   After consulting Marx and Engels and de Tocqueville, Davies of the California Institute of Technology concluded revolutions are likely when periods of development are followed by sharp reversals. Uses Russian Revolution.

8. Debray, Regis, "Revolution in the Revolution?" *Monthly Review*, XIX (July-August, 1967), 11-126.

   Controversial treatise on modern guerilla warfare by French journalist Debray. Trans. Bobbye Ortis.

9. Edwards, Lyford P., *The Natural History of Revolution*. New York: Russell & Russell Publishers, 1965.

   Edwards, a professor at St. Stephen's College in New York, first published this short but comprehensive treatment of revolution in 1927.

10. Falk, Richard A., "Revolutionary Nations and the Quality of International Legal Order," in *The Revolution in World Politics*, ed. M. A. Kaplan. New York: John Wiley & Sons, Inc., 1962, pp. 310-31.

    Prof. Falk of Princeton examined the effect that the instability of revolutionary nations such as the Soviet Union, Communist China, the United Arab Republic, and Cuba is having upon law in world affairs.

11. Hoffer, Eric, *The True Believer*. New York: Harper & Row, Publishers, 1951.

    Short, cryptic comments with the subtitle, "Thoughts on the Nature of Mass Movements," by an unconventional and controversial thinker.

12. Jameson, John F., *The American Revolution Considered as a Social Movement*. Boston: Beacon Press, 1961.

    Jameson, former history professor at Brown University and the University of Chicago, delivered this interpretation of the American

Revolution in the form of lectures to Princeton in 1925. Termed the "small book with the big title."

13. Johnson, Chalmers, *Revolution and the Social System*. Stanford, Calif.: Stanford University Press, Hoover Institution on War, Revolution, and Peace, 1964.

A short treatise by a political science professor at the University of California at Berkeley examines the causes and types of revolutions.

14. Larson, Arthur, "The Real Nature of the World Revolution," *Saturday Review*, L, 22 (June 3, 1967), 15-18.

Larson, director of the Rule of Law Research Center at Duke University and a foreign affairs adviser to President Johnson and the State Department, examined the ideologies pertinent to revolution.

15. Lubasz, Heinz, "Introduction," in *Revolutions in Modern European History*, ed. Heinz Lubasz. New York: The Macmillan Company, 1966, pp. 1-7.

In the introduction to a series of essays on the French, Russian, and English revolutions, Lubasz of Brandeis University presented the three stages into which a revolution can be divided.

16. Moorehead, Alan, *The Russian Revolution*. New York: Harper & Row, Publishers, 1958.

For annotation, see the Lenin bibliography.

17. Morris, Morris D., "Toward a Reinterpretation of Nineteenth-Century Indian Economic History," *Journal of Economic History*, XXIII (March, 1963), 606-18.

Morris of the University of Washington offered proposals to fill in what he termed a distressing gap in India's economic history between 1800-1947.

18. Rosen, George, *Democracy and Economic Change in India*. Berkeley and Los Angeles: University of California Press, 1966.

Rosen, former economic advisor to Nepal and the state of West Bengal, surveyed contemporary economic problems in India.

19. Shapiro, Leonard, "The Bolsheviks and their Rivals," in *Revolutions in Modern European History*, ed. H. Lubasz, New York: The Macmillan Company, 1966.

A somewhat negative article on bolshevism, first published in *History Today* (August, 1951) summarized Lenin's decisions made after mid-March, 1917.

20. Stephens, H. Morse, *A History of the French Revolution*, 2 vols. London, 1886-1891.

A basic work with an excellent appendix in volume two. Stephens' treatment of oratory was much more extensive in his two-volume work on the speeches of the revolution (see Danton bibliography), but he frequently commented on rhetoric in his general discussion of French history. No index.

21. Trotsky, Leon, *Lenin.* New York: G. P. Putnam's Sons, 1962.
For annotation, see Lenin bibliography.

John Hancock
(1737-1793)

A Revolutionary Grant from the Private Sector

The American myth has made John Hancock more closely allied to sales-manship than to statesmanship. These short remarks are necessary to restore Hancock as a revolutionist so that his speech of 1774 can be properly appreciated. Hancock has not been honored with a definitive biography, and the primary sources are so scattered that, without some assistance, the researcher would have serious difficulties penetrating the legendary Hancock to discover the agitator, the philanthropist, and the egoist that combined to make Hancock one of the chief contributors of the private sector to the American Revolution.

John Hancock, who was one of the colonists' few millionaires, who served as president of the Continental Congress, and who, except for one term, presided as governor of Massachusetts from 1780 to 1793, was born on January 23, 1737, the son of an undistinguished clergyman. When John's father died in 1744, he left his family home at Braintree to live on Beacon Hill with his rich uncle, Thomas Hancock. In July of 1745, Hancock entered the Boston Latin School; in 1750, he went to Harvard where he had a tutor, studied Greek, Latin, logic, rhetoric, and physics in his freshman year, followed by courses in the Bible, theology, mathematics, and geometry. On July 17, 1754, Hancock was graduated from Harvard at the age of seventeen.

Hancock began at once to assist his uncle in business. There were still remnants of a retail trade with which Uncle Thomas had begun his business, but now there was wholesaling of miscellaneous stocks and a lively shipping business. Soon the Hancock investments included large real estate holdings. Thomas Hancock's business may not always have been legitimate, but it was usually profitable.

When John was twenty-three, Uncle Thomas sent him to London to settle accounts with their British representatives and to make new contacts for the firm. Hancock saw the funeral of George II, observed Pitt as prime minister, and led a gay life, acquiring an elegant wardrobe. But, although Jack played, he also did his work well, arriving home on October 3, 1761, to be welcomed by his doting aunt and uncle.

How did such a dandified poor young rich man drift into becoming a revolutionist? Attempts have been made to base his actions on a search for wealth by removing the restrictions which the British were placing on business. But Hancock was already rich, and his existing wealth would have done him little good were he to have languished in a British prison. Hancock had become rich by cooperating with England in supplying the British armies, and he could have increased his fortune by continuing his support, once some inconveniences to his shipping had been solved. Attempts have also been made to explain his actions as a search for power, but Lorenzo Sears pointed out that Governor Hutchinson and King George could have offered him positions of importance and even a peerage (16, 336-37). Neither of these reasons, wealth or power, can explain the transformation of Hancock from what should have been a conservative businessman into a revolutionist. The search for the reasons for the transformation becomes more vital when Hancock develops into a man who encouraged lawlessness, incited men to violence, assisted in establishing a rebel government and used his personal fortune to oppose the Old Regime with force. In short there is no way around the fact that Hancock was an out-and-out revolutionary and his position in this respect must be understood if he is to be anything more than a cardboard dummy of a patriot.

What were the events that led to the violence that Hancock perpetrated on the Old Regime? They probably began soon after Hancock's return from England when he joined the Masonic lodge of which Paul Revere was a member. Shortly thereafter he probably became a member of a secret society known as the Long Room Club. At the same time business went on much as usual. In 1763, John was taken in as a full partner, assisting his uncle in attempts to corner the whale-oil trade, to supply the British with provisions and to employ the Hancock ships to maximum advantage. In 1764, Uncle Thomas died, leaving John a millionaire, but there is evidence that the event did not go to John's head. There is throughout Hancock's life a contrapuntal activity of a demonstration of humility and a brash display of wealth, evidently a genuine duality and one which endeared him to the common people of Massachusetts.

In 1764, the Sugar Act began the oppressive British taxes, and the Stamp Act followed in 1765. On August 14, 1765, the Sons of Liberty were partly responsible for organizing a mob that sacked the home of the British lieutenant governor. Hancock probably had mixed feelings about this act of civil disobedience. He opposed the Stamp Act, which was injurious to his business, but he did not like the lawlessness, which resulted in personal injury to the lieutenant governor.

Times got worse and worse for Boston. Resistance to the Stamp Act had paralyzed business, for ships could not load or unload without obeying the king's command and the colonists refused to obey. On November 7, 1765, Hancock took another step toward revolution by speaking at the Green Dragon Tavern on Pope's Day (Guy Fawkes' Day) and by paying $1,000 for the dinner at which open opposition to England was encouraged.

On May 6, 1766, Hancock was elected to the Massachusetts House of Representatives, a move greatly approved by Sam Adams. Hancock's wealth and social status could be very useful to Adams in opposing England. When, in that same year, the Stamp Act was repealed, Hancock gave a public display of fireworks in his yard, which lasted until midnight, and he had all 54 of his windows lighted to celebrate the victory over the British.

In 1767 Hancock bailed Sam Adams out of debt, showing the extent to which Hancock was dedicated to his radical friend. Furthermore Hancock was reelected to the House of Representatives. Then the Townshend Acts were passed, with duties on tea, glass, and lead, directly affecting Hancock's business and further provoking the colonist toward open aggression.

In 1768 Hancock openly challenged the right of inspectors to go aboard his vessel, the *Lydia*, in Boston harbor, to look for taxable items under the Townshend Acts. British customs officials tried to seize a second of Hancock's vessels on a technicality, but they had not reckoned with his popularity among the citizenry. A mob arose, forcing customs officials to flee to an island in Boston harbor. Hancock refused a compromise offered him by the customs officials. Inflammatory meetings were held by the colonists at Faneuil Hall and at the Old South Church.

By October 1, 1768, British troops had arrived in Boston, and on November 3, 1768, charges of wine smuggling were placed by the British against Hancock. Hancock hired John Adams to defend him. On January 1, 1769, a boycott on all Townshend items by Boston merchants went into effect. So great was the colonial resistance that on May 26, 1769, the Crown abandoned its case against Hancock, though he was obviously guilty. Hancock continued to be elected to the Massachusetts House of Representatives and became its presiding officer. On August 14, 1769, Hancock attended an elaborate celebration to commemorate the establishment of the Sons of Liberty and to rejoice in the departure of Governor Bernard who, having had enough, was returning to England. Hancock led the procession in his elaborate carriage, followed by 138 other carriages, making a procession a mile and a half long (2, 116).

The chief event of 1770 was the Boston Massacre. In retrospect it sounds like a squabble which, for lack of leadership, turned into a minor tragedy, but in 1770 it was an event that crystallized the spirit of revolt. Naturally there had been incidents between the British troops and Bostonians, often between the waterfront element and the soldier, but nothing serious had occurred. At nine o'clock on the snowy night of March 5, 1770, an urchin spotted Captain Goldfinch, and employed the common sport of making fun of the officer, in this case because the officer was in debt to the urchin's master. A sentinel slapped the impudent urchin. A crowd collected. The guard was called. The small detachment began to retreat to its barracks. One soldier was attacked by the crowd. The main guard was called. The crowd pressed. Someone gave the order to fire. Five Bostonians were killed. Lieutenant Governor Hutchinson appeared on his balcony, asking the crowd to disperse, promising that law would take its course and ordering the offending soldiers arrested. The next day Hancock headed a committee demanding that Hutchinson remove his troops from Boston. After some delay, the lieutenant governor agreed.

A glorious funeral was held for the five dead men, and the spirit of revolt in the colony reached a peak of excitement. That very day, news was received that all of the Townshend duties except the tax on tea were lifted, that tax being continued to show that Britain had the right to levy duties if it wished.

By the fall of 1770, Hancock and the two Adamses were appointed to a committee of five to achieve intercolonial liaison. The Massachusetts House named Hancock to the Governor's Council, but Hutchinson refused to seat him. At a conciliatory meeting Hutchinson offered Hancock his seat, but Hancock was not to be bought off with favors. During this period, Adams and Hancock had been slipping apart. Hancock was not sympathetic with the violence that Adams was recommending, but the rigidity of the Old Regime helped friends to patch up their differences.

In 1772 Hutchinson courted Hancock by appointing him a colonel and put him in command of a Corps of Independent Cadets. Hancock accepted the honor. The new colonel continued to endear himself to Bostonians by making donations to the town—a bandstand, a fire engine, a fence and walks for the park, and money for the Brattle Street Church.

By November of 1773 the *Dartmouth* had arrived in Boston with the first tea since the tax had been retained. The citizens ordered the consignees to refuse shipment. The merchants tried to stall, for they were caught between the colonists and the British. Two more tea ships arrived. The Sons of Liberty remained on guard to see that no tea was landed, and placards called Bostonians to action. Matters climaxed on December 17, 1773, when, following a meeting at the Old South Church where Hancock may have spoken, an undetermined number of "Mohawk Indians" threw 342 chests of tea overboard from the three ships and Governor Hutchinson found himself powerless to act against the offenders.

On the past three anniversaries of the Boston Massacre, a public ceremony had been held, featuring a speech by an outstanding Bostonian. The news that Hancock, one of the town's richest citizens, a respectable businessman, and a conservative, was to deliver the commemorative address on March 5, 1774, was greeted with considerable interest. The British interpreted the act as widening the gap between Hancock and the king, while the radicals celebrated. How much detail remains concerning how the fourth anniversary of the Boston Massacre was celebrated?

The committee appointed by the Massachusetts House to exchange information with other colonial grievance committees was in charge of the celebration. This committee, dominated by Whigs with Sam Adams as one of its members, felt it highly politic to enlist the services of an outstanding Boston merchant whose fellow shippers were suffering from the opposition of the radicals to the laws of England. This particular March 5 fell on a Saturday. Although a certain amount of business must have gone on as usual, much of the town's activity centered on the anniversary. The British stayed home, making themselves inconspicuous. The colonials and their dignitaries assembled at Faneuil Hall for preliminaries, but had to adjourn to the Old South Church since the crowd was so great. How many did Hancock address? The present seating capacity of Faneuil Hall is around 950, but prior to 1806 the building was only half as wide as it is now and the existing balconies were not present. Old Faneuil Hall did not have seats, so that, during Hancock's time, it could have accommodated around 1,000 persons standing. So there must have been more than 1,000 persons. How many more? At present the Old South Meeting House can seat 875, but the present fire regulations permit fewer pews than in 1774. Assuming maximum standees, close to 2,000 might have been accommodated in the Old South Church to hear Hancock.

After some introductory remarks by Sam Adams, Hancock, who had just recovered from the gout, delivered his blistering attack. The moment that Hancock took his position at the sacred desk must have been dramatic, and when the audience heard the vigorous way he attacked the British, there must have been an increase in the number who felt that a revolution was inevitable. It was one thing for Sam Adams and his crowd to agitate against the king; it was quite another for one of the town's most wealthy and beloved citizens to take an uncompromising position. Herbert Allan concluded: "It was a spell-binding tirade of inflammatory rhetorical questions, extravagant accusations, gore-dropping passages, and passion-rousing apostrophes that was received, even by intellectuals, with reverberating plaudits and with tears" (2, 144). Allan concluded that, once Hancock had made this speech, he had committed himself publicly to the revolution, and there could be no turning back.

After March 5, 1774, Hancock wavered no more. On June 1 to 14, the Port Bill prohibiting any unloading in Boston and moving the seat of government to Salem irritated Bostonians further. The humiliating provisions stipulating that jurors not be selected by the people and that capital offenses be tried in England or outside the colony were outrageous to Englishmen who had come to Boston to escape oppression. Yet some communication with the Old Regime continued. Gage replaced Hutchinson as governor, and Hancock's Independent Cadets with their colonel in charge formed part of the welcome party. Through a maneuver by which the assembly hall doors were locked, Sam Adams had Gage's first General Court at Salem name delegates to a Continental Congress to be held in Philadelphia on September 11, 1774. Gage took out his vengeance on Hancock by dismissing him from his colonelcy. When Adams went to Philadelphia for the first Congress, Hancock held General Court, dissolved the court into a Provincial Congress, and kept the transactions secret. On November 23, 1774, the Provincial Congress chose to recruit minutemen and the rhetoric of the Thanksgiving proclamation omitted the words "God Save the King."

In February of 1775, the second Massachusetts Provincial Congress began its meetings with Hancock presiding. The 1775 commemorative oration almost created a riot when the heckling of British soldiers crying "Fie, fie" was mistaken for "Fire, fire." Later, Hancock's mansion was the target of physical abuse by British officers. So much had transpired in a year's time that the respectful silence with which the British appear to have received Hancock's oration a year ago had given way to open hostility. By April, the Provincial Congress had gone so far as to call for an armed alliance of Massachusetts, Rhode Island, Connecticut, and New Hampshire. The stage was set for the shot heard around the world.

The tenseness after Lexington and Concord was insurmountable. Hancock was a delegate to the Second Continental Congress in 1775 and was elected its president. Sears commented that the way in which the Adamses backed Hancock for this post proved how he had already established himself as an effective speaker:

If Hancock had not already proved his ability as a parliamentarian neither of the Adamses would have risked his reputation as an adviser by advocating his election; but his experience and success as moderator in Boston town-meetings and as president of the Massachusetts Provincial Congress warranted his recommendation by his friends . . . (16, 179).

Soon after, Hancock fell out with the Adamses because they backed Washington for commander-in-chief instead of Hancock. The Adamses knew that Hancock was no deep thinker or strategist, but functioned very effectively as a symbol of patriotism. They did not hesitate to choose Washington.

On July 2, 1776, the Declaration of Independence was certain of adoption, and it was officially approved on July 4, bearing only Hancock's signature as president. In the fall of 1777, Hancock asked permission to return to Boston, and his request was too speedily granted to satisfy the Hancock ego. In 1777, he was back in Philadelphia briefly, but not before he had successfully wined and dined the French army and navy and smoothed over several disputes between the new allies. In 1780, Hancock was easily elected the first governor of the Commonwealth, serving under a constitution that he had been instrumental in drafting. On October 31, 1780, Hancock delivered his inaugural address. Only two years later he showed signs of his deteriorating health:

In June, 1782, Hancock had the appearance of advanced age, though only forty-five. He had been repeatedly and severely afflicted with the gout. . . . Governor Hancock was nearly six feet in stature, and of thin person, stooping a little and apparently enfeebled by disease. His manners were very gracious, of the old style. . . . His face had been very handsome. . . .Hancock was dressed in a red velvet cap, within which was one of fine linen. . . . He wore a blue damask gown, lined with silk; a white stock; a white satin, embroidered waistcoat, black satin small-clothes; white silk stockings, and red morocco slippers (17, 10).

In 1788 Hancock engineered Massachusetts's ratification of the Constitution in a famous speech, in which he came out of his sickbed to introduce nine amendments; the phraseology of these is evident in the Bill of Rights. In 1789, he was disappointed at not being named vice-president, but his continued success as governor was some consolation. On September 18, 1793, Hancock was too weak to deliver his own speech and had to have it read for him. On October 8, he died.

Fight and Even Die

March 5, 1774
Fourth Anniversary of the Boston Massacre
Old South Meeting House, Boston

Vendidit hic auro, patriam, dominumque potentem
Imposuit: fixit leges pretio atque refixit.
Non, mihi si linguae centum sint, oraque centum,
Ferrea vox, omnes scelerum: comprendere formas,
   possim.[1]

Men, brethren, fathers and fellow-countrymen:

The attentive gravity, the venerable appearance of this crowded audience; the dignity which I behold in the countenances of so many in this great assembly; the solemnity of the occasion upon which we have met together, joined to a consideration of the part I am to take in the important business of this day, fill me with an awe hitherto unknown; and heighten the sense which I have ever had, of my unworthiness to fill this sacred desk; but allured by the call of some of my respected fellow-citizens, with whose request it is always my greatest pleasure to comply, I almost forgot my want of ability to perform what they required. In this situation I find my only support, in assuring myself that a generous people will not severely censure what they know was well intended, though its want of merit, should prevent their being able to applaud it. And I pray, that my sincere attachment to the interest of my country, and hearty detestation of every design formed against her liberties, may be admitted as some apology for my appearance in this place.

I have always, from my earliest youth, rejoiced in the felicity of my fellow-men; and have ever considered it as the indispensable duty of every member of society to promote, as far as in him lies, the prosperity of every individual, but more especially of the community to which he belongs; and also, as a faithful subject of the state, to use his utmost endeavors to detect, and having detected, strenuously to oppose every traitorous plot which its enemies may devise for its destruction. Security to the persons and properties

---

The first edition of the speech (7) has been faithfully followed by reprintings (noted in 7 and *15*) with variations largely continued to differences in capitalization, spelling, and italics, except that Alden T. Vaughan offers a highly abridged version.

[1] Virgil's *Aeneid*, VI, 621-22; 625-26, 627.

of the governed, is so obviously the design and end of civil government, that to attempt a logical proof of it, would be like burning tapers at noonday, to assist the sun in enlightening the world; and it cannot be either virtuous or honorable, to attempt to support a government, of which this is not the great and principal basis; and it is to the last degree vicious and infamous to attempt to support a government, which manifestly tends to render the persons and properties of the governed insecure. Some boast of being *friends* to *government*; I am a friend to *righteous* government founded upon the principles of reason and justice; but I glory in publicly avowing my eternal enmity to tyranny. Is the present system, which the British administration have adopted for the government of the colonies, a righteous government? or is it tyranny? —Here suffer me to ask (and would to Heaven there could be an answer) what tenderness, what regard, respect or consideration has Great Britain shewn, in their late transactions for the security of the persons or properties of the inhabitants of the colonies? or rather, what have they omitted doing to destroy that security? they have declared that they have, ever had, and of right ought ever to have, full power to make laws of sufficient validity to bind the colonies in all cases whatever: they have exercised this pretended right by imposing a tax upon us without our consent; and lest we should shew some reluctance at parting with our property, her fleets and armies are sent to enforce their mad pretentions. The town of Boston, ever faithful to the British crown, has been invested by a British fleet: the troops of George the III have crossed the wide Atlantic, not to engage an enemy, but to assist a band of traitors in trampling on the rights and liberties of his most loyal subjects in America—those rights and liberties which, as a father, he ought ever to regard, and as a king, he is bound, in honor, to defend from violations, even at the risk of his own life.

Let not the history of the illustrious house of Brunswick inform posterity, that a king descended from that glorious monarch, George the II, once sent his British subjects to conquer and enslave his subjects in America, but be perpetual infamy entailed upon that villain who dared to advise his master to such execrable measures; for it was easy to foresee the consequences which so naturally followed upon sending troops into America, to enforce obedience to acts of the British parliament, which neither God nor man ever empowered them to make. It was reasonable to expect that troops, who knew the errand they were sent upon, would treat the people whom they were to subjugate, with a cruelty and haughtiness, which too often buries the honorable character of a *soldier* in the disgraceful name of an *unfeeling ruffian*. The troops, upon their first arrival, took possession of our senate-house, and pointed their cannon against the judgment hall, and even continued them there whilst the supreme court of judicature for this province was actually sitting to decide upon the lives and fortunes of the king's subjects. Our streets nightly resounded with the noise of riot and debauchery; our peaceful citizens were hourly exposed to shameful insults, and often felt the effects of their violence and outrage.—But this was not all: as though they thought it not enough to violate our civil rights, they endeavored to deprive us of the enjoyment of our religious privileges; to viciate our morals, and thereby render us deserving of destruction. Hence the rude din of arms which broke in upon your solemn devotions in your temples, on that day hallowed by heaven, and set apart by God himself for his peculiar worship. Hence, impious oaths and blasphemies so often tortured your unaccustomed ear. Hence, all the arts which idleness and luxury could invent, were used to betray our youth of one sex into extravagance and effeminacy, and of the other to infamy and ruin; and did they not succeed but too well? Did not a reverence for religion sensibly decay? Did not our infants almost learn to lisp out curses before they knew their horrid import? did not our youth forget they were Americans, and regardless of the admonitions of the wise and aged, servilely copy from their tyrants those vices which finally must overthrow the empire of Great Britain? And must I be compelled to acknowledge, that even the noblest, fairest part of all the lower creation did not entirely escape the cursed snare? when virtue has once erected her throne within the female breast, it is upon so solid a basis that nothing is able to expel the heavenly inhabitant. But have there not been some, few indeed, I hope, whose youth and inexperience have rendered them a prey to wretches, whom, upon the least reflection, they would have despised and hated as foes to God and their country? I fear there have been some such unhappy instances; or why have I seen an honest father clothed with shame; or why a virtuous mother drowned in tears?

But I forbear, and come reluctantly to the transactions of that dismal night, when in such quick succession we felt the extremes of grief, astonishment and rage; when Heaven in anger, for a dreadful moment suffered hell to take the reins; when Satan with his chosen band opened the sluices of New-England's blood, and sacrilegiously polluted our land with the dead bodies of her guiltless sons. Let this sad tale of death never be told without a tear; let not the heaving bosom cease to burn with a manly indignation at the barbarous story, through the long tracts of future time: let every parent tell the shameful story to his listening children 'til tears of pity glisten in their eyes, and boiling passions shake their tender frames; and whilst the anniversary of that ill-fated night is kept a jubilee in the grim court of pandaemonium, let all America join in one common prayer to heaven, that the inhuman, unprovoked murders of the fifth of March, 1770, planned by Hillsborough,[2] and a knot of treacherous knaves in Boston, and executed by the cruel hand of Preston[3] and his sanguinary coadjutors, may ever stand on history without a parallel. But what, my countrymen, withheld the ready arm of vengeance from executing instant justice on the vile assassins? perhaps you feared promiscuous carnage might ensue, and that the innocent might share the fate of those who had performed the infernal deed. But were not all guilty? were you not too tender of the lives of those who came to fix a yoke on your necks? but I must not too severely blame a fault, which great souls only can commit. May that magnificence of spirit which scorns the low pursuits of malice, may that generous compassion which often preserves from ruin, even a guilty villain, forever actuate the noble bosoms of Americans! But let not the miscreant host vainly imagine that we feared their arms. No; them we despised; we dread nothing but slavery. Death is the creature of a poltroon's brains; 'tis immortality to sacrifice ourselves for the salvation of our country. We fear not death. That gloomy night, the pale faced moon, and the affrighted stars that hurried through the sky, can witness that we fear not death. Our hearts which, at the recollection, glow with rage that for revolving years have scarcely taught us to restrain, can witness that we fear not death; and happy it is for those who dared to insult us, that their naked bones are now piled up an everlasting monument of Massachusetts' bravery. But they retired, they fled, and in that flight they found their only safety. We then expected that the hand of public justice would soon inflict that punishment upon the murderers, which, by the laws of God and man, they had incurred. But let the unbiassed pen of a Robertson, or perhaps of some equally famed American, conduct this trial before the great tribunal of succeeding generations. And though the murderers may escape the just resentment of an enraged people; though drowsy justice, intoxicated by the poisonous draught prepared for her cup, still nods upon her rotten seat, yet be assured, such complicated crimes will meet their due reward. Tell me, ye bloody butchers! ye villains high and low! ye wretches who contrived, as well as you who executed the inhuman deed! do you not feel the goads and stings of conscious guilt pierce through

[2] On January 20, 1768, Wills Hill, first marquis of Downshire and second Viscount Hillsborough, was appointed secretary of state for the colonies. It was he who on June 8, 1768, ordered a regiment to Boston to intimidate the colonists.

[3] Captain John Preston, officer of the day, had ordered his men to load and then placed himself before them to prevent unnecessary violence. It was evidently not Preston who gave the command to fire, for he was tried for his part in the massacre and acquitted.

your savage bosoms? Though some of you may think yourselves exalted to a height that bids defiance to human justice, and others shroud yourselves beneath the mask of hypocrisy, and build your hopes of safety on the low arts of cunning, chicanery and falsehood, yet do you not sometimes feel the gnawings of that worm which never dies? Do not the injured shades of Maverick, Gray, Caldwell, Attucks and Carr, attend you in your solitary walks, arrest you even in the midst of your debaucheries, and fill even your dreams with terror? But if the unappeased manes of the dead should not disturb their murderers, yet surely even your obdurate hearts must shrink, and your guilty blood must chill within your rigid veins, when you behold the miserable Monk, the wretched victim of your savage cruelty. Observe his tottering knees, which scarce sustain his wasted body; look on his haggard eyes; mark well the death-like paleness of his fallen cheek, and tell me, does not the sight plant daggers in your souls? unhappy Monk! cut off in the gay morn of manhood, from all the joys which sweeten life, doomed to drag on a pitiful existence, without even a hope to taste the pleasures of returning health! yet Monk, thou livest not in vain; thou livest a warning to thy country, which sympathizes with thee in thy sufferings; thou livest an affecting, an alarming instance of the unbounded violence which lust of power, assisted by a standing army, can lead a traitor to commit.

For us he bled, and now languishes. The wounds by which he is tortured to a lingering death, were aimed at our country! Surely the meek-eyed charity can never behold such sufferings with indifference. Nor can her lenient hand forbear to pour oil and wine into those wounds, and to assuage at least, what it cannot heal.

Patriotism is ever united with humanity and compassion. This noble affection which impels us to sacrifice every thing dear, even life itself, to our country, involves in it a common sympathy and tenderness for every citizen, and must ever have a particular feeling for one who suffers in a public cause. Thoroughly persuaded of this, I need not add a word to engage your compassion and bounty towards a fellow citizen, who, with long protracted anguish, falls a victim to the relentless rage of our common enemies.

Ye dark designing knaves, ye murderers, parricides! how dare you tread upon the earth, which has drank in the blood of slaughtered innocents, shed by your wicked hands? How dare you breathe that air which wafted to the ear of heaven, the groans of those who fell a sacrifice to your accursed ambition? but if the laboring earth doth not expand her jaws; if the air you breathe is not commissioned to be the minister of death yet hear it, and tremble! the eye of heaven penetrates the darkest chambers of the soul, traces the leading clue through all the labyrinths which your industrious folly has devised; and you, however you may have screened yourselves from human eyes, must be arraigned, must lift your hands, red with the blood of those whose death you have procured, at the tremendous bar of GOD.

But I gladly quit the gloomy theme of death, and leave you to improve the thought of that important day, when our naked souls must stand before that being, from whom nothing can be hid. I would not dwell too long upon the horrid effects which have already followed from quartering regular troops in this town; let our misfortunes teach posterity to guard against such evils for the future. Standing armies are sometimes (I would by no means say generally, much less universally) composed of persons who have rendered themselves unfit to live in civil society; who have no other motives of conduct than those which a desire of the present gratification of their passions suggests; who have no property in any country; men who have given up their own liberties, and envy those who enjoy liberty; who are equally indifferent to the glory of a George or a Louis; who for the addition of one penny a day to their wages, would desert from the Christian cross, and fight under the crescent of the Turkish sultan, from such men as these, usurping Caesar passed the Rubicon; with such as these he humbled mighty Rome, and forced the mistress of the world to own a master in a traitor. These are the men whom sceptered robbers now employ to frustrate the designs of God and render vain the bounties which his gracious hand pours indiscriminately upon his creatures. By these the miserable slaves in Turkey, Persia, and many other extensive countries, are rendered truly wretched, though their air is salubrious, and their soil luxuriously fertile. By these, France and Spain, though blessed by nature with all that administers to the convenience of life, have been reduced to that contemptible state in which they now appear; and by these Britain— but if I was possessed of the gift of prophecy, I dare not, except by divine command, unfold the leaves on which the destiny of that once powerful kingdom is inscribed. But since standing armies are so hurtful to a state, perhaps my countrymen may demand some substitute, some other means of rendering us secure against the incursions of foreign enemy. But can you be one moment at a loss? will not a *well disciplined militia* afford you ample security against foreign foes? We want not courage; it is discipline alone in which we are exceeded by the most formidable troops that ever trod the earth. Surely our hearts flutter no more at the sound of war, than did those of the immortal band of Persia, the Macedonian phalanx, the invincible Roman legions, the Turkish Janissaries,[4] the Gens des Armes of France,[5] or

[4] Until 1826, the name given to the standing army of the Ottoman empire.

[5] The regular French army was supplemented by *gens d'armes*, a sort of national guard from which came the word *gendarme*.

the *well known grenadiers of Britain.* A well disciplined militia is a safe, an honorable guard to a community like this, whose inhabitants are by nature brave, and are laudably tenacious of that freedom in which they were born. From a well regulated militia we have nothing to fear; their interest is the same with that of the state. When a country is invaded, the militia are ready to appear in its defence; they march into the field with that fortitude which a consciousness of the justice of their cause inspires; they do not jeopard their lives for a master who considers them only as the instruments of his ambition, and whom they regard only as the daily dispenser of the scanty pittance of bread and water. No, they fight for their houses, their lands, for their wives, their children, for all who claim the tenderest names, and are held dearest in their hearts, they fight *pro aris et focis,*[6] for their liberty, and for themselves, and for their God. And let it not offend, if I say, that no militia ever appeared in more flourishing condition, than that of this province now doth; and pardon me if I say—of this town in particular—I mean not to boast; I would not excite envy but manly emulation. We have all our common cause; let it therefore be our only contest, who shall most contribute to the security of the liberties of America. And may the same kind Providence which has watched over this country from her infant state, still enable us to defeat our enemies. I cannot here forbear noticing the signal manner in which the designs of those who wish not well to us have been discovered. The dark deeds of a treacherous Cabal, have been brought to public view. You now know the serpents who, while cherished in your bosoms, were darting their envenomed stings into the vitals of the constitution. But the representatives of the people have fixed a mark on these ungrateful monsters, which, though it may not make them so secure as Cain of old, yet renders them at least as infamous. Indeed it would be affrontive to the tutelar deity of this country even to despair of saving it from all the snares which human policy can lay.

True it is, that the British ministry have annexed a salary to the office of the governor of this province, to be paid out of a revenue, raised in America without our consent. They have attempted to render our courts of justice the instruments of extending the authority of acts of the British parliament over this colony, by making the judges dependent on the British administration for their support. But this people will never be enslaved with their eyes open. The moment they knew that the governor was not such a governor as the charter of the province points out, he lost his power of hurting them. They were alarmed; they suspected him, have guarded against him, and he has found that a wise and a brave people, when they know their danger, are fruitful in expedients to escape it.

[6] for their altars and hearths,

The courts of judicature also so far lost their dignity, by being supposed to be under an undue influence, that our representatives thought it absolutely necessary to resolve that they were bound to declare that they would not receive any other salary besides that which the general court should grant them; and if they did not make this declaration, that it would be the duty of the house to impeach them.

Great expectations were also formed from the artful scheme of allowing the East India company to export tea to America, upon their own account. This certainly, had it succeeded, would have effected the purpose of the contrivers, and gratified the most sanguine wishes of our adversaries. We soon should have found our trade in the hands of foreigners, and taxes imposed on every thing which we consumed; nor would it have been strange, if, in a few years, a company in London should have purchased an exclusive right of trading to America.—But their plot was soon discovered.—The people soon were aware of the poison which, with so much craft and subtilty, had been concealed: loss and disgrace ensued: and, perhaps, this long-concerted master-piece of policy, may issue in the total disuse of tea in this country, which will eventually be the saving of the lives and the estates of thousands—yet while we rejoice that the adversary has not hitherto prevailed against us, let us by no means put off the harness. Restless malice, and disappointed ambition, will still suggest new measures to our inveterate *enemies*.— Therefore let us also be ready to take the field whenever danger calls; let us be united and strengthen the hands of each other, by promoting a general union among us.—Much has been done by the committees of correspondence for this and the other towns of this province, towards uniting the inhabitants; let them still go on and prosper. Much has been done by the committees of correspondence, for the houses of assembly, in this and our sister colonies, for uniting the inhabitants of the whole continent, for the security of their common interest. May success ever attend their generous endeavors. But permit me here to suggest a general congress of deputies, from the several houses of assembly, on the continent, as the most effectual method of establishing such an union, as the present posture of our affairs requires. At such a congress a firm foundation may be laid for the security of our rights and liberties, a system may be formed for our common safety, by a strict adherence to which, we shall be able to frustrate any attempts to overthrow our constitution; restore peace and harmony to America, and secure honor and wealth to Great Britain even against the inclinations of her ministers, whose duty it is to study her welfare; and we shall also free ourselves from those unmannerly pillagers who impudently tell us, that they are licensed by an act of the British parliament to thrust their dirty hands into the pockets of every

American. But I trust, the happy time will come, when with the besom of
destruction, those noxious vermin will be swept forever from the streets of
Boston.

Surely you never will tamely suffer this country to be a den of thieves.
Remember, my friends, from whom you sprang.—Let not a meanness of
spirit, unknown to those whom you boast of as your fathers, excite a thought
to the dishonor of your mothers. I conjure you by all that is dear, by all that
is honorable, by all that is sacred, not only that ye pray, but that you act;
that, if necessary, ye fight, and even die, for the prosperity of our Jerusalem.
Break in sunder, with noble disdain, the bonds with which the Philistines have
bound you. Suffer not yourselves to be betrayed by the soft arts of luxury
and effeminacy, into the pit digged for your destruction. Despise the glare of
wealth. That people who pay greater respect to a wealthy villain, than to an
honest upright man in poverty, almost deserve to be enslaved; they plainly
shew that wealth, however it may be acquired, is in their esteem, to be
preferred to virtue.

But I thank God, that America abounds in men who are superior to all
temptation, whom nothing can divert from a steady pursuit of the interest of
their country; who are at once its ornament and safe-guard. And sure I am, I
should not incur your displeasure, if I paid a respect so justly due to their
much honored characters in this place; but when I name an *Adams*, such a
numerous host of fellow patriots rush upon my mind, that I fear it would
take up too much of your time, should I attempt to call over the illustrious
roll: but your grateful hearts will point you to the men; and their revered
names, in all succeeding times, shall grace the annals of America. From them,
let us, my friends, take example; from them, let us catch the divine enthusiasm; and feel, each for himself, the God-like pleasure of diffusing happiness
on all around us; of delivering the oppressed from the iron grasp of tyranny;
of changing the hoarse complaints and bitter moans of wretched slaves, into
those cheerful songs, which freedom and contentment must inspire. There is a
heart-felt satisfaction in reflecting on our exertions for the public weal, which
all the sufferings an enraged tyrant can inflict, will never take away; which
the ingratitude and reproaches of those whom we have saved from ruin,
cannot rob us of. The virtuous asserter of the rights of mankind, merits a
reward, which even a want of success in his endeavors to save his country, the
heaviest misfortune which can befall a genuine patriot, cannot entirely prevent him from receiving.

I have the most animating confidence that the present noble struggle for
liberty, will terminate gloriously for America. And let us play the man for our
God, and for the cities of our God; while we are using the means in our

power, let us humbly commit our righteous cause to the great Lord of the universe, who loveth righteousness and hateth iniquity. And having secured the approbation of our hearts, by a faithful and unwearied discharge of our duty to our country, let us joyfully leave our concerns in the hands of Him who raiseth up and putteth down the empires and kingdoms of the world as He pleases; and with cheerful submission to His sovereign will, devoutly say,

Although the fig tree shall not blossom, neither shall fruit be in the vines; the labor of the olive shall fail, and the field shall yield no meat; the flock shall be cut off from the fold, and there shall be no herd in the stalls; yet we [I] will rejoice in the LORD, we [I] will joy in the GOD of our [my] salvation.[7]

The Revolt Rhetoric of Hancock

Hancock is an excellent example of a man of stature turning into the man of words with a grievance. The colonies had experienced a wave of social, economic, and political prosperity that was threatened by the Old Regime. The nationalistic pride of the colonists was threatened by the insistence of the Old Regime on the right to tax. This focal point of dysfunction spread to multiple dysfunction when the courts were interfered with, when local government was threatened, and when additional legislation jeopardized economic prosperity. Under such circumstances even a rich tradesman could turn to a rhetoric which openly advocated lawlessness against the Old regime.

By 1774 Hancock had demonstrated that he could be an effective speaker. He had grown up in an atmosphere that commended rhetoric, for he remembered his own father in the pulpit and recalled his grandfather's preaching, since the "bishop" lived until John was 15. Furthermore the traditional New England town meeting placed prestige on oral communication, and Hancock's training at Harvard had given sufficient attention to oral discourse to assist him with the task he faced in 1774.

Therefore, although there is considerable smoke indicating that Hancock did not write his own Boston Massacre speech, there was sufficient fire in Hancock to enable him to have done so had he wished. The two sources that question Hancock's authorship are both based on hearsay. On July 29, 1840, Noah Webster wrote to Ebenezer Thomas:

In the year 1774, Mr. Trumbull was a student of law in the office of John Adams. Mr. Hancock was, at that time, a wavering character; at least he was so considered

[7]Habakkuk (King James Version) 3:17-18.

by the leading Whigs of that day. It was a matter of no small importance to bring him to a decision, as to the part he was to take in the crisis then approaching. To effect this object, the more staunch leading Whigs contrived to procure Mr. Hancock to be appointed to deliver an oration on the anniversary of the Massacre; and some of them wrote his oration for him, or a considerable part of it. . . . Judge Trumbull related to me these facts, as from his personal knowledge . . . (*19*, II, 169, *11* XLIII, 155).

The second piece of evidence is even more questionable:

It is known among a few that Samuel Adams composed nearly the whole of this oration for his friend. A letter asserting this as a fact, written in 1787, by one who personally knew both Adams and Hancock, was in existence a few years since, but has been lost. Mrs. Hannah Wells has repeatedly stated that she knew the time and place where her father used to meet Hancock while preparing the speech, but, as a girl, she had been cautioned not to mention it. Mr. Joseph Allen, a nephew and special favorite of Adams and a frequent visitor at his house, used to say that Hancock was long closeted with Adams on several occasions, a week or two before delivering the oration (*21*, II, 138).

Of course there are always persons who claim the successes of the deceased. Naturally Hancock consulted with Adams. The two were very intimate, and Adams may well have done all he could to influence what Hancock had to say. But both men would have appeared ridiculous had the speech resembled too much the sort of propaganda for which Adams was already famous. A proud Hancock would certainly have avoided the charge of borrowing too liberally from his interesting but seedy friend.

We have therefore a speech that advocated lawlessness, delivered by a man of words with a grievance, in a state of preservation that gives us considerable assurance of its authenticity. What can be learned from this speech and from Hancock's speaking in general about the rhetoric of revolt?

Invention

When Hancock delivered his speech of 1774 during stage one of the American Revolution, the age of the baroque had not ended. Wordsworth's preface to the *Lyrical Ballads* was still a number of years away. Therefore it is not surprising that the orators of the Boston Massacre began with a classical quotation, in imitation no doubt of a preacher's text and in an effort to impress the British that the colonists were not unlearned. Lovell, who delivered the first oration in 1771, began with short excerpts from Caesar and Cicero, while Joseph Warren, who followed in 1772, took his "text" from Virgil, as did Church in 1773. It was therefore natural for Hancock to open with a passage from the *Aeneid*. It must be assumed that all of these gentlemen recited their introductory quotations in Latin, even though many of those who attended could not comprehend. Communication can be effectively achieved, even if the words themselves are not understood. Hancock could say by quoting Virgil, that the sentiments of the colonists were not new but in keeping with classical tradition.

Hancock's continued classical references ("the Macedonian phalanx, the invincible Roman legions, the Turkish Janissaries") and his use of the Latin phrase *pro aris et focis* demonstrate that, although he was in the process of adopting the costume of words of the new revolutionary movement, he was not willing to surrender his identification with traditional symbols. Hancock's frequent borrowing from biblical phraseology and his innovation of concluding a Boston Massacre address with a biblical quotation[8] show also the equivocal position of his rhetoric and therefore of his status as an agitator. Of course Hancock knew of the religious zeal that still pervaded the descendants of Jonathan Edwards and Cotton Mather, and this facet of his audience analysis, coupled with the security he sought as a reluctant agitator, made biblical language and references very comfortable to him.

The degree of credibility that Hancock achieved by delivering a Boston Massacre address can be appreciated by considering the risks that were involved. The price that he paid for his commitment is dramatized by the fact that, when George III offered Massachusetts a general amnesty, he exempted only Hancock and Adams. A rich and influential conservative espousing a popular lawless cause at considerable inconvenience to himself—here is ethos in the making. If a speaker's intent materially affects his credibility—i.e., if the less he gains personally from his sentiments and if the more he inconveniences himself to express those sentiments, the less suspect is his intent—then Hancock as the man of words with a grievance held high ethos on March 5, 1774. How many felt at that time, that if a revolution actually did take place, it could succeed against powerful Britain? A free America could have resulted in prosperity for Hancock's business enterprises, but the reality of what actually did happen—that Hancock suffered large financial losses by espousing the revolutionary cause—was much more dominant in the minds of his audience. The reconstituted diary of Dorothy Dudley noted on May 20, 1775, how patriotic Hancock was considered to be when, addressing the North End Club of Mechanics, he cried: "Burn Boston and make John Hancock a beggar if the public good requires it" (5, 22). Burning was just as repulsive in 1775 as it is in the 1970s in which the phrase "Burn, baby, burn"

---

[8]Neither Lovell in 1771 nor Warren in 1772 had concluded with a quotation. Church had ended with poetry. Hancock was to follow the same format in 1782 for his Thanksgiving Day address, quoting the twenty-ninth verse of Psalm 100 (6).

fills many with horror. The public knew that Hancock had left the security of his mansion on Beacon Hill and inconvenienced himself to come to the Old South Church to advocate lawlessness, an event that would further divorce him from the favor of the British. The inconvenience caused to men of prestige in espousing lawless causes is a major factor in placing the leadership for agitation in the hands of men of stature. A Sam Adams, a John Brown, or a Huey Long have their intent strongly suspect, for they appear to stand to gain much more through destroying the Old Regime than they have to lose.

As an emotional harangue, the speech compares favorably to Castro's address on May Day, 1960. Its inflammatory nature shows a disdain for the British equal to Castro's disdain for the Yankee. A wide variety of emotions are exploited. The speech began with an artificial bid for humility ("feel sorry for me because unaccustomed as I am to public speaking"), a sentiment which was probably more acceptable in 1774 than it would be today. It proceeded swiftly into the emotion of indignation, progressing into anger during the discussion of the bad influences that the British had had upon Boston's youth. The anger continued into the discussion of the Massacre, climaxing when Hancock addressed the British as "ye bloody butchers! ye villains high and low! " Hancock then took advantage of the presence of the mutilated Monk to mingle his anger with pity.[9] The British, as is so often true of the Old Regime, had not taken those extra precautions to avoid an incident that would allow the agitator to make legitimate use of *argumentum ad misericordiam.* A massacre is so frequently stumbled into by the Old Regime—in the colonies, in Russia, in India, in Cuba—that Hancock not only could make legitimate use of *argumentum ad misericordiam* in his speech, but could turn the whole commemorative ceremony into a glorified appeal to pity. Hancock's discussion of the role that the militia should play and his call for a continental congress permitted him to progress into pride. The pride of the colonists, he concluded, was such that they would perish rather than submit to British tyranny. Although Hancock did not exhort his crowd to "Patria o Meutre" as did Castro, the sentiment was much the same.

The speech is based on several premises. First Hancock proposed that the colonists, "ever faithful to the British crown," were men whose rights and liberties had been impinged upon, not by the House of Brunswick but by the villians who advised the king. This is hardly original thinking, but it was undoubtedly the sentiment that Bostonians wanted to hear. It allowed them to be both loyal and disloyal. Hancock's second premise proposed that the men who committed the Boston Massacre were men who were falsely acquitted. Again a popular argument. Unless Hancock could establish this

[9]Did Hancock know that Monk would be present or is this passage extemporaneous?

proposition, all of his sympathy for the five deceased patriots and for the maimed Monk would not have come off. Hancock's third premise was that nations that act as Britain was then acting are nations that eventually lose their power. Fourth, to answer the British argument that troops were needed to protect the American colonists from foreign aggression, Hancock offered the opinion that the American colonies were territories that could be adequately defended by a locally recruited militia, and furthermore that the American colonists were a people with such common bonds that they could best combat their enemies by a form of unified resistance, i.e., a continental congress.[10] Fifth, Hancock argued that activism required that the people of Boston evade both the usurpation of their local government and the British taxation, and that passivism had caused the colonial judges to decline monies offered by the Crown.

As with many men of words during the first stage of a revolt, Hancock's goals are not altogether clear. Like Mirabeau in 1789, he was the reluctant revolutionist. On the one hand he argued that the colonists are loyal to the king in spite of the bad advice he is receiving; on the other hand he urged the colonists to use both active and passive measures of lawlessness. Sam Adams would probably have been as blunt as Gandhi and said that it was independence that the colonies wanted, i.e., nationalism was their true theme and the source of their dysfunction. But at this point Hancock was not prepared to do so. Fortunately, Hancock had time from 1774 to 1789 to develop a philosophy in support of American nationalism. Castro did not have such a period to develop a political philosophy to supplement his urge for human rights. Suddenly, in 1959, before he was ready, Castro was forced to inaugurate a political philosophy; the American colonists had several years to formulate theirs.

Organization

As is so frequently true of revolt rhetoric, there are no signposts in the Hancock speech. Nothing is numbered. There are no transitions, no summaries, no recapitulations, all indicating that the speech was written into manuscript form without an outline having first been drafted. The speech does follow a loose chronological pattern, beginning with the invasion of Boston by the British troops, proceeding to the way these troops influenced

[10]That Hancock mentioned such a possibility early in 1774 when it was to be proposed later that year by Adams and was to take place in Philadelphia on September 1, 1774, shows the extent to which the two men were in agreement at this point.

the life of Boston, dwelling upon the failure of the British to punish the guilty, discussing how the problem could be solved by the creation of a militia, and proposing that the restrictive measures of the British could only lead to continued resistance on the part of the colonists. The casual organization of the speech is one of its chief weaknesses.

Style

There are two aspects of Hancock's style that deserve attention: first, the degree to which he uses the costume of words and second, the tumidity of his language.

The costume of words will be more easily detected among the extemporaneous remarks of agitators than it will be in manuscript speeches where there has been time and effort expended to polish and thereby to avoid repetition. Furthermore, the only infallible method of establishing a lexicon of the costume of words of a revolution as long past as the American revolt would be to feed numerous texts into a computer program that would index words and phrases alphabetically. Such texts should include not only speeches but pamphlets, newspaper accounts, songs, poetry, and other literature of the period.

There being no such study available, one can, however, make interesting subjective observations. Moreover, one can role-play with the Old Regime and, in the case of Hancock's speech, ask what particular passages would be most likely to provoke the British to say: "Yes, I read the Hancock speech. It's just like all the others. He keeps talking about . . . I'm tired of those same old things. You'd think he could come up with something new."

An interesting case study of the use of the costume of words in the Hancock speech involves his use of *liberty* which appears eight times in some form:

    formed against her liberties
    those rights and liberties
    men who have given up their own liberties
    and envy those who enjoy liberty
    for their liberty and for themselves
    security of the liberties of America
    security of our rights and liberties
    the present noble struggle for liberty

Not one of these usages is striking. In fact, as is often the case, the more dependency there is on the costume of words, the less effective the style appears in retrospect. Yet this use of the word *liberty* was probably highly annoying to the British who would have said over their tea tables that the colonists already had more liberty than they deserved; it appears throughout the speech and not just in one section; it was so dominant in the minds of the colonies that its frequent use either escaped Hancock or was approved by him; it made a prominent appearance in the Declaration of Independence; and it was undoubtedly received with tremendous enthusiasm by Hancock's audience.

As a second case study, let us examine Hancock's use of the word cluster *tyranny* and *slavery*. These two phrases, in some form, appear ten times in the Hancock speech. Only once do they occur in proximity, and their appearance, like that of the word *liberty*, is spaced rather evenly throughout the speech. They are something like synonyms and provide Hancock with a variety that he apparently sought throughout the speech. Certainly George III's ministers, in reading the speech, would have reacted: "Tyranny indeed! Slavery is it? Rubbish! Something must be done to stop this idle talk." The student of rhetoric can be certain that the agitator's use of the costume of words will receive an immediate negative reaction from the Old Regime.

The exercises at the conclusion of this chapter will encourage the student to seek further examples of the costume of words in the Hancock speech.

As a second facet of Hancock's style, let us evaluate its tumid or flowery aspect. Hancock's speech, coming from the baroque era, is highly figurative. In addition to commonplace usage of anaphora, epistrophe, and asyndeton, Hancock made striking use of several figures. First, there are an unusual number of two and sometimes three step alliterations, such as "felicity of my fellow men," "persons and properties" that Hancock uses three times, "traitors in trampling," and "the people soon were aware of the poison which, with so much craft and subtilty, had been concealed: loss and disgrace ensued; and, perhaps, this long-concerted masterpiece of policy . . ." These sequences employ a wide variety of initial sounds, almost as if Hancock had gone through his manuscript and made certain that no one sound dominated his alliteration. Even more interesting is his use of "syncopated" alliteration, in which an initial sound is followed or preceded by the repetition of that initial sound in a medial or terminal position: "assist the sun"; "easy to foresee"; "unfeeling Russian"; "we then expect." Such a syncopation softens the sound repetition, so that Hancock, who needed to conceal the extent to which he used sound repetition, may have followed this offbeat pattern deliberately.

In addition to his striking use of alliteration, Hancock used one outstanding anastrophe wherein he said that he would not predict the future of a powerful kingdom such as Britain when he had only just finished making such a prediction. For personification, charity is termed "meek-eyed", while justice is called "drowsy" and nodding upon her rotten seat.

There are surprisingly few metaphors, and only one extended use of a comparative figure, namely, "like burning tapers at noonday, to assist the sun in enlightening the world."

There are a number of words that must have been unfamiliar to many of his listeners: *allured, viciate, poltroon, manes, assuage, salubrious, jeopard, tutelar, besom, emulation* and *diffusing.* But Hancock was addressing more than one audience, and he knew that his speech would appear as a pamphlet to be read by enlightened members of the Old Regime and by educated colonial sympathizers in England and America. The numerous biblical allusions, e.g., den of thieves, the Philistines, loveth righteousness and hateth iniquity, were communicable to his audience so steeped in religious tradition. How convenient it was for Hancock to find that the new spirit of revolt could find support in the philosophies of the oldest of the Old Regimes, namely, the church.

Delivery

The newspapers of the day are terse in comment and discouragingly in agreement. The *Boston Gazette* and *Country Journal* of Monday, March 7, 1774, noted the three items reported by all newspapers: (1) the celebration began at 10:00 A.M. at Faneuil Hall, where Sam Adams was chosen moderator; (2) the assembly moved to the Old South Meeting House or Church, where "a prodigious crowd of people" heard the speech; and (3) the oration was received with "universal applause." The *Gazette* noted that, since the anniversary of the massacre fell on a Saturday evening, i.e., the Sabbath eve, the exhibition of the portraits of the murderers and the slaughtered citizens would be put off until Monday evening when they would be displayed at Mrs. Clapham's in King Street. As the meeting broke up, a generous collection was taken up for Christopher Monk (*21*, II, 140). The *Massachusetts Spy* of Thursday, March 10, 1774, reported that "a vast concourse of people attended the oration, which lasted about three quarters of an hour, and was received with . . . approbation."[11] The *Royal American Magazine* of March,

---

[11] The *Spy's* comments were evidently copied from the Boston *Evening Post* of March 7, 1774, or else the two newspapers shared the same reporter for accounts were identical. The Boston *Post-Boy and Advertiser* reported largely what had been noted in the Boston *Journal*, and the Massachusetts *Gazette* and *Boston Weekly News Letter* followed suit.

1774, reprinted the speech but added nothing of importance except to say that Hancock "very affectionately addressed the audience" in Monk's behalf. The only eyewitness who appears to have noted the occasion was John Adams who made the following diary entry for March 5, 1774:

> Heard the oration, pronounced by Colonel Hancock in commemoration of the massacre. An elegant, a pathetic, a spirited performance. A vast crowd, rainy eyes, etc. The composition, the pronunciation, the action—all exceeded the expectations of everybody. They exceeded even mine, which were very considerable. Many of the sentiments came with great propriety from him. His invective, particularly against a preference of riches to virtue, came from him with a singular dignity and grace (1, II, 332).

Thomas, who spoke from personal experience about Hancock's later speeches, noted that a man who had heard Hancock's Boston Massacre speech told Thomas "that the multitude who listened to it, were wrought up to such a pitch of phrenzy, that a single sentence from the oration, calling upon them to take arms, and drive the murderers from their town, would have been at once carried into effect. Such was his control over them, many could not keep their seats,[12] from indignation" (19 I, 245). Thomas recalled Hancock's form as "elegant" and his facial expression as "beautiful, manly, and expressive." Hancock was capable of exciting his audience to "the highest pitch of phrenzy" or he could "sooth them into tears" as he wished. Thomas's description of Hancock's last speech before the Massachusetts Legislature[13] is particularly vivid:

> A town meeting was called, upon a question of great excitement. Old Faneuil Hall could not contain the people, and an adjournment took place to the Old South Meeting-house. Hancock was brought in, and carried up to the front gallery, where the Hon. Benjamin Austin supported him on the right, and the celebrated Dr. Charles Jarvis upon the left, while he addressed the multitude. The governor commenced, by stating to his fellow citizens, that "he felt" it was the last time he should ever address them—that "the seeds of mortality were growing fast within him." The fall of a pin might have been heard such a death-like silence pervaded the listening crowd, during the whole of his animated and soul stirring speech, while tears ran down the cheeks of thousands. The meeting ended, he was conveyed to his carriage, and taken home, but never again appeared in public—his death followed soon after (19, I, 244).

[12] A puzzling reference to "seats," since the audience was supposedly standing.

[13] Although Thomas referred to a "town meeting," the nature of the message concerned not Boston alone but the whole State of Massachusetts and contributed to the passage of the Eleventh Amendment to the Constitution of the United States. The matter of an alien having the right to sue a state had gained such public attention that an open meeting of the assembly was probably called.

Conclusion

John Hancock is an outstanding example of the prosperous benefactor of the Old Regime who, because of multiple dysfunction, relinquished his security to become a revolutionary. His role in the fight for freedom should not be forgotten in contemporary America.

Bibliography

1. Adams, John, *Works* ed. C. F. Adams, 10 vols. Boston: Little, Brown and Company, 1965.
   Index in volume 10 contains numerous references to Hancock.
2. Allan, Herbert S., *John Hancock: Patriot in Purple.* New York: The Macmillan Company, 1948.
   One of the more thorough biographies of Hancock, with excellent bibliography. Massacre is discussed on pp. 144-49.
3. Baxter, W. T., *The House of Hancock.* Cambridge, Mass.: Harvard University Press, 1945.
   Limited to the Hancock business enterprises between 1724 and 1775, based on manuscripts in library of Harvard Business School.
4. *Dictionary of American Biography*, VIII, 211-19. New York: Charles Scribner's Sons, 1932.
   A short biography. Bibliography with references to manuscripts.
5. Dudley, Dorothy, "Dairy", ed. Mary Williams Greely in *Theatrum Majorum: the Cambridge of 1776*, ed. Arthur Gilman. Cambridge, Mass., 1876.
   The source of several incidents and comments about Hancock. This second edition confesses that the diary is a composite derived from original letters and other documents.
6. Hancock, John, Manuscript of Thanksgiving Discourse, 1782. New York: The Pierpont Morgan Library, 16 pp.
   Autographed copy with some corrections.
7. Hancock, John, *An Oration: Delivered March 5, 1774, at the Request of the Inhabitants of the Town of Boston to Commemorate the Bloody Tragedy of the Fifth of March, 1770.* Boston: Edes & Gill, 1774, 20 pp.
   The Library of Congress, Rare Book Room, has two copies, E215.4.H2262 and E215.4.H226. The former call number may be to

a second printing, although both are dated 1774. The Library of Congress also has a copy from the library of Thomas Jefferson, marked 2nd. ed., dated 1807, presented to Jefferson by the editors and bound with the other March 5 commemorative addresses. The first edition of the collected orations was published by Peter Edes in Boston in 1785. A copy of the speech is also located in *The Magazine of History*, XXIV, #3, extra no. 95 (1923), pp. 31-42 and in *Modern Eloquence*, XIII, 1125-36, edition of 1903.

8. Higginson, Stephen, *Ten Chapters in the Life of John Hancock*. New York, 1875.

   A short biography, but no discussion of Hancock's speaking.

9. Hutchinson, Thomas, *Diary and Letters*, ed. P.O. Hutchinson. Boston, 1884-1886.

   The great-grandson of the former governor of the Massachusetts Bay Colony offers the British point of view toward the Revolution.

10. Lancaster, Bruce, *From Lexington to Liberty*. Garden City, N. Y.: Doubleday & Company, Inc., 1955.

    A readable and up-to-date account of the American Revolution from 1764 to 1783, with numerous references to Hancock.

11. Massachusetts Historical Society, *Proceedings*, 3rd series, XLIII (1910), 155. Boston: Massachusetts Historical Society, 1910.

    Reprints the letter from Noah Webster to Ebenezer Smith Thomas of July 29, 1840, about authorship of Hancock's Boston Massacre address.

12. Miller, John C., *Sam Adams: Pioneer in Propaganda*. Boston: Little, Brown and Company, 1936.

    A thorough treatment of Sam Adams as a propagandist, with footnote references, detailing the influence that Adams had on Hancock.

13. Musick, John R., *John Hancock: A Character Sketch*. Chicago: The University Association, 1898, 116 pp.

    A very short biography, general in nature, with some good photographs.

14. *National Cyclopaedia of American Biography*, I, 103-4. New York: J. T. White & Co. 1893.

    A short biography, helpful in establishing dates. No bibliography.

15. Niles, Hezekiah, ed. *Principles and Acts of the Revolution*. Baltimore, 1882.

    Niles, editor of the *Baltimore Register*, presented randomly "speeches, orations, and proceedings, with sketches and remarks" to preserve data on the American Revolution. The first entries are the Boston Massacre orations. Brief index. Commager said in a 1965 reissue of Niles's work [*Chronicles of the American Revolution*, ed. A. T. Vaughan (New York: Grosset & Dunlap, Inc.), which abridges Hancock's speech (pp. 76-80) but which offers a reminiscence of the Boston Massacre (pp. 31-33)] that Niles's work was valuable for three reasons: first of its kind; material well selected; and covered entire Revolution. See also an 1876 reissue of Niles, ed. S. V. Niles (Cranbury, N. J.: A. S. Barnes & Co., Inc.), which regrouped material under colonies.

16. Sears, Lorenzo, *John Hancock: The Picturesque Patriot.* Boston, 1912.

Factual. Good footnote references. No bibliography. Index.

17. Sullivan, William, *Familiar Letters on Public Characters . . .* Boston, 1834.

Largely reminiscences about Jefferson; valuable for Hancock's appearance in 1782.

18. Thacher, Peter, *Sermon Preached to the Society in Brattle Street, Boston, and Occasioned by the Death of His Excellency John Hancock . . .* Boston: Alexander Young, 1793.

A 30-page sermon by Hancock's pastor portraying the official attitude toward Hancock at the time of his death.

19. Thomas, Ebenezer Smith, *Reminiscences of the Last Sixty-Five Years,* 2 vols. Hartford: Case, Tiffany & Burnham, 1840.

In addition to reprinting the letter from Noah Webster to Thomas (see #11 sup.), Thomas offers (I, 243-47) a brief sketch of Hancock with references to his abilities as a speaker.

20. Wagner, Frederick, *Patriot's Choice: The Story of John Hancock.* New York: Dodd, Mead & Co., 1964.

The most recent biography of Hancock, short, good bibliography divided into primary and secondary sources. See chapter entitled "The Bloody Scuffle in King Street . . . and a Party on Griffin's Warf."

21. Wells, William V., *The Life and Public Services of Samuel Adams,* 3 vols. Boston: Little, Brown and Co., 1865.

Index in volume 3 has numerous references to Hancock and in particular, authorship and delivery of Boston Massacre address (II, 137-40.).

Questions for Discussion

1. How do the themes of nationalism, religion, human rights, and internationalism appear in Hancock's speech?

2. What words and phrases in the Hancock speech do you consider examples of the use of the costume of words? Consider his usage of the words *patriot*(ism), *villain, justice, besom, righteous government,* and *rights and liberties.*

3. Examine the Boston Massacre speeches of 1771, 1772, and 1773 to see how closely their use of the costume of words resembles Hancock's.

4. Compare Hancock's Boston Massacre address with an occasional speech by a contemporary senator speaking on a cause to which he is highly dedicated.[14] Discuss why Hancock's rhetoric is revolutionary and the senator's is not.

5. Compare the account of the Boston Massacre in Thomas (*24,* II, 212-18) with the description in Chapter VII of Miller's *Sam Adams* (*14,* 166-92). Note additional details that would increase the emotional impact of Hancock's speech.

6. To what extent did Hancock advocate lawlessness in his Boston Massacre address?

7. Examine three of the five Hancock biographies listed in the bibliography and discuss why you think Hancock turned into a revolutionist.

8. Compare unlawful acts of today with the unlawful acts of the Bostonians during the American Revolution (i.e., the Tea Party, the sacking of the lieutenant governor's mansion, the running of the customs officials out of Boston, and so on).

9. Read Thomas's descriptions of John Hancock (*19,* I, 243-47) and of Sam Adams (*19,* I, 252-55) and be prepared to add from these accounts any items that you think contribute to the credibility of either man.

10. Contrast the emotional impact of the Hancock speech with the emotional impact of the Castro speech, particularly concerning the manner in which the speakers employ *argumentum ad misericordiam* and *argumentum ad hominem.*

[14] Examine the *Appendix* to the *Congressional Record, Vital Speeches, The Chicago Tribune, The New York Times* and similar sources for your occasional address.

Exercises

1. Imagine that you are a member of one of the Communist European satellite countries and that freedom of speech is permitted. Write a speech to be given to a group of patriots as much in the Hancock tradition as possible, protesting Soviet occupation.

2. Rewrite the introduction and the conclusion, composing a transition to go between the Virgil quotation and the introduction, and between the conclusion and the biblical quotation.

3. Choose 500 words from the speech and practice delivering them from manuscript. Note the adjustments in delivery that you feel you must make in order to do an effective presentation. How much like a revolutionist do you feel?

4. Rewrite the speech, keeping the rhetoric tumid but using flowery language that is modern in character. Use the Kennedy inaugural as an example of a contemporary style that approaches the tumid.

5. Select from the Declaration of Independence and the Constitution five examples of the costume of words of the American Revolution and rewrite the Hancock speech, using each of those five examples at least six times in the speech.

Georges Jacques Danton
(1759-1794)

A Friend and Foe Alike

This brief preface to Danton's speech of March 27, 1793 will summarize the primary sources that many libraries will not have available and/or that, because they are in French, would prove a hardship to some readers. There are two obstacles to doing adequate background research on Danton: first, because Danton was not a philosopher like Robespierre, research on his career has been sporadic, has been largely limited to materials in French, and has appeared in rare publications; second, Danton's strange mixture of personality characteristics biased many scholars into making him either a friend or a foe. These few pages summarizing obscure French sources will take the position that Danton was both friend and foe—a friend in that he almost succeeded in establishing democracy in Western Europe at a most critical period; and a foe because his lusty and raucous personality, coupled with a penetrating wit, made him use such fear tactics as an adversary that the degree to which he ridiculed his opponents seems too harsh to be constructive.

George Jacques Danton was of peasant stock from Arcis-sur-Arbe in Champagne. Two encounters with bulls and one with smallpox had left him disfigured, but his height, broad shoulders and bull neck gave him a forceful appearance. After getting a rudimentary education at Troyes, Danton was apprenticed in Paris to study his father's profession of law. Six years later, in 1785, Danton was admitted to the bar at Rheims.

In 1787, his father-in-law assisted Danton in purchasing the right to become one of the 73 *advocates aux conseils du roi*, entitling him to act as public prosecutor as well as defense attorney. His marriage to the daughter of an influential cafe owner of the Cordeliers district had also cast his lot with an area populated with petit bourgeois and laborers, flavored with actors and journalists. Although the district meetings in Danton's section of Paris may have been frequented by some persons of questionable repute, they were led by well-educated, liberal-minded bourgeois.

The history of the Cordeliers Club and Danton's role as district leader are somewhat obscure. Danton spoke as early as July 13, 1789, calling his district to arms to protect themselves from the troops Louis was supposedly assembling at Versailles, but there is no mention of him at the Bastille on the following day. Again, on the third of October, an eyewitness described Danton's harangue on the eve of the march to Versailles, but there is no eyewitness to Danton at Versailles. In January of 1790, Danton defied Lafayette's troops sent to his district to arrest Marat. In November of 1790, Danton was named Commandant of the Cordeliers Batallion of the National Guard. By January 31, 1791, he was one of thirty-six administrators to the Department of Paris. It was in this dual capacity of military man and administrator that Danton defied Lafayette in April of 1791 by organizing the crowd that prevented the king from spending Easter at Saint Cloud. Again it was Danton and the Cordeliers who led the signing of the petitions on the *Champ de Mars* after the king's flight to Varennes.

A general amnesty for the perpetrators of the July petitions avoided a decision on his arrest. However, Danton's radicalism limited his popularity to his own district, as is evidenced by his defeat for a seat in the Legislative Assembly in October of 1791. But, by December of the same year, the Commune of Paris had elected him joint *député-procureur* (or prosecutor). The Brunswick Manifesto was followed by the mob attack on the Tuileries of August 10, 1792. The leadership of Danton as integrator of the attack is evidenced by his appointment to the six-man provisional executive council named by the Legislative Assembly on August 11, 1792. As minister of justice in a country whose civil institutions were in turmoil, Danton was virtual ruler of France, a situation that aroused jealousies and that forced Danton to exclude himself from subsequent ministries to avoid the stigma of *dictateur*. On August 11, 1792, Danton set about preparing France for invasion by the Prussians. His conduct during the prison massacres of September 2-6 has been largely exonerated. His election to the National Convention, which opened on September 20, 1792, forced Danton to submit his resignation as minister.

Danton's energies from August 10, 1792, until his arrest on March 31, 1794, were expended in trying to prevent invasion from without and dissention from within, so he spoke little and then only tersely. To create a strong executive, Danton sponsored the appointment of the Committee of Public Safety, and, on April 7, 1793, became a member of the first committee. His tendency toward moderation kept him from being named to the second Committee of Public Safety of July 10, 1793. In September, after six weeks in Arcis, he returned to find the extremists more firmly entrenched. Weary of bloodshed Danton approved of Desmoulins's publication of the *Vieux Cordelier*, a series of pamphlets that deplored the excesses of the Revolution and asked for a return to the spirit that had prompted the Cordeliers district to rebel back in 1789. The first issue appeared on December 5, 1793; the last was written by Desmoulins from prison in April of the following year.

From August 10, 1792, until April 5, 1794, Danton's speeches were recorded in the newspapers of Paris. Although he occasionally spoke before the Jacobins, he spoke more frequently to the assembly which met in the *Salle du Manège*, a former riding academy converted haphazardly into a legislative hall. To understand the significance of Danton's remarks on March 27, 1793, we must first understand the physical surroundings in which they were given. Reports on the *Salle du Manège* complained of poor acoustics, and it was only the orator with sufficient volume who could command attention. Speeches were therefore likely to be explosive in nature and were filled with the outbursts that characterized not only Gallican oratory in general but also that particular brand of Gallican oratory that makes sweeping pronouncements to attract attention. The plan of the former riding academy shows that its inordinate length and narrow width made it compare favorably with a small-town basketball court. The deputies sat on six tiers of seats in amphitheater style, forming a complete oval. In the center was a pit (*la piste* or riding track) where, until late 1791, there were two stoves. The president's box with places for his assistants was in the middle of the tiers of seats on one side, and directly opposite it were the tribune and the bar, with the pit, of course, in between. Arched windows, stretching from somewhat above the top tier of seats to the high ceiling, ran down the long sides of the rectangular structure. Flags hung down from the buttressed ceiling, which was 27 feet high. Balconies were at both ends, and others hung suspended over the side tiers.

Poor lighting, ventilation, and heating, coupled with ominous galleries for journalists and spectators, made the incubator for French democracy more like a boiler factory than a deliberative assembly. The *Journal de Paris* of November 10, 1789, reported that the voices of the speakers were absorbed rather than being projected and that the best of the orators could hardly be heard at the far ends. The *Journal de Paris* blamed the vaulted roof for the problems and was hopeful tht changes could be made. The Girondist orator Vergniaud, as chairman of a committee which reported to the assembly in

August of 1789 concerning a suitable meeting place for the legislature, recommended that another location be found and pointed out how much the hall affected the deliberations:

> I wish to say that it is impossible to establish order and to maintain silence in the present chamber. . . . There are many seats from which one cannot see the presiding officer nor be seen by him. It therefore follows that, if certain members forsake the important business of public interest to enter into private conversations, the presiding officer finds it impossible to interrupt them by a call to order, that if one wishes to get the floor, he must either inconvenience himself and trouble his neighbors to go take a place from which he can demand the floor from the president, or gain the president's attention by calling out loudly which interrupts the discussion and provokes new disturbances. . . . You have already noted, gentlemen, how our chamber is unpleasant and fatiguing for the orator. It condemns to a deadly silence . . . any man who does not have in his vocal organs the same depth and expanse of feeling that he has in his soul . . . and perhaps gives too much advantage to those who, with less intelligence, have a more sonorous voice and a more striking physical make-up *(19)*.

Not only did the physical characteristics of the *Salle du Manège* require an orator of particular abilities, but the nature of the gallery was highly instrumental in the way a speaker formed his remarks. Just before the overthrow of the king in August of 1792, Vaublanc complained bitterly about interference by the Parisian populace: "I beg you, Mr. President, to recall bluntly to the members of the assembly, who are responding by shouting to those whose shouting is more indecent yet, their duties as members. . . . If then these outbursts continue, I will make, not in a shouting mood, but coldly, the motion to leave Paris. . . . I maintain that it would be an act of courage for you to leave Paris, if you come to the conclusion that the people of this city wish to rule you, and if the galleries continue to insult, by their shouts, the national sovereignty . . ." *(13,* X, 334).

Danton developed a technique permitting him to command respect by making impressive pronouncements in a loud tone of voice. Danton's colleague Garat observed that Danton knew well how terrifying his person and his voice were and that Danton's style of speaking was singularly appropriate to his deportment and his voice quality *(8,* 188-90). Danton was described as having the voice of a Stentor. Certainly it took an orator with unusual abilities to electrify the deputies and the galleries in the incongruous *Salle du Manège,* and a speaker who succeeded might well have appeared as an ogre to a more dignified and shy deputy who realized with a sinking heart the hopelessness of his position.

To understand the significance of Danton's remarks on March 27, 1793, we must comprehend not only the characteristics of the hall but also the political game that Danton played. The Jacobins in general and Danton in particular had opposed declaring war on Austria, but the Girondists had prevailed, so that on April 20, 1792 the infant nation found itself at war. The strategy of the French general and would-be diplomat, Dumouriez, was to isolate Austria by keeping the other major powers neutral while France was achieving her long-lived ambitions in Flanders and in Northern Italy. However, the émigrés succeeded in enlisting the aid of the King of Prussia, and on July 25, 1792 the Duke of Brunswick issued his threatening manifesto in behalf of the allied armies of Austria and Prussia. The manifesto was a major factor in the overthrow of the king on August 10, 1792, and in the prison massacres in early September. England had wanted to remain neutral, but the execution of Louis in January of 1793 made Pitt's position very difficult. The French forced the hand of the British by declaring war on England on February 1, 1793. Spain joined the war against France on March 7, 1793. Dumouriez's strategy, therefore, was unsuccessful.

At the outset of the war, there were both successes and failures for the French, but the successes were sufficient to hearten Paris and the assembly. Once war was declared, Danton threw aside his opposition and exerted his energies in securing victory. But the armies of the new Republic, in spite of some excellent leadership and some valiant fighting, had retreated, so that by early March gains in Flanders and the Rhineland had been largely erased. As usual, events at the front had an immediate effect upon Paris. On March 8, Danton had made a great speech trying to reconcile the unhappy General Dumouriez at the front with the unhappy assembly in Paris. But the general remained skeptical and the assembly decided to redouble its efforts against counter revolutionaries by creating the Revolutionary Tribunal, later to become the chief instrument of the terror. Danton knew well that jealousy, suspicion, anger, and hate were not the best weapons with which to fight the allies. Because of the refusal of the assembly to follow British tradition in allowing members of the assembly to serve as ministers, Danton had had to give up his post as attorney general in the fall of 1792. What means did he have at his command to set the affairs of government straight? As a deputy on mission to the front, he could do all in his power to coordinate affairs in Paris with the desires of Dumouriez; as a member of the assembly, he could caution about the inevitable outcome of the dissent and confusion he saw on all sides. But this is all he could do, and his frustration equaled Mirabeau's at not being able to put things straight when he knew so well how to do so. On November 7, 1789, Mirabeau saw how to reconcile the king and the assembly, but the assembly refused to allow him a ministerial post where he could effect the union. As a deputy on mission, Danton had done what he could with Dumouriez earlier in the month at Antwerp. Now he had returned to

Paris to try to bolster the assembly and to reduce its bickering. Because of the nature of the assembly, he could not confront it directly with its shortcomings. He could, however, indulge in self-criticism that would indirectly reflect upon the delegates; he could attack persons not in the assembly for the same shortcomings he wished to call to the attention of the delegates; and he could grandstand to the galleries by proposing some extravagant gesture which would make it appear that, since the deputies could not be counted upon to do the job, the good people of France would do it for them. So Danton pointed out that he did not object to personal criticism as long as he knew he was serving his country (and therefore that the deputies should not object to criticism if they were doing the same); he pointed to Roland, who was not a member of the assembly, to illustrate what dissention could do; he called for the issuance of pikes to threaten the delegates with a peasant-based opposition. But the call for pikes would also offer the delegates the support of an armed populace, and it would make sufficient headlines in foreign newspapers to illustrate the determination of the French to resist. Danton knew with what horror the British would view this proposition to make an armed mob out of the French peasants. It was not until their desperation after the fall of Dunkirk that the British under Churchill were to make a similar gesture toward Hitler. Just as Churchill wanted everyone to feel a part of the resistance to Hitler, in spite of the fact that the population's efforts could really do little to stop a modern army, so Danton wanted the peasant to feel an integral part of the resistance to the allies. In World War II, Americans made similar gestures by buying war bonds, wrapping bandages, practicing blackouts, and holding mock air raids.

Danton made three important speeches in March on the same theme. His attempts to unite the assembly and the army on March 8 have already been noted. He made a second attempt on March 10. But his efforts of March 27 were chosen for this volume because they represent so clearly Danton at his best and at his worst, the friend and foe alike. The treason of Dumouriez to the Austrians was only a few days away. Danton had just returned from the front where he saw much to be desired, and now he had rejoined the assembly where things were going equally bad. Danton was close to desperation. He knew what had to be done. Neither Danton nor Mirabeau was a political theorist as was Robespierre. They were both pragmatists. Politics was the science of the possible. Danton knew that the French could stop their bickering and defeat the allies, so he exerted all of his energies to that end. The result was not a philosophical discourse, but political common sense. The French Assembly needed a pep talk, and Danton gave them a magnificent one. Pep talks, although they may have been magnificent in their time, are mundane in retrospect, unless the dynamic situation in which the pep talk was given can be recreated. We must recall that the enemy was on the frontier and advancing, that the French commander was on the brink of treason, that the assembly was more often consumed with recrimination and jealousy than with pursuing the war, and that only a handful of people saw what had to be done to save the day. If one can role play these pressures, he can sense how important it was for a person with a dynamic personality to step in with as blunt a costume of words as the situation would allow and make a dynamic gesture like a flag behind which the French could rally.

Perhaps Danton's rhetoric has suffered because the force of his words was not great enough. He did win that particular battle, because the Revolutionary Tribunal that he and others were calling for was established and the resolution to authorize the distribution of pikes was passed. The tribunal, of course, did prosper, to the extent that it eventually took Danton's life. The exact effect of the legislation on pikes is difficult to determine. Although it was meant more as a gesture than as a military maneuver, it is interesting to explore the extent to which the decree was put into effect. The pikes that Danton was talking about were not to go to any of the four existing types of soldiers[1] but to peasants. How many pikes were issued? Some, because on May 3 and July 15, 1793, the assembly was asked for funds to pay for pikes authorized on March 27; and on July 24, funds were voted to pay for their manufacture.[2]

Even though Danton did win the immediate battle by motivating the assembly into concerted action against the enemy, he lost the war against disunion and ended up giving his life for France. How much stature his words of March 27 would now have had he succeeded in stabilizing France is difficult to determine. How different Europe would have been had Danton established in France a democracy to which other European countries could have looked for guidance! It is highly likely that Danton understood better than anyone since Mirabeau what had to be done to save the French Revolution and that he used all his powers to achieve those ends. He failed. Danton is dead. Long live the Republic!

[1] At the time Danton spoke, there were four types of French soldiers: the remnants of the royal mercenary armies then fighting under revolutionary generals; the national guardsmen; the *fédérés*; and the volunteers that had enlisted to defend their country. It was not until June 2, 1793, that the Convention approved "une armée révolutionnaire." However, because of fear as to who would control such an army, it was not until the following September, after the treason at Toulon, that approval was given to the creation of a force of 30,000 men (*4*, II, 40-58).

[2] On July 24, Minister of Interior Garat was reminded that the assembly wanted an accounting of what happened to the much larger sum appropriated for pikes by the Legislative Assembly to implement a similar law of April, 1792.

How Can France Be Saved?
Comment sauver la France?

March 27, 1793
The National Convention
Salle du Manège,
Paris

[From his seat] I want to say that absolutely nobody can influence the decisions of the minister [of war] [3] I acknowledge that I myself have recommended to the minister some excellent patriots who will serve the Republic well in the posts that will be entrusted to them. There is no law which can take a representative's opinion away from him. The old law that has been brought up was absurd. It has been revoked by the Revolution. The National Convention must be a revolutionary body. It must be peopled like the people themselves, if it wants to save the people.

It is time for us to declare war on our enemies within. What's this, citizens, civil war has broken out everywhere and the National Convention remains immobile! Indeed yes, citizens, everywhere the old aristocracy is insolently rearing its head. You have approved a tribunal to cut off the heads of the guilty, and your tribunal is not even organized yet? [4] What are the people going to say about this, because they are ready to rise up *en masse*? [Prolonged applause from the galleries and from the Mountain (the left). Some murmurs to the contrary from the right. "Oui, oui, oui" came from all parts of the chamber, followed by applause and again, "oui, oui."] [Danton coming up to the speaker's stand.] What are the people going to say about this,

This translation follows the version in the Paris newspaper, *Le Logotachigraphe*, with amendments from versions reported in *Le Journal des Débats et des Décrets*, *Le Républicain Français*, *l'Auditeur National*, *Le Moniteur Universel*, and the reconstituted version in vol. LX, 1st ser., pp. 603-5 of *Archives Parlementaires*.

[3] The minister of war was Pierre de Bournonville who had taken office on February 4, 1793. He left office on March 28, 1793, two days after this speech. Albitte had moved that the minister of war submit an account of all flag officers. Ducos, a Girondist, had moved to amend by asking for a statement of the recommendations on file for each such officer, to see if the deputies had been influencing the minister of war in his appointments. Since Danton was highly involved in vitalizing the army, he knew the references were partially aimed at him. Therefore, he answered his critics.

[4] The Revolutionary Tribunal of Paris was decreed on March 10, 1793, but was not appointed until shortly after Danton's speech. In April of 1793, it executed nine persons, the first on April 15.

because they see it and they feel it. [More cries of "Oui, oui." Outburst of applause.] They are going to say: "What's going on here! Some pretty miserable passions are influencing our representatives while they ought to be directing their energy against both the enemy within and the enemy abroad."

Citizens, I must at last tell the truth, and I'm going to say it right out. What do all these trifles anyone can think up mean to me, as long as I can serve my country! Yes, citizens, you are not doing your duty. You say that the people are being led astray? Yes, without doubt, there are men wicked enough to lead them astray. But if, when you are not at your desks, if you would go out all over Paris, this same people would listen to reason. Because, mark it well, the revolution could not have been accomplished except by the people themselves. They are its instrument, and it is up to you to direct that instrument.

It's vain for you to say that the popular societies are swarming with citizens who are busy denouncing everyone in an absurd way, in an atrocious way. Well, why don't you go and remind them of their confusion? Do you think you can do it by describing the overzealous patriot as a fool? Revolutions stir up every passion. A great nation in revolution is like a metal seething in the furnace; the statue of liberty is not yet cast, the metal is in a state of flux; if you do not know how to handle the furnace, you will all be devoured by it. [Renewed applause].

Why can't you sense that this very day we must enact a decree that will cause all the enemies of the nation to tremble? We must declare that, in every municipality, there will be given to all citizens at the expense of the rich who shall make a contribution (and they must pay up, private property will not be violated), we must, I say, decree that every citizen have a pike paid for by the nation.

Don't ever forget that at Orleans, if there had been pikes, your commissioners would never have been assassinated.[5] You have been told (the record attests to it[6]) that there were not twenty just plain armed people to repulse those who tried to kill Bourdon.[7] Well, citizens, we must see to it, as I have

<hr>

[5] Vos commissaires n'auraient pas été assassinés. A puzzling use of the conditional, since the commissioners were only beaten, not killed.

[6] See the *séances* of March 18 and March 23, 1793, for accounts of the debates on Orleans.

[7] On March 15, 1793, Léonard Bourdon was sent on business by the Convention to his own department. Walter stated that, one evening, when Bourdon was drunk, he picked a quarrel with a sentry. A scuffle ensued involving passersby, and Bourdon received some nasty licks. As a result, Orleans was declared in a state of rebellion and 40 of its citizens were brought to Paris before the Revolutionary Tribunal (*13*, II, 1239-40).

just said, that every citizen has a pike. We must declare that, in the towns, in the departments where the revolt is manifesting itself, that whosoever is audacious enough to call for the counterrevolution, to manifest perverse ideas, to invoke every possible misfortune on his country, is an outlaw. [Applause.] At Rome (and, at that epoch, the republic was in no greater danger than is ours), Valerius Publicola had the courage to have a law passed that permitted any Roman citizen to execute anyone who might propose to reestablish the tyranny.[8] Well, as for me, I want to point out that, since counterrevolution has been publicly proposed— in the streets, in public places, patriots are being insulted—that since at all types of entertainment the misfortunes of the country are being furiously applauded, I want to make it clear, I tell you, that anyone who has the audacity to vow before me to forward the counterrevolution and to upset, as has been done, those who are in power, he will have to pay for it at my hands, and, afterwards, let my head fall—at least I shall have given a great example of virtue to my country. [Universal applause.]

I ask that we pass on to the orders of the day concerning the motion which has given rise to this unprepared speech that I am making, that every citizen, every individual, no matter how little favored by fortune, be armed with a pike at the expense of the nation. I ask that the tribunal, established to strike down the counterrevolutionaries, be put without delay into full force. I ask that the Convention declare to the French people, to Europe, to the universe, that it is a revolutionary body, that it is resolved to maintain liberty, to stamp out all the serpents which are rendering its bosom asunder, to stamp out every monster, by virtue of an extremely revolutionary law, if that be necessary. I ask that this not be a proclamation of little significance, but a declaration made by men who sense vividly the mission that the people have bestowed upon them. You yourselves declare war on all the aristocrats. Say that the public welfare requires laws over and above all ordinary measures. Show that you are revolutionary, show that you are a nation, and then liberty is no longer in peril.

Well then, nothing will really be lost, because, do not mistake it, citizens, nations who wish to be truly great, must be, just like individuals, brought up through the school of misfortune. No doubt we have had some reverses, but, mind you, at the time when everything in Europe was combining to destroy you, at the time when the old despotism was using the people themselves in

---

[8]Valerius Publicola (the people's friend) was instrumental in the overthrow of the Tarquins. When the king and his allies moved against Rome in 509, Valerius met and defeated them. He then had a law passed providing that one who attempted to become king could be killed by anyone.

order to delay the time of their fall; if, back in September, when all appeared so desperate, someone had said to you, the tyrant is going to perish under the sword of the law, the enemy will be routed, you will have 100,000 men at Mayence,[9] you will occupy a portion of the enemy territory,[10] you will also be in Tournay,[11] who would not have believed that the liberty of France was forever assured by such rapid successes. Well, in spite of our reverses, this is again our position. Is it so desperate?

Consider what our resources are now! But, as for our resources, it's up to us to direct them. You have lost some precious time in vain debating; you will have to make it up; you have allowed yourselves to be led astray by a very cruel scheme. You have been told that the Revolution had been completed, that the only thing left were more *désorganisateurs* and more *factieux*.[12] Well, these very same *factieux* are falling under the blows of the assassins. And thou, Peletier,[13] while thou wert perishing for thine hatred for tyrants, thou wert also a *factieux*. Thou hast been painted as such, and the monsters have pierced thy side.

We must get out of this political lethargy which has made us lose our way. A scheme worse than aristocracy has portrayed to all of France any man who has had character as a monster, as a scoundrel. France has been powerless. She has not known to what individuals, to what ideas she ought to turn. Happily, enlightenment is spreading among all men. Marseilles already knows that Paris has never sought to crush the Republic, as one would like you to believe, that Paris has only sought liberty. Marseilles is known as the Mountain of the Republic. She will swell, this Mountain, and she will roll the rocks of liberty over all the monsters who are seeking tyranny and oppression.[14] [Universal applause.]

[9] On October 21, 1792, the French general Custine conquered Mayence, a town on the left bank of the Rhine, but on March 3, 1793 it was besieged and finally surrendered to the allies on July 13, 1793.

[10] Presumably a reference to the annexation of the provinces of Nice and Savoy.

[11] After the battle of Jemnapes, the French General La Bourdonnage entered Tournay on November 8, 1792. The Austrians reentered Tournay on April 30, 1793.

[12] The words *désorganisateur* and *factieux* are only partially translated by the English word *dissenter*. They pertain to persons interested in splintering movements into smaller and smaller parts.

[13] Louis Michel le Peletier de Saint-Fargeau (1760-1793), a liberal nobleman who embraced the Revolution, was murdered by a royalist as he was eating dinner in a restaurant in the Palis Royal.

[14] Lyon, Bordeaux, and Caen as Girondist strongholds were suspicious of Paris, while the Vendée was in open revolt. Marseilles, with a strong Jacobin element, had begun to cooperate more fully with Paris, until the arrest of the Girondists on June 2, 1793, again made them rebel.

I do not want to revive the unfortunate debates, I do not want to recount the history of the persecutions that patriots have had to suffer through. We all have our own shortcomings. For, if it were in my nature to enter into detail, I could tell you myself that a general who has been so much praised [15] has been subsequently led toward his ruin, and has been made to lose his popularity by stirring him up against the people themselves. Roland [16] (I shall cite you only a single fact, and then I beg you to forget it)—Roland wrote to Dumouriez (and it is the general himself who showed it to me and Lacroix [17]): "You must join with us to destroy that party of Paris and especially that Danton." [Stir of indignation.] Consider, citizens, how similar examples, consider how an imagination, smitten to the point of producing such opinions, how a man located at the core of the Republic, must have had such a deadly influence. But let us pass on and pull the curtain over these things.

We must reunite. And this reunion must establish liberty from one pole to the other, in both hemispheres, and throughout the Convention. Well, let us stamp out our differences. I do not ask for half hearted embracing—individual antipathies are indestructible—but rather what is basic to our welfare, and I am so convinced that it is an atrocious crime to cast aspersions on the National Assembly that I take a solemn oath to die to defend my most cruel enemy.

I ask that this sacred sentiment enkindle all souls, that for himself at least, or for his own safety, that each member of the Assembly believe that, above all, we must kill the enemies within, because we must be victims either of our passions or of our ignorance, if we do not save the Republic.

What am I trying to say! The Republic is immortal. Certainly the enemy could very well make some progress, he could well seize some more territory, but he would be destroyed in the heart of France. I have seen the new reinforcements which are being led to the frontier. Here we have the true children of liberty. In the departments that I have been passing through, I have found that measue of devotion which presages terrible things for our enemies. They have had some successes. Right now, while we are deliberating, their despots have strengthened their forces and have made us recoil. But, in

[15] A reference to General Charles Dumouriez who later defected to the Austrians.

[16] Jean Marie Roland was, with one small interruption, minister of the interior from March 23, 1792, until March 14, 1793. There was no love lost between Danton and Roland and his famous wife, Manon.

[17] Jean François Delacroix who went on mission with Danton to Belgium in the winter of 1792 to 1793. Note that Danton refers to Delacroix and Le Peletier by their most plebian names.

recoiling and falling back onto the land of their own country, the French, like the giant in the fable, are gaining renewed vigor.[18] [Applause.]

I ask you to pass this law, citizens, that I have proposed to you. But I insist on something more than just a law, on just what necessity commands you to do. It is imperative that you be the very people themselves; it is imperative that every man in whom there rests some spark of patriotism, that every man who still wishes to show that he is a Frenchman should not remove himself from the people. It is the people who have produced us. We are not their father; we are rather their children. [Applause.] Well, this father, if he should be led astray, we owe him our understanding, our affection, and our attention. Let us reveal to him what we want, our means of defense, our resources. Let us say to him (not just to flatter him) that he will become invincible if he should become united.

In this regard, I will cite a single fact. Let us recall the terrible revolution of August 1.[19] Then all Paris was afire. All passions were stirred. Paris did not wish to leave her walls. Excellent patriots dreaded to abandon their homes because they feared the enemy and conspirators within. All seemed to presage a tearing asunder. I myself (because it is sometimes highly necessary to refer to yourself), I, as I said, brought the Executive Council, the sectional councils, the municipality, the members of the Commune, the members of the committees of the Legislative Assembly together in a friendly reunion at the town hall.[20] We were then a very sizable assembly. We devised there, in concert, the measures that had to be taken. Each section commissioner carried them back to his people. The people applauded them, backed us up, and we were victorious.

Citizens, let us communicate our knowledge to one another. Let us not swerve from our duties. Let us not hate one another. Let us mingle our feelings with those of the people! If we draw near to them, if we can feel affectionate toward the popular societies, in spite of what may be defective

[18]The giant Alcyoners who, after being shot with an arrow by Hercules, was dragged outside Pallene to die, because he was immortal in the land in which he had been born.

[19]The day on which Louis XVI was overthrown and the Republic founded.

[20]The cabinet of ministers appointed on August 10, 1792, by the Legislative Assembly; the leaders of the 48 sections into which Paris had been divided in 1790; the municipality of Paris, presumably the remnants of the old Paris Commune that had governed the city since May 21, 1790; the *commune insurrectionelle* or Revolutionary Commune inaugurated by the more radical sections of the city during August 9 and 10, 1792, and which replaced the old commune shortly thereafter; the Committee of Twenty-One, an arm of the Legislative Assembly that began as 12 members, was increased to 18 and finally to 21, a forerunner of the National Convention's Committee of Public Safety and the ruler of Paris from August 10, 1792, until the opening of the National Convention on September 21, 1792.

about them (because nothing human is perfect), well, we would thereby develop a union of forces, of actions, of support against the enemy, which would assure to the nation new triumphs and new successes.

I insist then on the necessity of this measure (all errors and all passions put aside) to reach this salutary goal. France will regain its force, France will return victorious, and soon the despots will be sorry for having pushed us back, because a defeat more complete and more terrible is awaiting them.

I ask that my proposition to arm all Frenchmen, at least with a pike, be put to a vote[21]; that the Revolutionary Tribunal be put into action; and that you make a manifest declaration which will be sent to all the departments, by which you will announce to the French people that you will be as terrible as they, that you will enact every law necessary to abolish slavery forever, and that there is no longer either peace nor truce between you and our enemies. [Outburst of applause.]

The Revolt Rhetoric of Danton

Danton delivered few formal speeches. He was not Hoffer's man of words and was therefore not dominant in the first stage of the French Revolution. There are no records of speech notes of manuscripts. Danton boasted that he wrote nothing at all, that he detested writing.[22] What speeches remain are not eloquent. They are purposefully inelegant. Perhaps his speeches to the Cordeliers during the first stage of the revolt were eloquent, but they have been lost. Danton's rhetoric demonstrates the ambivalence of a man of action during the second stage of a revolution who has had to interrupt his absorbing administrative duties in an attempt to bridge the gap between a revolution ruled during peacetime by deliberation and a revolution ruled during wartime by executive action. The honeymoon stage of the French Revolution had ended, requiring that philosophical thought be replaced with efficient administration. However the assembly was jealously guarding its rights. Danton made strange noises for a compromiser, but that is what he was. The men of words and the men of action were not to be successfully reconciled. No wonder that Danton's rhetoric was doomed to failure.

In what state of repair has Danton's rhetoric been preserved? The only

[21]The three Danton resolutions were decreed immediately.

[22]The French National Archives have only two letters that are probably in Danton's handwriting. Even his characteristic signature was often stamped on documents, a custom not widespread in the years 1792 and 1793.

record of his speeches consists of newspaper coverage. But there was not much type space available for the debates in the best of the journals, for they consisted of only a few pages. Occasionally a new journal would appear, such as the *Logotachigraphe* (January 1-May 10, 1793), which, by extending its coverage of the assembly, would force the other newspapers to improve their reporting. But economy always dictated restraint.

Furthermore Danton spoke only when provoked so that, with few exceptions, his speeches were not planned but formed a part of a general debate. Such short and blunt comments could be slighted by reporters who were not furnished copies of Danton's remarks, in contrast to many of the other orators whose speeches had been planned in advance. Danton's patience was sorely tried by his contemporaries. He was a man of action first and a man of words second. He had little tolerance with continual bickering and personal animosity. He was not able to understand how men could quibble when foreign armies were invading France and when the fate of the Revolution was at stake. When he had had more of the insinuations and innuendos than he could take, he gave his own inimitable brand of the pep talk.

Danton's rhetoric was suitable to the *Salle du Manège* with its shape of a basketball court. His remarks on the floor are highly comparable to the rhetoric used by the coach in the locker room between halves, when the play has been choppy, when each player has tried to be a star, and when the players cannot meet the attack of the opposition. The team needs upbraiding; it needs complimenting; it needs to be provoked; it needs to find an excuse for its mistakes. To achieve such a multiplicity of contrary purposes, who could ask for a consistent, logical, and straightforward approach? The coach senses what he has to do. Danton knew what it would take to arouse the legislature, and he spoke until he sensed that his job was done.

In retrospect Danton often appears blustering, vain, and erratic. His harangues cannot be outlined. But they are bold, brash, and brilliant. What then is to be learned about the rhetoric of revolt from Danton?

Invention

Danton's agitation is multiphasic. He is in so many places at once and is using so many aspects of rhetoric at once that he is difficult to attack. He is like the *guerrilla* who strikes quickly and then eludes the regular troops who are following the established rules of warfare.

Danton's multiple arguments, so triggerlike in character, illustrate three aspects of his revolt rhetoric. First, during stage one of the French Revolution, Danton had grown accustomed to advocating lawlessness. Then, during the second stage, he found that he himself was the law. How therefore could he advocate lawlessness to himself? This adjustment from the oppressed to the oppressor is generally difficult for revolutionists. In arguing for the issuance of pikes, Danton could sense the vigor of his former cries for destruction without calling for his own destruction. The Old Cordelier could ride again. Patriots who had been effective against the Old Regime by promoting lawlessness before the revolution were patriots who could be effective against the Old Regime by taking the law into their own hands after the Revolution. The issuance of pikes to the general public was tantamount to making every Frenchman a vigilante. Hence lawlessness par excellence.

Second, Danton argued heavily for nationalism. What had been a revolution for human rights modified itself quickly into a revolution for nationalism once France had been attacked by the allies. The human rights that had been gained were to be maintained ("I ask that the Convention declare . . . that it is resolved to maintain liberty . . ."), but the integrity of France had to be preserved ("The Republic is immortal"). A similar shift of emphasis occurred also in the American and Russian revolutions when the struggle for human rights had to be superseded by a struggle for nationalism. Only in America was the emphasis returned to human rights once the outside threat had been relieved. France went from 1795 to 1871 before a sustained attention to human rights was possible, while Russia has gone from 1917 to the present without making the transition. Perhaps if the tsar had been overthrown in peacetime, the rhetoric of the Russian Revolution would have reflected the theme of human rights without its being superseded by nationalism.

Third, Danton's rhetoric did not assist him in clarifying his long range goals. He wanted France free, but he failed to clarify how a free France should be governed. In this respect he was both a victim of his times and a victim of his own rhetoric. So fierce were the jealousies in the assembly, so ingrained were the inferiority complexes of the bourgeois so long treated as second-class citizens by the aristocracy, and so threatening was Danton's powerful personality on men who were inexperienced in governing and often of mediocre ability that Danton would have been highly suspect had he proposed anything more than situational politics. Furthermore Danton's rhetoric had taught him to take one hurdle at a time, to storm one bastion and then look at tomorrow. Now that we have a full perspective on the Revolution and the way the war was progressing, it seems ungrateful to ask for more. But because Danton did not do the next to impossible, he permitted the creation of a committee that destroyed him and the Revolution itself.

Danton's emotional persuasion is as guerrilla-like as are his arguments. His multiphasic approach included fear—the enemy is in our territory; pride—Frenchmen are impregnable on their own soil; pity—poor Peletier died for his country and I am willing to do the same; anger—how could Roland have said such a despicable thing; disgust—why cannot the assembly get about its important work; hate—down with the counterrevolutionaries; love—our regard for France and the Revolution, and so on.

There is some evidence. It is not free from bias, but Danton has seen the troops going to the front and he does know their demeanor. He does quote (?) from Roland's letter. He does have the latest information from the war front.

Danton's ethical appeals are as numerous and varied as are his arguments and his emotions. He acknowledges that he has recommended appointments to the minister of war, that he has to talk about himself, and that he is impervious to petty attack, improving his credibility through confession. He surrounds his entire speech with an aura of honesty, as if to say that these words have cost him a great deal, but that there was nothing else he could do. He qualifies himself as an expert, as having the latest information from the fronts and possessing intimate knowledge of what is transpiring in the government. His intent, he says, is unselfish and laudable. All he wishes is for France and the Revolution to prosper.

Organization

With such a variety of emotions and arguments to handle, it is to be expected that Danton's organization was unorthodox and elusive. How annoying it must have been to those Frenchmen of the Age of Enlightenment who wanted a deliberate treatment of the problem. But Danton knew that, for many in the assembly, deliberation was not called for. The assembly had to be cajoled into action. What it had to do was so elementary that to point it out in an organized way would have been insulting. Therefore, although Danton may well have had a plan of attack, he was going to make certain that his victims could not perceive it and thus not trace his course of action.

Style

Danton's use of language illustrates four aspects of the rhetoric of revolt: first, a prolific use of the costume of words; second, an effective employment during the second stage of the revolution of *argumentum ad hominem;* third, the fear of Thermidor; and fourth, the impatient, conversational style of the man of action who is tired of words and wishes to substitute deeds instead.

In volume three of *A History of the English Speaking Peoples* entitled "The Age of Revolution," Winston Churchill said, in what could be construed as a condescending manner, that the radical element in America began to call themselves "patriots." And so they did in the French Revolution as well. Danton's positive phraseology of identification included the frequent use of the following terms: *patriots, Republic, Revolution, people, citizens,* and *liberty.* His negative cluster of terms involved *tyranny, monster, despots, slavery, scoundrels, counterrevolution,* and *enemies.* The positive terminology outnumbered his pessimistic terms 67 to 27, demonstrating that Danton was trying desperately to emphasize the favorable aspects of the Revolution. It is not surprising to find that "citoyens" appears as a part of Danton's costume of words, but it is surprising that the Revolution had not created a term similar to "fifth column" to replace Danton's clumsy expressions such as "nos ennemis intérieurs" and "les conspirations intérieures." A good example of how frequently the orator can use his costume of words without risking boredom is the sentence: "elle doit être peuple comme le peuple luimême, si elle veut sauver le peuple." References such as "le salut public" and "notre salut" show the influence of Rousseau. One of the passages in which Danton concentrated his phraseology of identification demonstrates how the costume of words can be used effectively and artistically:

> Je demande que le tribunal établi pour frapper les *contre-révolutionnaires*, soit, sans délai, mis en pleine activité. Je demande que la Convention déclare à l'univers entier, au *peuple français*, qu'elle est *révolutionnaire*, qu'elle maintiendra la *liberté*, qu'elle a resolu d'étouffer tous les *serpents* qui déchirent son *sein*, d'écraser tous les *monstres*, en vertu d'une loi extrêmement *révolutionnaires*, si cela est nécessaire.

As will be noted later with Castro, Danton speaking extemporaneously used the device of anaphora to link his ideas. He utilized four sequences of ideas beginning with "je demande" until he elected to modify his pattern. Danton's use of the costume of words is no more dramatic or spectacular than is to be expected, but it was undoubtedly effective with a target that had long been deprived of using his positive terminology and that had long desired to use his negative terminology against the Old Regime.

The two examples of *argumentum ad hominem* directed at Roland and at Dumouriez are considered by some as part of that evidence that proves that Danton was never a statesman but only a politician. The fact that both men deserved to be attacked—that Roland was encouraging dissention and that Dumouriez did defect—softens only partially Danton's use of name-calling. So strong is the association between *argumentum ad hominem* and the unfavorable connotations of revolution that even today efforts by legislative bodies to reprimand or punish specific individuals are met with the accusation that the guillotine is being replaced in the *Place de la Concorde*. Therefore, although one journal records a "stir of indignation," it cannot be assumed that all of this emotion stemmed from sympathy toward Danton. A sizable portion of the indignation probably came from the Girondists who resented a public attack on one of their chief members. The fact that Danton had a long-outstanding feud with Roland and his wife Manon Roland did not increase the credibility of his attack. Why did Danton on one hand call for union and on the other partially destroy that call for union by using *argumentum ad hominem* against one of the major factions required to achieve union? The answer does not lie in Danton's particular personality, but in the inability of those revolutionaries unaccustomed to power to restrain from personal invective. Only tradition can prevent excesses of personal attack—the sort of tradition that has been established in London, Washington, Canberra, Toronto, etc. The National Convention did not have that tradition to lean on.

Danton's speech also shows in its style the fear of Thermidor. The monsters, the tyrants, the despots, the scoundrels (*les scélérats*, a word Danton liked to use), the enemies from without, and the enemies from within were all trying to produce counterrevolution, and even such extreme measures as making a vigilante of every citizen were justified to prevent a return to the Old Regime. For the most part, at this stage of the revolution, Danton appears justified in fearing Thermidor. The enemy from without and from within was genuinely threatening the Revolution. But his information on the incident at Orleans involving Bourdon was not correct and is illustrative of how quickly the revolutionary can overreact to a minor counterrevolutionary incident.

Danton's impatience with rhetoric during this second stage of the revolution is illustrated by his highly conversational style, bearing a few remnants of the figurative language of the man of words to satisfy the many representatives of the first stage of the revolution who were still active in the National Convention. Since Danton did not edit the newspaper accounts and since every effort has been made to keep his direct, informal style in the translation, even though it resulted in some substandard English with lapses in syntax and structural disturbances, the mixture of the man of action of the second stage of the revolution with the man of words of the first stage is readily apparent. Even though Danton protested that he detested to write and even though he preferred action to meaningless rhetoric, he could turn out a polished phrase when expediency required.

Delivery

Danton was anything but a polished orator. But he had learned how to move a crowd. He had a physique and a vocal apparatus that permitted an explosive delivery. Picture Danton seated to one side of the assembly, glowering, off by himself, surrounded by a few of his cronies. The room was stuffy. The debate was brittle. A few innuendos were passed. A few stupid statements were made. A few more deputies showed their desire to run the army. Everyone was protecting his own interests. Danton could take it no longer. He spoke out sharply from his place, not intending to get embroiled but unable to restrain himself. After some cryptic remarks from his seat, he strode up to the tribune, glaring around fiercely, allowing a dramatic pause here and there to let his words sink in, changing his pace abruptly from the bombastic to the subdued. His powerful voice filled the hall, so that the deputies who were accustomed to talking among themselves had to pay attention. Danton may well have been interrupted several times at those points where the speech exhibits a *non sequitur*.

There is no comment on how Danton spoke on March 27, 1793, but two eyewitnesses to Danton's earlier efforts before the Cordeliers justify him as both friend and foe. Lavaux described Danton speaking on July 13, 1798:

> It was Danton, my colleague, in whom I had always noted a just mind, a gentle, modest, and quiet demeanor. Imagine my surprise, in seeing him standing up on a table, shouting frantically, calling the people to arms, to repulse 15,000 brigands assembled at Montmartre, and an army of 30,000 men, ready to wipe out Paris, to lay it open to pillage, and to slaughter its inhabitants (9, 4).

Thibaudeau's description of October, 1789, is more complete:

> In the evening I went to the Cordeliers district. Danton was presiding. I had often heard him spoken of. I saw him for the first time. . . . I was struck by his height, by his athletic build, by the irregularity of his features slashed with smallpox, by his speech, biting, brisk, and resounding, by his dramatic gestures, by the mobility of his countenance, by his confidence and penetrating look, by the energy and the audacity with which his whole attitude and all his movements were stamped. . . . Danton . . . surrendered to the emotions, impetuosity was allowed free reign. The effect of this was prodigious. He presided with the resolution, the ability and the authority of a man who knew his power (17, 110).

Levasseur described Danton's demeanor later, during an attack by the Girondists in the assembly:

> Danton, immobile in his place, stuck out his lip with a scornful look which suited him and inspired terror; his countenance portrayed at the same time his anger and his disdain; his general demeanor contrasted with the movements of his face, and you could see in this bizarre mixture of calm and agitation that he did not interrupt his adversary because it would be easy for him to answer, and that he was certain of repudiating him (*10*, I, 138-9).

When the speaker had finished and was returning to his seat, Levasseur reported that Danton muttered under his breath: "the scoundrels! They want to foist off their crimes on us." "It was easy," continued Levasseur, "to see that his impetuous eloquence, so long held back, was about to break through all the dikes, and that our enemies had reason to tremble" (*10*, 138).

Conclusion

Had France been able to maintain a democracy from 1789 through 1870, a democracy which Danton knew how to lead to prosperity and stability, the British reforms of 1832 might have come easier and the European revolts of 1848 might have been moved up a number of years and had their chances for success materially increased. Such a vision of a nineteenth-century Europe enlightened not just by philosophical thought but by political action dramatizes the stakes for which Danton was fighting and brings us closer to a man who dedicated his life to the cause of freedom from tyranny.

Bibliography

1. Aulard, François Alphonse, *L'Eloquence Parlementaire pendant la Révolution Française: les Orateurs de la Législative et la Convention*, 2 vols. Paris, 1885-1886.

    Companion volume to *L'Eloquence Parlementaire pendant la Révolution Française: les Orateurs de l'Assemblée Constituante* (1882), by one of the outstanding historians of the French Revolution. A detailed account of Danton's rhetoric. No English translation. Reissued complete. Paris: E. Cornély, 1907, Avoid abridged edition *Les Grands Orateurs de la Révolution*. Paris: F. Rieder, 1914.

2. ——, "Le texte des discours de Danton," *La Révolution Française*, II (1882), 929-46.
   Discusses how Danton's speeches appeared in the French press.

3. Beesly, A. H., *Life of Danton*, 3rd ed. New York, 1899.
   Discusses March 27, 1793 speech (pp. 190-92) and his oratory (pp. 331-33).

4. Cobb, Richard, *Les Armées Révolutionnaires*. Paris: Mouton, 1961.
   A two-volume set giving some detail of how Danton's recommendation about pikes could be implemented.

5. Danton, Georges Jacques, *Discours*, ed. A. Fribourg, édition critique. Paris: E. Cornély, 1910.
   Augmentation of earlier article, "Méthode pour une édition critique des discours de Danton," *La Révolution Française*, LVI (1909), 105-13, explaining how Fribourg established definitive texts of Danton's speeches. The only reliable source for speech texts other than the Revolutionary journals. Avoid abridgment. Paris: Librairie Hachette, 1910.

6. ——, *Speeches*, translation not given, introduction Paul Frolich. New York: International Publishers, Co., Inc., 1928.
   Excerpts in English from several of Danton's speeches. Translation sometimes clumsy. Frequent abridgments not noted.

7. ——, Three speeches, translation not given. *Modern Eloquence*, XII, 799-803. Philadelphia, 1903.
   Short English excerpts from three of Danton's speeches: September 2, 1792; March 10, 1793; Apr., 27, 1793.

8. Garat, D. J., *Mémoire sur la Révolution*. Paris, 1795.
   Garat, journalist and lawyer, elected to the States General, succeeded Danton as minister of justice in 1792, discusses personal relationships with Danton.

9. Lavaux, Christophe, *Les Compagnes d'un Avocat* . . . Paris, 1815.
   Obscure memoirs valuable only for description of Danton before Cordeliers.

10. Levasseur, René, *Mémoires*, 4 vols. Paris, 1829.
    Levasseur, a physician elected to the Convention in 1792, gives interesting descriptions of Danton as orator. Authenticity of memoirs questioned.

11. Madelin, Louis, *Danton*, trans. Lady Mary Lloyd. London, 1926.
    Prosaic biography of Danton. Pp. 149-55 discuss Danton's oratory.

12. Michelet, Jules, *Histoire de la Révolution Française*, 2 vols., ed. Gérard Walter. Paris: Editions Gallimard, 1952.

Michelet, while at *Collège de France* between 1838 and 1851, published his history. It was reissued in 1952 with valuable notes by Walter, plus a list of Revolutionary personages and places. Since Michelet had access to sources since destroyed, history is considered a quasi-primary source.

13. *Moniteur, Réimpression de l'Ancien,* 32 vols. Paris: Réné, 1840-50.

Most famous of Revolutionary newspapers, reissued with introduction and table of contents. Since *Moniteur* itself began publication on November 24, 1789, issues between May 5 and November 24 are a compilation by editors.

14. Robinet, Jean François Eugène, *Danton, Homme d'Etat.* Paris, 1889.

The physician Robinet became Danton's champion, wrote widely in an effort to refute claims that Danton was responsible for prison massacres and that he stole money from state. Frequently discusses Danton as orator.

15. ——, *Danton, Mémoire sur sa Vie Privée.* Paris, 1865.

Vigorous defense of Danton's character. Contains interesting items, such as inventory of books in Danton's library (pp. 238-42.)

16. Stephens, H. M. ed., *The Principal Speeches of the Statesmen and Orators of the French Revolution, 1789-1795,* 2 vols. Oxford, 1892.

After Aulard's two volumes (sup. no. 1), most valuable source on rhetoric of French Revolution. Gives important speeches in French by eleven orators, with long introductory chapter in English and substantial chapters in English on most of the orators whose speeches are included.

17. Thibaudeau, Antoine Claire, *Mémoires, 1765-1792.* Paris, 1875.

Thibaudeau, son of a deputy to the States General and himself a deputy to the Convention, published these memoirs along with a two-volume set, *Mémoires sur la Convention et le Directoire.* Offers valuable detail.

18. Thompson, James M., *Leaders of the French Revolution.* Oxford, 1932.

Thompson published a series of works involving Danton, including his well-known *The French Revolution* (1945). Chapter on Danton (pp. 115-34) is particularly oriented toward Danton's speaking, but unfortunately no source is given for some of the most valuable quotations and their source cannot be located.

19. Vergniaud, Pierre Victurnier, *Rapport Fait par M. Vergniaud au Nom de la Commission Extraordinaire du* [13e] *Août, l'an 4e. de la Liberté ... sur le Changement de la Salle des Séances de l'Assemblée Nationale.* Paris: Imprimerie Nationale, 1792, 10 pp.

The Girondist orator Vergniaud, chairman of a special committee to seek a better meeting place than the Salle du Manège for the assembly, described in detail the difficulties in meeting in a converted riding academy and how these difficulties affected the process of democracy.

20. Wendel, Hermann, *Danton*, translation not given. New Haven, 1935.
Biography, originally published in German, valuable for its account of how Danton failed in protecting France against attacks by the allies.

Questions for Discussion

1. Trace the aspects of nationalism and human rights as themes in the Danton speech. Is either more dominant than the other?

2. Explain the absence or presence of the theme of *revolutionary export* in Danton's three speeches delivered during March of 1793 (see bibliography nos. 5 and 13).

3. Name five contemporary speech situations involving possible lawlessness in which you think a "pep talk" such as Danton's would be effective today.

4. Justify the assumption that Danton's speech is reflective of both the second and the third stages of the French Revolution.

5. To what extent does Danton's career justify the contention that it is men of stature with a grievance who produce the rhetoric to forward a revolution (see bibliography nos. 1, 3, 11, 16, 18 and 20).

6. Compare Stephens's description of Danton (*15*, II, 165-68) with Danton's remarks of March 27. What passages in the speech support Stephens's conclusions?

7. Danton's analogy about the statue of liberty shows how the rhetoric of stage one can continue into stage two. Is this figure too tumid for a Danton?

8. Why does not more of the revolutionary slang appear in the speech as a part of Danton's costume of words?

9. Note the difficulties in trying to outline the Danton speech. Was his lack of organization purposeful or could it be developed as a characteristic of the rhetoric of stage two of a revolt?

10. Contrast the amount of emotional appeals in Danton's speech with those in the four speeches by Hancock, Lenin, Gandhi, and Castro. Can you develop a common denominator among the four speeches regarding emotion that would permit generalization about the rhetoric of revolt?

Exercises

1. Prepare a short "pep talk" to a group suffering from defeat. Imitate Danton's approach, avoiding structure, employing a variety of emotional appeals, and using a highly personalized approach.

2. Plan a bold address to a body that you think is losing its way. Choose a subject about which you have deep convictions (or role-play conviction). Use no notes. Measure your success by the degree of motivation you achieve.

3. Imagine yourself on television, asking the country to forget its bickering in order to join a crash program for social welfare. Upbraid your audience severely for laxness, but give it hope. Conclude with some drastic proposal (in imitation of Danton's call for pikes and a tribunal).

4. Rewrite the Danton speech, using a current costume of words associated with a revolutionary movement. Retain Danton's ideas but update his style.

5. Calculate how many structural disturbances there are per 100 words in Danton's speech in an effort to determine the degree of extemporaneousness of his style.

Vladimir Ilich Ulianov-Lenin
(1870-1924)

The Professional Revolutionary

Researching the background for Lenin's speech of June 17, 1917, is difficult because not only are sources on Lenin (a) biased; (b) difficult to obtain; and (c) often only in Russian, German, or French, but the confused manner in which the Soviet Union has released Lenin's papers makes an investigation of Lenin's rhetoric perplexing. This brief description of the events that led up to the revolution of 1917 should provide sufficient background so that, with the assistance of the annotated bibliography, additional research can be fruitfully undertaken.

Vladimir Ulianov was born on April 22, 1870, in Simbirsk on the Volga, that natural dividing line between Europe and Asia. Serfdom had been abolished in 1861 and the Franco-Prussian War was about to begin. While Europe was enjoying relative prosperity, Russia was only beginning to progress from an archaic social order to the initial stages of a modern technological society. Lenin and Stalin were to fulfill Peter the Great's dream of bringing Russia from the medieval shadows into the light of the twentieth century.

As can be expected of revolutionary leaders, Vladimir was reared in relative prosperity. His father was school inspector for the province and his mother was the daughter of a physician. When Vladimir was 17, his elder brother was executed for trying to assassinate Alexander III. This tragedy set the mission in life for the man whom we know as Lenin and also for his younger brother and three sisters, all of whom became "men" of words with a grievance.

Ulianov entered the university at Kazan in 1887, but was soon banished because of Marxist involvement. The following year he was permitted to return to Kazan but not to enter the university. In 1891, thanks to Alexander Kerensky's father who had been named a guardian in Vladimir's father's will,

Ulianov was admitted to the university at Saint Petersburg where he passed his law examinations with honors. By 1893, Ulianov had joined the underground in Saint Petersburg, distributing propaganda among industrial workers. He also practiced law, but was spending too much of his time agitating to give attention to his practice. In December of 1895, Vladimir was arrested and put into prison, where he (1) set up a strict routine for study and exercise; (2) used the prison library, rich in ideological material left by former inmates; and (3) kept up a secret correspondence by writing in milk to organize Russian workers.

After 14 months in prison, Ulianov was banished for three years to Siberia, where he boarded with a peasant family, hunted, fished, played the guitar and chess, and read Russian classics. When he was released in 1900, he left for Germany to establish an underground newspaper. The first issue of *Iskra* appeared on December 21, 1900, printed in Munich on thin paper so it could be smuggled into Russia. The *Iskra* staff never knew how much of their material got through, and, since they were highly desirous of feedback, they questioned carefully each visitor from Russia. In 1901, Krupskaya arrived in Munich to assist with the newspaper, and she became Lenin's wife and remained his loyal supporter. In 1902, when the Munich publisher complained that it was too risky to continue, Lenin moved *Iskra* to London, where he had his first visit from Trotsky.

In 1903, against Lenin's judgment, *Iskra* was moved to Geneva. The Second Party Conference of the Social Democratic Party, which opened in Brussels in 1903 and which, because of harassment, had to be moved to London, showed how weak the coalition was that had supported the development of *Iskra*. The Bolsheviks (meaning majority) and the Mensheviks (meaning minority) quarreled bitterly and Lenin resigned the editorship of *Iskra*.

In 1904, with packs on their backs, Lenin and Krupskaya tramped through the Swiss mountains to restore Lenin's shattered nerves. On January 22, 1905, a priest led workers to the tsar's palace in Saint Petersburg to ask for a redress of grievances. Troops fired on the crowd, killing 500 and creating Bloody Sunday, the Boston Massacre of the Russian Revolution. Therefore the Third Party Congress held in London in April, 1905, was lively. On August 19, 1905, to restore order, the tsar announced the creation of a powerless national assembly known as the Duma. Worker strikes continued, so on October 30, 1905, the tsar issued a new manifesto that maintained the Duma, permitted freedom of speech, and initiated a liberal suffrage. Shortly thereafter the first issue of the Soviet newspaper *Izvestia* appeared. On November 8, the sailors at the Kronstadt naval base mutinied. Lenin arrived in Russia; street barricades appeared in Saint Petersburg and Moscow; and the

Soviets called for a revolution and a constituent assembly. The tsar suppressed the Soviet newspapers, and, on December 16, 1905, to prevent revolution, the Executive Committee of the Soviets was arrested. Lenin escaped into Finland.

In 1906 the first Duma was dominated by the Cadets (Constitutional Democratic Party), an enlightened group headed by the liberal professions, by delegates from the Russian regional assemblies, and by the intelligentsia. The Bolsheviks opposed the Duma largely because they could not control it, so the secret police, the Okhrana, gave the Bolsheviks freedom to harass the new assembly. The tsar almost agreed to a constitution, but retreated and tried to undermine his concessions of 1905. Stolypin became the tsar's prime minister and tried to restore order. Under his guidance, however, the Okhrana was enlarged so that it contained 20,000 members (13, 86), many of whom were Bolsheviks who had sold out to the tsar.

In 1907 the second Duma was dissolved because it would not obey Nicholas; and Lenin's enemies within the Social Democratic Party were sent to Siberia, leaving him a much freer hand. A Party Congress in London in April of 1907 included Mensheviks, Bolsheviks, the Jewish Socialist Bund, and Polish, Latvian and Lithuanian Social Democrats (19, 94-95). As soon as the Russian delegates had returned home they were arrested through betrayal and sentenced to hard labor in Siberia. Lenin's group, which had boycotted the Dumas, largely escaped, leaving Lenin to pursue his relentless opposition to gradual reform.

In 1910, Lenin was bitterly opposed at the International Socialist Congress in Copenhagen. In 1911, Stolypin was murdered at the opera, and one of the few men who might have controlled Russia was removed as an obstacle to revolution. In 1912, at an important conference of Bolsheviks in Prague, of the 13 voting delegates, three were spies of the Okhrana (19, 117). The daily newspaper *Pravda* first appeared on May 5, 1912. A strike in the Lena goldfields resulted in a second massacre, greatly agitating Russian workers. Stalin, who had been apprehended five times before, was again arrested and sent to Siberia, where he remained until the revolution began. Lenin moved to Krakow, sensing revolution and wanting to be as close as safety permitted.

When World War I began, Austrian police arrested Lenin, but he was released through the efforts of the Austrian Socialists and returned to Switzerland. During the first days of the war, a surge of patriotism swept Russia uniting the people, so that a capable government could have avoided revolution. But the army was corrupt, the tsar was weak, the neurotic empress was dominated by Rasputin, and the government found itself in desperate financial straits. Disillusion was not long in coming.

On September 5, 1915, in Zimmerwald, Switzerland, a conference of European antiwar Socialists was held, resulting in a loose confederation known as the Zimmerwald Union, a forerunner of the Communist International. The war was to be opposed in all countries by all groups represented. After some initial successes the woefully equipped army suffered disastrous casualties and began a steady retreat. Four million men under General-in-Chief Grand Duke Nicholas were killed. By 1916, food and fuel shortages in Russian cities became acute. The tsar dismissed the grand duke and took charge of the front, leaving domestic policy to the empress and Rasputin. On December 30, Rasputin was murdered, but this deed, like all counterrevolutionary moves in Russia, came much too late.

By 1917, the chairman of the Duma called the impending disaster to the tsar's attention, but the tsar was determined to continue absolutism. Yet his rule could last no longer than spring. The events of March, 1917, were too many and too complicated to be detailed here. On March 8, the Saint Petersburg workers struck. Between March 12 and 14 a coalition government was formed of parties amendable to an evolutionary progression toward constitutional government. The revolution, so long awaited by so many, came unobtrusively. On March 15, the tsar abdicated. Prince Lvov became prime minister and attempted to set up a constitutional monarchy. Lenin knew he had to get from Switzerland to Russia. But how? The allies would have detained him because he wished to remove Russia from the war. Germany agreed to transport him by rail in the hope of closing the eastern front. Lenin knew that he would be criticized for selling out to the German imperialists, but he took the chance. On April 9, 1917, he left Bern, and, on April 16, 1917, he was received by a huge crowd at the Saint Petersburg railway station.

Lenin's anarchism was well known to other Bolsheviks early in 1917 because he made it clear on April 17, at a conference of Social Democrats, that a hard line was to be followed, that cooperation with other parties was unheard of, and that civil war was inevitable. Between May 7 and 12, the All Russian Bolshevik Party Conference adopted Lenin's April theses as the basis for action. On May 17, a new coalition cabinet included five socialists with Kerensky as minister of war and navy.

On June 16, the All-Russian Congress of Soviets opened in Saint Petersburg. Lenin and his followers did all they could to increase the dissention between moderates and radicals. Moderates, heartened by the proclamations of President Wilson, asked for restraint; Lenin, pointing to the misery of the soldiers and the wretchedness in the cities, called for abrupt change with violence. Under what conditions did this vital conflict take place?

The congress was held in a complex of structures, called the Tauride Palace which had been the home of the Dumas. All liberal socialist elements were represented, so there were many curious to hear this legendary Lenin. The Bolshevik party had felt the impact of Lenin one month earlier when it adopted his April theses; now the whole socialist movement was to feel the force that eventually overwhelmed it. Maynard points out that, although it is now known how dangerous Lenin was to the liberal aspects of the Russian Revolution, he was hardly taken seriously at the time (*12*, 186). His strength was largely among industrial workers, with some following in the army and rising support among the peasants. He was, after all, an outsider, a newcomer on the scene, expressing lawless ideas that might have gone well in the garrets of London, but that were not to be taken seriously in Saint Petersburg. Therefore, when the first séance of the congress opened, Lenin did not occupy a place of importance. The leader of the Mensheviks, Tsereteli, who had been given a cabinet post under Lvov on May 17, was a much more important man. But Lenin knew where he had to go and he used the congress to establish the cognitive dissonance that led him to success.

On June 17, Tsereteli defended the provisional government, claiming it was the only solution and that no one party was then ready to assume control. From out in the crowd of delegates Lenin interrupted to say: "There is such a party! " When the time came for Lenin to speak, the delegates prepared themselves for an extremist—about whom the provincials, the businessmen, the intellectuals and the bourgeois had heard so much—now not in pamphlet or newspaper form but in the flesh; a compact little man with a large bald head, a reddish goatee, properly but simply dressed (*22*, 323), who had left his underground cave for the light of day (*20*, 380). Sukhanov, a member of the Executive Council seated on the platform close to the orators, recalled that "in unaccustomed surroundings, face-to-face with his ferocious enemies, surrounded by a hostile crowd that looked on him as a wild beast, Lenin clearly felt himself insignificant and had no special success. In addition, the cruel fifteen minutes allotted to a fraction speaker[1] weighed on him. . . . His speech was not very well arranged and had no central pivot, but it contained some remarkable passages for whose sake it must be recalled" (*20*, 380). Even Sukhanov, the intellectual, the Social Democrat, cantankerous and opinionated, had to recognize that the opening statements comprised "a complete political system that now replaced, developed, and interpreted Lenin's original schema of April" (*20*, 381). Sukhanov reported that Lenin's call for absolute power for his own faction only baffled the extreme left and was untenable to the central factions. But the gauntlet had been thrown

---

[1] A speaker representing one of the many parties present.

down, and the open battle between Lenin and the other liberal elements had begun in earnest.

Shub reported that Lenin began his speech of July 17 "without looking at his audience, his eyes fixed on a distant point at the far end of the hall" (19, 199). As the speech progressed, Lenin undoubtedly became more animated. Shub wrote: "One Socialist writer, recalling Lenin's speech, reported: 'When he suggested the arrest of fifty or one hundred capitalists . . . he paced the platform like a caged beast, squinted his eyes as if delighting in the imaginary sight of fifty capitalists taken through the streets in cages, and uttered his words rapidly, like one possessed,'" (19, 201).

Lenin's speech received applause from his most staunch followers and from the gallery of soldiers and sailors, but there was open hostility from others. Moorehead reported: "One man got up and declared that such a speech was 'the ravings of a madman' " (13, 190). Kerensky answered Lenin, warning of the fate that befell France in 1795 and calling for a preservation of the very freedom that allowed Lenin to return from exile. Prophetically Kernesky said: "We must see to it that the historic mistakes do not repeat themselves, that we do not bring on a situation that would make possible the return of reaction, the victory of force over democracy" (19, 201). At one point he so provoked Lenin that Lenin called out: "You should call him to order! "

A turbulent debate followed Kerensky's remarks. The session ended with a blanket rejection of Lenin's philosophy (13, 190). But Lenin had clarified his extreme position, not only for the Bolsheviks but for the entire Socialist movement. The entropic qualities of his speech shook the congress. His solutions hardly offered sufficient negative entropy to calm the consternation of his fellow leftists. But, following this speech, Lenin's position became a point of reference around which the events of the next five months were to revolve. Lenin's practical application of cognitive dissonance eventually won over many and the remainder were eliminated by alienation or force.

Premature moves of the Bolsheviks in the summer of 1917 failed to overthrow the government, but they forced Kerensky to assume an offensive against Lenin. Lenin was ordered arrested. On July 21, Lvov was succeeded by Kerensky as prime minister. Lenin went into hiding in Finland. The new Kerensky government had as its chief liability the war. On September 12, Kerensky became supreme commander to bolster a faltering offensive and to prevent an ambitious general from assuming dictatorial powers. On September 14, Russia was declared a republic. On October 20, a provisional parliament began meeting. Trotsky announced the withdrawal of the Bolsheviks from the assembly, claiming that its bourgeois elements were preventing a constituent assembly. The preparations for an armed uprising began. Lenin returned from Finland. On November 5, Kerensky declared an emergency; on November 6, Red Guards began a take-over; on November 7, the provisional parliament was dismissed; and on November 8, the historic night session of the Congress of Soviets began. Lenin was proclaimed chairman of the Soviet of People's Commissars and a Bolshevik cabinet was announced. The extremists had seized power. Could they keep it?

Kerensky, who had tried unsuccessfully to rally troops to his support at the front, fled into exile. A constituent assembly, whose election had been provided for under the provisional government, was elected on November 25. Of the 36 million votes cast, only 9 million were for Bolsheviks. Obviously Lenin was not firmly in the saddle. The plague of war must be lifted. The parliament must be disposed of. Trotsky was dispatched to Brest Litovsk to negotiate with the Germans.

The Constituent Assembly began its meetings on January 18 at 4:00 P.M. but was not allowed to continue past that night. Bolshevik soldiers and sailors invaded the hall, and it was with great courage that the delegates continued their futile session. Although they were willing to approve land reform, to proclaim a republic and to approve an armistice, "the one thing the Assembly would not do was to acknowledge the dictatorship of the Bolsheviks" (13, 269). As a result the Executive Committee of the Congress of Soviets dissolved the assembly and the doors to the Tauride Palace were barred so that the deputies could not return. Democracy in Russia came to an abrupt end.

On January 26, Trotsky reported the drastic terms demanded by the Germans. Lenin wanted to accept, but he was overruled. Trotsky was asked to stall. On February 22, the Germans proposed even more severe stipulations and on March 3, 1918, Trotsky signed the treaty of Brest Litovsk, an agreement that Lenin had no intention of fulfilling. He needed time. On March 6, those Bolsheviks who had voted against acceptance resigned, leaving Lenin in charge.

Counterrevolution was put down with difficulty; the Romanov family was shot in a basement in Siberia; the capital was moved to the Kremlin; war with Poland in 1920 and a revolt of the Kronstadt sailors in 1921 were among the post revolutionary highlights. In 1922, Lenin suffered a stroke. A second stroke caused Stalin to be named chairman. Lenin died on January 21, 1924.

Advance or Retreat
Vperiod ili Nazad

June 17, 1917
The First All-Russian Congress of Soviets,
Tauride Palace, Leningrad

Comrades, in the brief time at my disposal, I can dwell—and I think this best—only on the main questions of principle raised by the speaker [dokladchik] and by those orators [orátory] who commented on his report.

The first and basic issue before us was: *What is this assembly* we are attending, what are these Soviets now gathered at the All-Russian Congress, and what is this revolutionary democracy that people here speak so much about to conceal their utter misunderstanding and complete repudiation of it? For to talk about revolutionary democracy at the All-Russian Congress of Soviets and to overlook the character of this institution, its class composition and its role in the revolution—not to say a word about all this and yet lay claim to the title of democrats is really strange. They map out a program to us of a bourgeois parliamentary republic, the sort of program that has existed all over Western Europe; they map out a program to us for reforms which are now acknowledged by all bourgeois governments, including our own, and yet they speak about revolutionary democracy! And whom are they speaking to? To the Soviets.[2] But I ask you, is there a country in Europe—bourgeois, democratic, republican where anything like these Soviets exists? You have to admit there isn't. Nowhere is there, nor can there be, a similar institution because you must have one or the other—*either* a bourgeois government with "plans" for reforms like those just mapped out to us and proposed dozens of times [in Russian, tens of times] in all countries and which have remained on

The present official government version of this speech in Russian appeared in *6*, XXXII, 263-76. There appear to be no changes in this Russian version and that published earlier by the Russian government in 1952 in *7*, XXV, 3-14. The Marx-Lenin Institute noted that both of these versions had been taken from *Pravda* (*17*) following collation with a verbatim report edited by Lenin, the latter presumably being housed in the Institute. Three differing English translations were of assistance in establishing this translation: *5*, XXV, 17-28; *9*, 74-85; and *11*, 159-70. The version in *9* is the same as that in XX, part 2, 195-205, of the first English translation of Lenin's works, noted in the annotation to entry *5* in the bibliography at the end of this treatment of Lenin. The English version presented here is markedly different from earlier English translations.

[2] These short replies are affirmative in nature.

paper; or you have the institutions to which they are now appealing, that new type of "government" which has been created by the revolution and examples of which are found only in the history of the greatest rise in the tide of revolutions, for instance, in 1792 in France, in 1871 in France, in 1905 in Russia. The Soviets are an institution which, in any usual type of bourgeois-parliamentary state, do not exist and which, side by side with a bourgeois government, exist they cannot. They constitute that new, more democratic type of government which we in our Party resolutions have called a peasant-proletarian democratic republic, in which the sole power should belong to the Soviets of Workers' and Soldiers' Deputies.[3] In vain do they think that this question is a theoretical one; in vain do they attempt to present the matter as if it can be avoided; in vain do they offer excuses that at present certain institutions do exist together with the Soviets of Workers' and Soldiers' Deputies. Yes, they do exist together. But just that very thing is giving rise to countless misunderstandings, conflicts and disagreements. Just that very thing is causing the shifting of the Russian Revolution from its first peak [or upswing], from its initial advances, toward its stagnation and toward those steps backward which we now see in our coalition government,[4] in its entire domestic and foreign policy, in connection with the imperialist offensive under preparation.

One of two things: either[5] the usual bourgeois government—and then the peasants, workers, soldiers and other Soviets are not needed, then they will either be scattered by the generals, the counterrevolutionary generals, who hold the army in their hands, not paying any attention to the oratory of Minister Kerensky, or either they will die an inglorious death. There is no other alternative for these institutions, which can neither retreat nor stand still, and which can only exist by going forward. This is a type of state which was not invented by the Russians, but invigorated[6] by the revolution, for the

---

[3] The First All-Russian Congress of Soviets of Workers' and Soldiers' Deputies met in Saint Petersburg from June 16 to July 7, 1917. It was attended by more than 1,000 delegates, only 105 of whom were Bolsheviks. In spite of the Bolsheviks, the Congress passed resolutions favoring the provisional government and its preparations for an offensive and took a stand against the transfer of power to the Soviets.

[4] On May 17, 1917, the Socialist-Revolutionaries Kerensky and Chernov, a quasi-Socialist-Revolutionary Pereverzev, the Mensheviks Skobelev and Tsereteli, and the Popular Socialist Peshekhonov formed the first coalition government under Prince George Lvov.

[5] Note that Lenin does not complete this thought. It appears to be one of the few *non sequiturs* which he or his editors did not delete from this speech. Because of the rapidity with which he was thinking, it is highly likely that there were others which may become apparent in whatever transcripts of the speech are in the Institute.

[6] "Advance" would be a simpler, more Lenin-like word than "invigorate," but it

revolution can win in no other way. In the soul [nedra] of the All-Russian Soviet, the inevitables are disagreement and the battle of parties for power. But this will mean that the masses themselves are overcoming possible mistakes and illusions through their own political experience [commotion], and not by those speeches of the ministers, who quote what they said yesterday, what they will write tomorrow and what they promise the day after tomorrow. This is ridiculous, comrades, from the standpoint of that institution which is created by the Russian Revolution and which is now faced with the question: to be or not to be? To continue to exist in the way they now exist—that the Soviets cannot do. Mature people, workers and peasants are obliged to meet, adopt resolutions, and listen to reports without being able to verify them by studying the original documents! This institution that we have right here is the transition to the republic which will create a stable power, without police and without standing armies, not in words but in deeds—the kind of power that cannot exist as yet in Europe, the kind of power without which there can be no victory for the Russian Revolution—if we mean by it a victory over the landowners, a victory over imperialism.

Without such a power there can be no talk of our obtaining such a victory ourselves. And the deeper we penetrate into that program which is being urged upon us here, and into those facts which confront us, the more glaringly the fundamental contradiction stands out. They tell us—the chief speaker and other speakers tell us—that the first Provisional Government[7] was a bad one! But when the Bolsheviks, the unhappy Bolsheviks, said: "No support for and no confidence in this government! "—how many accusations of "anarchism" were hurled down upon us. Now everybody says that the former government was a bad one. But what about the coalition government with its Pseudo-Socialist ministers— how does it differ from the previous one? Hasn't there been enough talk about programs, about projects? Hasn't there been enough of this? Is it not time to get down to business? Here a month has passed since the sixth of May when the coalition government was formed. Just take a look at the facts, just take a look at the ruin which prevails in Russia and in all the countries which have been involved in the imperialist war. What is the ruin due to? The greediness of the capitalists. That is where the real anarchy is! And this according to admissions which are

---

would not allow the three-letter alliteration which Lenin provides in the Russian with the words [vydumat] and [vydvinuy]. "Invent" and "invigorate" preserve the alliteration in the English.

[7] The Provisional Government was formed on March 15, 1917, upon the abdication of the tsar, by an agreement between the Duma and the Soviets. It included Cadets, Socialist Revolutionaries, and members of the bourgeoisie and landed gentry.

published not in our newspaper, not in any Bolshevik newspaper—God forbid! —but in the ministerial *Rabochaya Gazeta*,[8] which said that industrial prices for coal deliveries were *raised* by the "revolutionary" government!" And here the coalition government has changed nothing. They tell us, can socialism be introduced in Russia, or can any radical changes, generally speaking, be made at once? That is all empty talk, comrades. The doctrine of Marx and Engels, as they always made clear, says: "Our doctrine is not a dogma, but a guide to action."[9] Nowhere in the world is there pure capitalism passing into pure socialism, nor can there be in time of war. But there is something in between, something new, unheard of, because hundreds of millions of people who have been involved in the criminal war of the capitalists are perishing. It is not a question of promising reforms—that is mere talk. It is a question of taking the steps we now need to take.

If you wish to refer to *"revolutionary"* democracy, then distinguish this concept from *reformist* democracy under a capitalist ministry, because, after all, it is time to quit talking about "revolutionary democracy," from handing ourselves congratulations on "revolutionary democracy," and get on with a *class* definition, as we have been taught to do by Marxism and by scientific socialism in general. What they are proposing to us is a transition to reformist democracy under a capitalist ministry. That may be excellent from the standpoint of the customary Western European models. Right now a whole group of countries are on the eve of destruction, and those practical measures which are supposedly so complicated that it is difficult to introduce them, and which must be especially worked out, as the previous speaker, the Citizen Minister of Post and Telegraph,[10] said, are perfectly clear. He said that in Russia there is no political party which would express its readiness to assume ful power. I say: "There is! " No one party can turn it down and our Party certainly doesn't. It is prepared at any time to take over full power. [Applause and laughter.] You may laugh as much as you please, but if the Citizen Minister confronts us with this question at the same time he proposes it to a party on the right, he will receive appropriate replies [from both]. No party can turn it down. And at a time when freedom still prevails, when threats of arrest and exile to Siberia—threats made by the counterrevolutionaries, with whom our pseudo-Socialist ministers are sitting in the government—are still only threats, at such a time every party says: "Extend

[8] The Workers' Gazette, a daily newspaper published by the Mensheviks in Saint Petersburg from the overthrow of the tsar until its suppression by Lenin on December 13, 1917

[9] K. Marx and F. Engels, *Selected Correspondence*, Moscow, 1955, p. 469.

[10] Tsereteli.

your confidence to us, and we will give you our program." Our conference of April 29[11] gave us such a program. To our regret it is being ingnored and not taken as a guide. It is obvious that it needs a more widespread understanding. I shall try to give the Citizen Minister of Post and Telegraph a popular explanation of our resolution, our program. Our program, in reference to the economic crisis, is immediately—no delays are necessary to do this—to demand the publication of all the unheard-of profits, reaching 500% and 800%, which the capitalists are taking in, not as capitalists on the open market, under "pure capitalism," but on war supplies. This is exactly where workers' control is inevitable and feasible. Here you have the kind of measure which, if you call yourselves "revolutionary" democrats, you should carry out in the name of the Soviet and which can be realized overnight. This is not socialism. This is opening the eyes of the people to that real anarchy, and to that real playing with imperialism, the playing with the wealth of the land, with hundreds of thousands of lives which tomorrow will perish so that we may continue to gobble up [smother] Greece. Publish the gains of the gentlemen capitalists [in Russian: *gospoda kapitalisty*; in French, it would be *Messieurs les Capitalistes*], arrest fifty or a hundred of the most important millionaires. It will be enough to keep them in custory for a few weeks, if only under the conditions as those under which Nicholas Romanov is being confined, with the simple purpose of compelling them to reveal the network, the fraudulent practices, the filth and the selfishness which even under the new government are costing our country thousands and millions daily. There you have the basic cause of anarchy and ruin. And that is why we say: to us everything has remained just the same, that the coalition government has changed nothing, it has added only a heap of statements and pompous declarations. However sincere the people may have been, however sincerely they may have desired the welfare of the toilers, matters have not changed—*the same class* has stayed in power. That policy which is being followed is not a democratic policy.

They tell us about "democratizing the central and local power." Don't you know that these words are something new only in Russia, and that in other countries dozens [tens] of pseudo-Socialist ministers made similar promises to their countries. What value do they have in face of a concrete fact like this: while the local population elects its own government, the ABC's of democracy are being violated by the claims of the central government to appoint or confirm the local officials. The plundering of the nation's wealth is continued

---

[11] Lenin is referring to the resolutions of the Seventh All-Russian Conference of the Bolshevik Party held in Saint Petersburg on May 7 to 12. Lenin is using the old Russian Calendar before it was brought up-to-date.

by the capitalists, the imperialist war is continued, yet they promise us reforms, reforms, and reforms, which cannot at all be realized under the present framework, for the war crushes, weighs down everything, dictates everything. Why do you not agree with those who say that the war is *not* being waged on behalf of capitalist profits? What is the criterion? It is, first of all, what class is in power, what class continues to be the master, what class continues to reap hundreds of billions in banking and financial operations. It is the same capitalist class, and the war therefore continues to be an imperialist war. Both the first Provisional Government and the government of the quasi-Socialist ministers have not changed anything. The secret treaties remain secret. Russia is fighting for the Straits and to continue Lyakhov's policy in Persia, and so on.[12]

I know that you do not want this, that the majority of you do not want it, and that the ministers do not want it, because it is impossible to want it, since it means the slaughter of hundreds of millions of people. But take that offensive about which the Milyukovs and the Maklakovs are talking so much at present. They understand full well what it means; they know that it is connected with the question of power, with the question of the revolution. They tell us that we must distinguish between political and strategical questions. It is ridiculous to even bring this up. The Cadets[13] know full well that this is a political question.

That the grass-roots revolutionary battle for peace could lead to a separate peace is sheer slander.[14] The first step which we would take if we had power would be: arrest the most important capitalists, to rip out the threads of their intrigues. Without this, all talk about a peace without annexations and indemnities is sheer piffle. Our second step would be to declare to the peoples, apart from their governments, that we regard all capitalists as robbers—Tereshchenko, who is not a whit better than Milykov, only a little more stupid—the French capitalists, the English capitalists, and all the rest.

Your own *Izvestia*[15] has got into a muddle and, instead of peace without annexations and indemnities, it proposes the *status quo*.[16] No, that is not the

[12]V. P. Lyakhov, a colonel in the tsarist army, led the Russian troops which put down the Persian Revolution of 1908.

[13]The Cadets, a nickname for the Constitutional Democratic Party, were the leading party of the liberal bourgeoisie. Founded in October, 1905, it consisted of landowners and intellectuals who wished to retain the monarchy.

[14]Lenin's adverb is [snizu], which means literally "from below." Lenin is therefore not figurative, but "grass-roots" translates best.

[15]*Bulletin of the Petrograd Soviet of Workers' and Soldiers' Deputies,* a daily newspaper founded on March 13, 1917.

[16]It was rare that Lenin used a Latin phrase.

way we understand a peace "without annexations." And there is where the Peasant Congress[17] comes nearer the truth when it speaks of a "federal" republic, thereby expressing the idea that the Russian republic does not want to oppress any nation, either in the new way or in the old way, and does not want to live on a basis of coercion with any people, neither with Finland nor with the Ukraine, with which the war minister is trying so hard to pick a quarrel and with which unallowable and inadmissible conflicts are being created. We want a single and indivisible Russian republic with a firm central authority; but a firm central authority can be secured only by the voluntary agreement of all peoples. "Revolutionary democracy" —these are big words, but they are being applied to a government that, by petty faultfinding, is complicating relations with the Ukraine and Finland, which do not even want to secede but only say:—don't postpone the application of the ABC's of democracy until the Constituent Assembly!

A peace without annexations and indemnities cannot be concluded until you have renounced your own annexations. You see, it is ridiculous, it is a game, at which every worker in Europe is laughing. He says: "They talk very eloquently and call upon the nations to overthrow the bankers, but they put their own bankers into the cabinet." Arrest them, expose their tricks, get to know their ins and outs. But that you do not do, although you have powerful organizations which are overpowering. You have lived through the years of 1905 and 1917, you know that revolution is not made to order, that revolutions in other countries were made by the hard and bloody path of revolt, while in Russia there is no such group, no such class that could resist the power of the Soviets. In Russia, an exception to the rule, this revolution can be a peaceful revolution. Let this revolution propose peace to all the nations today, or tomorrow, by making a breach with all the capitalist classes, and in the shortest time, both France and Germany, their people, that is, would agree in a very short time, because these countries are perishing, because the position of Germany is hopeless, because she cannot save herself, and because France . . .

Chairman: Your time has expired.

Lenin: I shall finish in half a minute , . . [Commotion; requests from the floor that time be extended; protests and applause.]

Chairman: I am to inform the congress that the presidium [the central committee] proposes that the speaker's time be extended. Any objections? The majority are in favor of an extension.

[17]The First All-Russian Congress of Peasant Deputies was held in Saint Petersburg from May 17 to June 10. 1917. It was attended by 1,115 delegates, of whom a number were Bolsheviks.

Lenin: I stopped at the point that if revolutionary democracy in Russia were democracy, not in word but in action, it would proceed to move the revolution forward and not to agree with the capitalists, not to talk about a peace without annexations and indemnities but to abolish annexations in Russia, and toward a direct declaration that it considers all annexations criminal and predatory. It would then be possible to avoid the imperialist offensive, which is threatening the lives of thousands and millions of people in order to partition Persia and the Balkans. The way to peace would then be open, not a simple way—we do not say that—a way which would not preclude a really revolutionary war.

We do not put the question in the way Bazarov puts it in today's *Novaya Zhizn.*[18] All we say is that Russia is placed in such circumstances that at the end of the imperialist war her tasks are easier than might have been thought. Her geographical position is such that if any powers would risk depending on capital and its greedy interests and would rise against the Russian working class and the semiproletariat associated with it—the poorest peasantry—if they went that far, it would be for them a most difficult task. Germany is on the brink of ruin, and since the entry of America which wants to gobble up Mexico and which any day, probably, will start a fight with Japan, after their entry, the position of Germany is hopeless; they will destroy her. France, whose geographical position is such that she is suffering more than the others, and whose state of exhaustion is reaching her limit, this country, although suffering less from starvation than Germany, has lost immeasurably greater manpower than Germany. And so, if, as your first step, you would restrict the profits of the Russian capitalists and deprive them of all possibility of raking in hundreds of millions in profits, if you were to propose to *all* the nations a peace directed against the capitalists of *all* countries and bluntly declare that you will not enter into any negotiations or relations with the German capitalists and with those who directly or indirectly support them or are involved with them, and that you refuse to speak with the French and English capitalists, you would be acting in such a way as to condemn them in the eyes of the workers. You would not regard it as a victory that a passport had been granted to MacDonald,[19] who has never waged a revolutionary struggle against capital and who is being allowed in because he has never

[18]*New Life,* a Social Democratic daily with Menshevik leanings. It was suppressed in July of 1918.

[19] Ramsay MacDonald, leader of the British Labour party, was invited to Russia by the Executive Committee of the Saint Petersburg Soviet of Workers' and Soldiers' Deputies. The trip was frustrated by the British Seamen's Union which refused to man the ship in which MacDonald was to sail.

expressed either the ideas, or the principles, or the practice, or the experience of that revolutionary struggle against the English capitalists for which our Comrade MacLean[20] and hundreds of other English Socialists are in prison, and for which our Comrade Liebknecht[21] is confined at hard labor for saying, "German soldiers, turn your guns on your Kaiser! "

Wouldn't it rather be right to consign the imperialist capitalists to that hard labor which the majority of the Provisional Government, together with the Third—but I really do not know whether it is the Third or the Fourth—Duma especially re-established for that purpose, have daily been preparing for us and promising us, and about which new bills are already being drafted in the Ministry of Justice? MacLean and Liebknecht—here are the names of those Socialists who are putting the idea of a revolutionary struggle against imperialism into practice. That is what we must say to all governments, in order to fight for peace! They must be condemned then before all peoples. You will then put all the imperialist governments in a difficult position. But now you have got yourselves in a difficult position by addressing your Manifesto of Peace of March 14[22] to the people, saying: "Overthrow your tsars, your kings and your bankers"—while we, who possess an organization of such untold wealth of numbers, experience, and material strength in the Soviet of Workers' and Soldiers' Deputies, conclude an agreement with our bankers, institute a coalition, pseudo-Socialist government, and draft reforms which have been drafted in Europe for decades and decades. Over there, in Europe, they laugh at such a method of fighting for peace. There they will understand us only when the Soviets take over the power and act in a revolutionary way.

There is only one country in the world which just now would be able to take steps to terminate the imperialist war on a class scale, against the capitalists, without a bloody revolution. There is only one country, and that country is Russia. And it will remain such as long as the Soviet of Workers' and Soldiers' Deputies exists. For very long, side by side with a provisional government of the ordinary type, it cannot exist. And it will remain what it is only as long as the initiative is not undertaken. The initiative will mark a turning point in the whole policies of the Russian Revolution, that is to say, it will be a movement from a state of waiting, of preparing for peace by

[20]John MacLean, Glasgow schoolteacher and member of the British Socialist Party, was sentenced on April 12, 1916, to three years of penal servitude for making statements calculated to discourage recruiting.

[21]Karl Liebknecht, an outspoken German antimilitarist.

[22]The manifesto, drafted and adopted by the Saint Petersburg Soviet of Workers' and Soldiers' Deputies on March 27, 1917, called for working people in all belligerent countries to rise up in favor of peace.

means of a grass-roots revolutionary uprising, to the resumption of the war. Initiative bringing fraternization on one front to fraternization of all fronts, from the rudiments of fraternization, when people exchange a crust of bread with a hungry German proletarian for a penknife under menace of penal servitude, to conscious fraternization—such was the path indicated.

When we take the power into our hands, we shall bridle the capitalists, and then the war will *not be the kind* that is being waged now—because a war is determined by the class which wages it, and not by what is written down on paper. You can write down what you like on paper. But as long as the capitalist class is represented in the government by a majority, no matter what you write, no matter how eloquent you are, no matter how many pseudo-Socialist ministers you have, the war will remain an imperialist war. This everybody knows, and everybody sees. And the case of Albania, the case of Greece and Persia[23] have demonstrated this so clearly and strikingly that I am astonished that everybody is attacking our written declaration on the offensive,[24] and not a single word is being said about specific cases! It is easy to promise bills, but specific measures are being continually put off. It is easy to write declarations about a peace without annexations, but the case of Albania, Greece and Persia took place *after* the coalition government was formed. You see, the *Dela Naroda*,[25] which is not an organ of our Party, but a governmental organ, a ministerial organ, wrote about them that it is the Russian democracy that is being subjected to this humiliation, and that Greece is being throttled. And this Milyukov—whom you imagine to be God-knows-who, when he is only an ordinary member of his party, and Tereshchenko in no way differs from him—he wrote that pressure by the allied diplomats was exerted on Greece. The war remains an imperialist war, and

[23] Following an uprising against the Turks in 1912, Albania underwent a period of turmoil. Italy subjugated the country in 1917 and remained in control until 1920. The Greeks also won their independence from Turkey in the Balkan Wars of 1912 and 1913. Greece's king who had ruled under the protectorate of the sultan was assassinated in 1913, and his son Constantine I became king. In World War I, the royal family was pro-German, but the people were pro-Ally. In 1917, with the aid of the Allies, Venizelos overthrew Constantine, made his son Alexander king, and brought Greece into the war on the side of the Allies. Persia, now known as Iran, had been ruled by the Qajar dynasty since the late 1700s, but was under the domination of Russia and Great Britain. In World War II, Russian and British troops fought Turks and German-inspired tribes for the oil fields.

[24] A reference to the declaration that the Bureau of the Bolshevists and the Bureau of the Social Democrats made at the First All-Russian Congress of Soviets, opposing the offensive that the Provisional Government was preparing.

[25] *The People's Cause*, a Socialist-Revolutionary daily which appeared between March, 1917, and June, 1918.

however much you may desire peace, however sincere may be your sympathy for the toilers, and however sincere may be your desire for peace—I am fully convinced that it cannot but be sincere in the majority of cases—you are impotent, because the war cannot be terminated except by the further development of the revolution. When the revolution began in Russia, it also began a grass-roots revolutionary struggle for peace. If you took the power into your hands, if the power passed to the revolutionary organizations for battle against the Russian capitalists, then the toilers of other countries would believe you, then you could propose peace, then our peace would be assured at least on the part of two, on the part of two nations, who are shedding their blood and whose cause is hopeless—from Germany's side and from France's side.

And if circumstances then obliged us to wage a revolutionary war—nobody knows about this, and we do not rule out the possibility—we would say: "We are not pacificists, we do not renounce war when the revolutionary class is in power and when it has really deprived the capitalists of the opportunity to exercise any influence on the state of affairs, on the increase in the ruin which enables them to gain hundreds of millions." The revolutionary force would explain and say to all the nations without exception that all nations should be free, and that just as the German people dares not fight to retain Alsace-Lorraine, so the French people dares not fight for its colonies. For, if France may fight for her colonies, Russia has Khiva and Bokhara, which are also in the nature of colonies, and then the division of colonies will begin. And how are they to be divided, on what basis? According to strength. But the forces have changed, the situation of the capitalists is such that there is no solution but war. When you take over revolutionary power, you will have a revolutionary way toward peace: by addressing a revolutionary appeal to the nations and explaining your tactics by example. Then the way to securing peace by revolution will open before you, with the greatest likelihood that you will avert the deaths of hundreds of thousands of people. Then you may be certain that the German and French people will back you up. And the capitalists—English, American, and Japanese—even if they wanted a war against the revolutionary working class—the strength of which will be multiplied tenfold when the capitalists are bridled and removed and the control passes into the hands of the working class—the chances would be ninety-nine out of one hundred that they would be unable to carry it out. It will be enough for you to declare that you are not pacifists, that you will defend your republic, your working proletarian democracy, from the German, French, and other capitalists. This will be enough for peace to be secured.

That is why we attributed such radical importance to our declaration on the offensive. The time for a break in the entire history of the Russian Revolution has arrived. The Russian Revolution began with the assistance of the imperialist bourgeoisie of England, which thought that Russia was something like China or India. Instead of this, side by side with the government in which there is now a majority of landlords and capitalists, there arose the Soviets, a representative institution of unheard-of, unseen force, which you are destroying by taking part in the coalition cabinet of the bourgeoisie. Instead of this, the Russian Revolution has achieved that grass-roots revolutionary struggle against the capitalist governments which everywhere began to meet with threefold greater sympathy. The question is: shall we go forward or backward? It is impossible to stand still during the time of revolution. That is why the offensive will be a thorough breakthrough in the Russian Revolution, not in the strategical sense of the offensive, but in the political, the economic. An offensive now would mean the continuation of the imperialist slaughter and the loss of hundreds of thousands, millions of people—objectively speaking, independently of the will or purpose of any minister—because of gobbling up [or smothering] Persia and other weak nations. The transfer of power to the revolutionary proletariat, supported by the poor peasanantry, means a transfer to a revolutionary struggle for peace in the surest and most painless forms known to mankind, a transfer to a state of affairs in which the power and victory of the revolutionary workers will be ensured in Russia and all over the world. [Applause from a part of the audience.]

The Revolt Rhetoric of Lenin

The practicality of studying the rhetoric of revolt is apparent because the effects of 1917 are still so influential. Contemporary official Soviet rhetoric continues to exhibit overkill toward even the most evolutionary forms of counterrevolution, and the extended overreaction of capitalist rhetoric to the Soviet costume of words demonstrates how self-perpetuating the effects of revolt rhetoric can be, particularly when peoples and movements lose perspective on their own use of words.

In one sense Lenin's June 17, 1917, speech occurred during stage one of the Russian Revolution because the November coup by the Soviets was five months away. Therefore his speech should, as it does, show the man of stature with a grievance[26] using phraseology of identification against the Old

---

[26] Lenin's grievance was not only political but personal, resulting from the execution of his brother for an attempt on the life of the tsar.

Regime. In a second sense the speech occurred during stage two of the revolution because the tsar had already been overthrown and the young Socialist revolution was under armed attack. Therefore the speech should, as it does, show the man of action impatient with talk, ready to dismiss words and to start pursuing a relentless attack on the enemy.

What particular contributions did Lenin make to revolt rhetoric, both as a man of words with a grievance and as a man of action?

Invention

Better than Hancock or Danton, Lenin knew how important it was to research a topic thoroughly. The hours he had studied in detention and in exile gave him the confidence that comes with limitless evidence and ideas. No one could cite theories with which he was not acquainted. When a contrary argument was raised, Lenin did not need to develop an answer. He had formulated his reply long ago.

Lenin reinforced his research with effective ethical, emotional, and logical appeals. "His hearers," said Kerzhentsez, "were gripped by his iron logic, his passion and conviction, and his brilliant mind. They saw from the first words that his speeches were not calculated to draw [applause] . . . but were the speeches of a fighting leader, addressing the broad masses of the people . . ." (2, 109). How did Lenin develop his logical, ethical, and emotional appeals?

First, to what extent did Lenin's rhetoric ask for the freedom that was required in the definition of revolution presented in the preface? Lenin frequently spoke of "democracy" and of the "people," but there were repeated slips in his democratic facade—capitalists were to be seized, the Republic of Russia had to have a "firm government," and the Soviets had to "act in a revolutionary way." Lenin put on the gospel armor of freedom, but his watchword was not democracy but dictatorship.

Second, Lenin's arguments for lawlessness reveal that Lenin was carefully analyzing his audience to see how much violence they were prepared to accept. At this point, when the Bolsheviks were only a small Socialist minority, Lenin felt he could only hint at the extreme measures he thought necessary. Therefore he contented himself with generalities, such as clarifying what revolutionary democracy should really mean and reminding the Socialists that the Bolsheviks had been right in using passive resistance against the first coalition government. Lenin's slip about putting the capitalists in custody to make them reveal the sources of their profits must have received a mixed reaction from the many in his audience who had experienced detention themselves. Profits were not yet illegal and the delegates were struggling for freedom from detention while, on the other hand, the desire for vengeance by even a Kerensky, who had briefly experienced solitary confinement, was hard to resist.

Lenin's reference to the Peace Manifesto of March 14 demonstrates that the international aspects of communism, clarified at Zimmerwald, were to be a basic argument of the new revolution. In 1917 the working classes on both sides of the war were weary and felt oppressed. Lenin knew of these sentiments from his contacts in Switzerland, and, although he did not feature revolutionary export in this speech because of the necessity to consolidate gains at home, his references kept it alive as one of the major Socialist contentions.

Lenin's chief argument involving cognitive dissonance was his claim that the Bolsheviks were ready to assume power. The disdain with which this argument was received shows the amount of dissonance it created.[27] Could Lenin have been a victim of his own rhetoric, proposing a measure so extreme that he talked himself into seeing supreme control when he himself did not think the Bolsheviks could rule Russia by themselves? The answer must be negative. Although hearing himself make such extreme statements undoubtedly reinforced his determination to assume dictatorial powers, Lenin had felt since 1905 that it should be his party and his party alone with Lenin at its head that should rule Russia. Lenin formulated his propositions to take advantage of cognitive dissonance. His ideas were more radical than the traffic would bear and were presented in such a blunt, antagonistic manner as to enhance the distance between him and his audience. Mor observed that "the speeches of Lenin were impregnated with a combative, militant spirit" (*14*, 23). Lenin hammered at his militant philosophy until its very controversial qualities lent it attractiveness.

Like Robespierre's, it was Lenin's infallible logic that dominated his invention. Witnesses are in agreement. Sukhanov said that where Lenin excelled was in "breaking down complicated systems into the simplest and most genuinely accessible elements, and hammering, hammering, hammering them into the heads of his audience until he took them captive" (*20*, 280). Trotsky observed:

The leading feature in Lenin's speeches . . . is his directness of purpose. . . . He

---

[27]Sukhanov said of Lenin's June 17, 1917 speech: "But as a program for a future government, both of Lenin's 'steps' were really absurd, and didn't seem the least bit attractive even to the tiny Left section, where both the faces and the talk reflected an absolutely unambiguous bafflement at Lenin's speech" (*20*, 381-82).

approaches his listeners in different ways: he explains, convinces, disconcerts, jokes, convinces again, and explains again. What holds his speech together is not a formal plan, but a clear aim forced for today, that pierces the consciousness of his listeners like a splinter (21, 169).

But Lenin supported his evidence and arguments with ethos and emotion. Lenin's reputation as a man of stature so long grieved enhanced his ethos. No one had inconvenienced himself more for the revolution than Lenin. He was a reputable curiosity. Sukhanov said that, on June 17, "Lenin wouldn't have been allowed to speak at all except for the enormous curiosity . . . felt for the notorious figure" (20, 380).

Moreover Lenin's speeches were packed with emotion, for, although he avoided theatrics (1), he was aware of the need for motivation. The fear of civil war, the fear of strikes, the fear of demonstrations, the fear of a powerful mind at work—but above all, the fear that Lenin might be right in how the revolution would develop, all these fears gripped his audience. Lenin's anger against the capitalists made his speeches captivating. Recrimination is a powerful magnet. Danton knew that well. Gandhi realized its strength, but resisted using recrimination against the British for ethical reasons. Lenin, however, did not hesitate to use it against his enemies.

Lenin could also be gay and humorous. He did not wish to appear contrived in his humor and therefore avoided light witticisms, puns, and plays on words for an "energetic joking, intelligible to the masses, popular in the true sense of the word" (21, 168). When Lenin felt at home with his audience he offered them and they gratefully accepted "the crafty, naive, witty remark, a good-natured, merciless characterization" (21, 168), i.e., the astute observation of the wily peasant.

Arrangement

How a contemporary speech professor would react to Lenin's outlining procedures is not difficult to imagine. He would suggest combining, regrouping, condensing, and consolidating. But Lenin would protest that he was not interested in a revolt rhetoric that exposed how he got from "A" to "Z." His goals were clear to himself, but he did not always want them clear to others. He only wanted his audience to feel the total impact of his arguments. Trotsky explained how this sort of outline could cause Lenin difficulties:

Now and then . . . the speaker raises the ladder of his thoughts too hastily and jumps up two or three steps at once; this is the case if the conclusions seem to him very clear and practically close at hand, and he wants to bring his hearers to it

> as quickly as possible. But he detects at once that the audience is not with him, that the connection with his hearers is broken off. Then he constrains himself at once, springs down at one bound and begins the ascent anew, but with a calm and more moderate step. . . . The construction of his speech naturally suffers from this backward leap. But is the speech made for its construction? Is any other logic of value . . . but that which compels action (*21*, 167-68)?

This second time, said Trotsky, Lenin carried his audience with him. Then came nailing down the conclusion, striking it two or three times so that it would hold, and then giving it "a simple, clear, and picturesque expression so that it may more easily be impressed on the memory . . ." (*21*, 168).

Lenin said that the only speech he had ever written out in advance was one delivered on April 2, 1922, to the Eleventh Soviet Congress (*16*, XXXVI, 477). His wife Krupskaya noted, however, that he invariably wrote down the theme of his speech and developed its plan. This outline was not revised, said Krupskaya, and was subject to very few corrections (*1*).

The latest translation of Lenin's collected works has two items that support Krupskaya's observations: first, a speech "outline" of December, 1922 (*5*, XXXVI, 588-89) and second, a set of speech "notes" of March, 1921 (*5*, XXXVI, 535-37). The "outline" is brief, listing 24 items, each numbered, with no subpoints. There are references to evidence Lenin planned to use, and one or two instances indicating phraseology. The "notes" list only 14 points. Several of these have two or three subpoints, while one has as many as four. The "notes" give more indication of exact phraseology and include marginal comments that could represent Lenin's notations of what other speakers said, for Krupskaya noted that Lenin made such addenda (*1*). The text resulting from these "notes" delivered on March 15, 1921, (*5*, XXXII, 214-15) follows the "notes" to a moderate degree.

Style

"Communism must be made comprehensible to the masses of the workers," said Lenin, "so that they will regard it as their own cause" (*5*, XXXI, 372). Therefore Lenin had slowly developed a style that would communicate with the largely uneducated workers, soldiers, and peasants.[28] Consequently his June 17 speech featured an elementary vocabulary hammering home his costume of words that he knew would be understood by those outside the assembly. "Capitalist" in some form is used 36 times; "soviets" 14 times; "imperialist" 13 times; and "bourgeois" 10 times. Occasionally Lenin would

[28] For Krupskaya's description of how Lenin developed a simple style see *3*, 197.

double the impact of his costume of words by speaking of "imperialist capitalists" or the "peasant proletarian." In 1917 the effect must have been deadening to his opposition, and it is certainly monotonous to us now. But Lenin's followers reveled in his use of "comrade," "citizen," "masses," "toilers," and "workers," while their frequent appearance, although annoying, increased the cognitive dissonance among his opposition.

The austerity of Lenin's style is striking. He not only uses simple words himself, but he makes fun of his opponents for using high-flown phrases such as "democratization of the central and local power." Although Lenin did not strive for elevated phraseology or witticisms (2, 109) because these would have been bourgeois, he did allow himself an occasional figure of speech, e.g., "America which wants to gobble up Mexico"; threefold anaphoras featuring "no matter" and "in vain"; and frequent usage of inverted sentence structure, which, although it is more common in Russian than in English, can still be classified as figurative.

Therefore Lenin's speeches were lean and wiry. He could sense an onomatopoeic word, and his delivery allowed him to capitalize on the explosive quality of the Russian language. Krupskaya noted that he did sometimes pace up and down, whispering to himself (1). Perhaps, during these times, he was searching for words.

Delivery

Although there is much about Lenin that detracted from his speaking—his short stature, his insignificant features, his ordinary voice—he was highly effective. His voice could crack and reach falsetto (21, 166), but the result was not ludicrous. "Lenin," said Sukhanov, "was in general a very good orator—not an orator of the consummate, rounded phrase, or of the luminous image, or of absorbing pathos, ... but an orator of enormous impact and power" (20, 280).

Krupskaya testified that Lenin was very nervous before he spoke, that he became uncommunicative and did not want to talk about other things. His method of delivery itself she found fast, simple, lacking in theatrics with "no artificiality or singing like in French, no monotony like in English, just typical Russian speech" (1). Once Lenin had begun, Krupskaya found that his words came without difficulty and with enthusiasm.

Trotsky is undoubtedly prejudiced, but his words have the ring of truth: "When I try mentally ... to see and hear Lenin on the platform," said Trotsky, "... I see a strong and supple figure of medium height, and hear a smooth, rapid, uninterrupted voice, rather striking, almost without pauses, and at first without special emphasis" (*21*, 162). During the initial period of a speech, Trotsky found Lenin introverted, "the gaze . . . turned inward, the face . . . sullen and even vexed" (*21*, 162).

When attacked, Lenin's eyes began to glow in their deep sockets. The anticipation of the audience quickened. His oriental cheekbones began to shine and his reddish gray beard became less important than his eyes. The voice lost its hardness and became flexible, soft and insinuating (*21*, 163).[29]

There is no detailed account of how Lenin spoke on June 17. However the Bolshevist Shottman does describe Lenin's appearance before the All-Russian Bolshevik Party Conference a month earlier:

> Lenin modestly seated himself on a low stool at the end of the room. He pulled out some closely written notes from his pocket and . . . began by saying that the Party was now immediately confronted with the question of seizing political power. . . . At first Lenin spoke in a calm and restrained tone, but later he warmed up and continued in his habitual style, interspersing his arguments with sallies of wit and hard blows at his opponents. . . . Sometimes he would get up from his seat and pace up and down the room, thumbs stuck in the armholes of his vest, stopping now and again to emphasize a particularly important point. His speech lasted two hours and was listened to with breathless attention. When he finished, several seconds passed in absolute silence. The comrades seemed to have been hypnotized. During my twenty years' acquaintance with Lenin I had occasion to hear many of his reports and speeches, but this was the best . . . (*18*, 314-15).

Conclusion

Sukhanov observed that Lenin's later speeches did not retain the intense flavor of his speeches of stage one and stage two. "Afterwards, about a year and a half later," said Sukhanov, "hearing him as head of the Government, one was bound to regret the former orator, the 'irresponsible' agitator and demagogue. After Lenin had changed from a demagogue and insurrectionary into a statesman, Lenin the orator became flat, faded, and trivial, losing both his power and his originality" (*20*, 280). The man of action, working against counterrevolution, had less and less need for the man of words. Free speech had been abolished. There was no one to oppose Lenin in the open forum and force him to keep alive his rhetoric. Thus the orator in Lenin died several years before his first stroke and long before his tired body was put to rest in the Kremlin.

[29] For additional descriptions of Lenin speaking, see *21*, 164 and 170-7.

Bibliography

1. Ermolovich, N., "Smel i otvazhen; chto rassakazyvala N. K. Krupskaia uchenym o V. I. Lenine" [Brave and daring; what did N. K. Krupskaia tell the scientists about Lenin], *Izvestia*, April 7, 1963, p. 5.

   The Institute of the Brain, established to dissect Lenin's brain, addressed questions to his wife, the replies to which were published in 1963. Krupskaya used "brave and daring" to describe Lenin.

2. Kerzhentsev, Platon M., *Life of Lenin*. New York: Blue Ribbon Books, 1925.

   Short biography by former commissar of education would be more valuable if quotations were documented.

3. Krupskaya, Nadezhda, *Memories of Lenin*, trans. E. Verney. London, 1930.

   Translation of the enlarged Russian second edition about the years 1894 to 1907 by Lenin's wife, with appendix on "Lenin's Method of Work."

4. Krupskaya, Nadezhda, *O Lenine* [About Lenin]. Moscow: State Publishing House for Political Literature, 1960.

   Essays on Lenin by his wife published between 1917 and 1938, containing sections on Lenin as propagandist and agitator. Translated into German, not into English.

5. Lenin, V. I., *Collected Works* vols. 1-38. Moscow: Foreign Languages Publishing House, 1960-.

   Translation of fourth edition (see No. 7). An English translation, authorized by Lenin Institute and begun in 1927 (New York: International Publishers Co., Inc.) issued only volumes 4, 13, 18, 19, 20, 21, and 23.

6. Lenin, V. I., *Polnoe Sobranie Sochinenii* [Complete Works], 5th ed. Moscow: Marx-Lenin Institute, 1958-.

   Fifty-five volumes of this latest Russian edition have appeared. Its claim to be complete appears more justified than similar claims of prior editions, where amendments for politican reasons were frequent.

7. Lenin, V. I., *Sochineniia* [Works], 4th ed., 44 vols. Moscow: Marx-Lenin Institute, 1941-1950.

   Interruptions caused by domestic turmoil and war complicated publication of Lenin's works. Citations of dates and numbers of volumes conflict. However, the following information should be reasonably accurate. The first edition of 20 volumes appeared between 1920 and 1926 and contained Lenin's writings and speeches, with valuable notes. The second edition of 32 volumes (1926-1932) expanded on the first edition by adding unpublished memoranda and continued excellent explanatory notes, but the work was never completed. The third edition of 30 volumes (1932-1935) was only a reprint of the second edition. When internal politics liquidated old Leninists, the fourth edition was published to correct errors of previous editions. Many of Lenin's letters and much commentary were omitted. See No. 6 for fifth edition and No. 4 for translation of fourth edition.

8. Lenin, V. I., *Speeches.* introduction A. Kurella. New York: International Publishers Co., Inc., 1928.

   Small volume of 13 of Lenin's speeches in English, forming volume 8 of *Voices of Revolt*, clumsily done with no acknowledgment of frequent abridgments.

9. Lenin, V. I., and J. Stalin, *The Russian Revolution: Writings and speeches from the February Revolution to the October Revolution, 1917.* New York, 1938.

   Contains five Lenin speeches, translated into English, dated February to October, 1917. No notes, no bibliography, and no source of translator.

10. *Lenin and Stalin on Propaganda*, vol. 24 of 27-vol. series, The Little Lenin Library. London: Lawrence & Wishart Ltd., 1931-1949.

    Volume 24 of this edition, which is difficult to obtain (copy in Library of Congress is lost), differs from volume 24 of second edition.

11. *Lenin, Stalin, 1917: Selected Writings and Speeches.* Moscow: Foreign Languages Publishing House, 1938.

    Contains four major Lenin speeches, dated May 12, 1917 to January 19, 1918, as well as several less important statements and proclamations.

12. Maynard, John, *Russia in Flux.* New York: The Macmillan Company, 1955.

    Fabian and Labour politician who spent the years from 1886 to 1926 in India. From there he made two extensive trips to Russia. He wrote two analyses of the Russian Revolution, both of which are condensed into this one volume.

13. Moorehead, Alan, *The Russian Revolution*. New York: Harper & Row, Publishers, 1958.

Moorehead's "brief, simple, and straightforward account of the Russian Revolution" is valuable because it reflects the work of Stephan Possony whose research into captured German army files attempted to disprove the spontaneity of the Russian revolt.

14. Mor, N. M., "La Preparación del Discurso" in *El Arte Leninista de la Propaganda y la Agitación*. Buenos Aires: Editorial Anteo, 1965.

Mor, a Soviet writer who assisted in publishing Lenin's collected works, outlines Lenin's propaganda technique. Russian title *Leninskoe isskustvo propagandy i agitatsii*. No English translation could be found.

15. Moscow: Institute Marksizma-Leninizma, *Vospominaniia o Vladimire Il'iche Lenine* [Recollections about Vladimir Ilich Lenin], 23 vols. Moscow: Marx-Lenin Institute, 1956-.

A series collecting personal reminiscences of Lenin by his family, fellow party members and officials, and statesmen. Two parts: before 1917 and after 1917. No English translation.

16. Moscow: Institute Marksizma-Leninizma, *Leninskii Sbornik* [Lenin's Miscellany], vols. 1-36. Moscow: Marx-Lenin Institute, 1925-1959.

A collection of miscellaneous materials by and relating to Lenin to supplement the collected works.

17. *Pravda*, nos. 82 and 83 (June 28 and 29, 1917), pp. 2-3 and 2-3.

Pravda, an organ of the Central Committee of the Communist party, first appeared in Saint Petersburg in 1912.

18. Shottman, A. V., *Memories of the Fight*. Moscow: Cooperative Publishing Society of Foreign Workers in the USSR, 1935.

Pages 314-16 give a description of Lenin speaking.

19. Shub, David, *Lenin*. Garden City, N. Y.: Doubleday & Company, Inc., 1948.

Well-indexed biography, excellent notes, by a Russian who knew Lenin, who was in the 1905-1906 revolt, and who, since 1908, kept up contacts with Russia from the United States.

20. Sukhanov, Nicolai N., *The Russian Revolution: 1917*, ed. Joel Carmichael. New York: Oxford University Press, Inc., 1955.

Abridgment of seven-volume memoir, first published in Russia in 1922, by a Russian intellectual who was in the revolutions of 1905 and 1917.

21. Trotsky, Leon, *Lenin.* New York: G. P. Putnam's Sons, 1962.
   Short but cryptic memoirs on Lenin by Trotsky, who fell from power after Lenin's death and went into exile. Written in 1924.
22. Walter, Gérard, *Lenine.* Paris: Éditions René Julliard, 1950.
   Lengthy bibliography by historian-librarian at *Bibliothèque Nationale.* Excellent notes. Bibliography by languages. No English translation.

Questions for Discussion

1. Divide Lenin's costume of words into four themes: negative Old Regime; positive New Regime; tributes to freedom; governmental jargon. Which set of word clusters is dominant?

2. Was Lenin's proposal that the Bolsheviks were prepared to assume leadership of the government an example of a call for lawlessness?

3. Read Kerensky's description of Lenin's older brother (Alexander Kerensky, *The Crucifixion of Liberty*, pp. 10-12). To what extent do you think that Lenin's political and social grievances were accelerated by his personal grievance?

4. Cite examples to show that the speecn of June 17 exemplifies the man of action of the second stage of a revolution impatient to get his work done.

5. Is there any evidence in the speech of June 17 that Lenin let himself become the victim of his own rhetoric?

6. Discuss what you consider to be the role of cognitive dissonance in Lenin's rhetoric.

7. To what extent did Lenin use *argumentum ad misericordiam* in his speech?

8. Be prepared to discuss Trotsky's chapter, "Lenin on the Platform" *(21,* 162-71).

9. What disappointments did you experience from studying Lenin as a revolt rhetorician?

10. Read the accounts of Lenin's speech at the Saint Petersburg Railway Station on April 16, 1917 (*19*, 187-88; *22*, 282; *20*, 269-70) and consult the speech in his collected works. How effectively do you think this speech has been preserved?

Exercises

1. Compare descriptions of Lenin's speech of June 17, 1917 (*2*, 179; *19*, 199-203; *20*, 380-84; *21*, 70-72). Write a description of the occasion in your own words.

2. Violate Lenin's speech technique by writing an effective conclusion for this speech, summarizing the ground that it has covered and underlining the main themes of the speech.

3. Insert organizational flags into the Lenin speech to punctuate its structure. Use such phrases as "in the second place," "now that we have explained," "there are several reasons why," and so on. Then write a short essay opposing or favoring the inclusion of such flags.

4. What voices are there now in the United States that may be attempting to make the same use of cognitive dissonance as Lenin did in 1917? Support your conclusions with examples taken from contemporary revolt rhetoric.

5. Compare Lenin's speech of June 17 with a speech delivered by a contemporary revolt rhetorician, preferably a Communist advocate, to see whether the degree to which Lenin depended upon a costume of words has continued to the present.

Mohandas Karamchand Gandhi
(1869-1947)

Law and Order, Love, and Let My People Go

Many of the sources on Gandhi and the Round Table Conference of 1932 have the advantage of being in English, but they have the disadvantage of often being obscure, rare, and biased. This brief introduction will present to the reader the research that will place Gandhi's revolt rhetoric in its social and historical perspectives.

Gandhi was born at Porbandar, India, to devout merchant-caste Hindus. Although the family had traditionally been grocers, Gandhi's father and grandfather had been prime ministers of their small princely state north of Bombay. At thirteen Gandhi married Kasturbai, daughter of a merchant family.

After completing school examinations and passing an unsuccessful year in college, Gandhi went to London to study law. He gained his mother's permission to leave by swearing to abstain from women, alcohol, and meat while abroad, but he was banished from his caste because he left India. In England Gandhi's problems included finding vegetarian food and dressing in what he then considered proper clothes. Shy, small, and ugly, he must have appeared ungainly at the Inner Temple where he studied. He attempted to read his first speech before a small meeting of vegetarians, but, because of extreme stage fright, he had to have a friend read it for him (10). After three years in London, Gandhi was admitted to the bar and passed the London University examinations.

Gandhi attempted to practice law in Bombay, but, in his first case, he had such stage fright that he could not speak and retreated to the position of law clerk. In 1893 he was offered an opportunity to go to South Africa to settle a suit for a rich Indian. The discriminatory practices of the English in Natal and the Dutch in Orange Free State forced Gandhi into politics. Although he was the first educated Indian wearing English clothes who had appeared in Natal, he nevertheless found himself called a "coolie." Indians brought to South Africa as indentured servants were virtually slaves. During twenty-one years in South Africa, which ended with the passage of the Indian Relief Bill of 1914, Gandhi developed the following philosophies:

(1) satyagraha—passive resistance or nonviolence (ashima)
(2) brachmacharya—continence in sex
(3) the ashram—communal living in relative poverty
(4) fasting—initiated to atone for the sins of others or for his own purification
(5) dieting—abstinence from cow or buffalo milk, plus previous abstinence from meat and eggs.

In 1893 Gandhi found the Indian minority helpless; in 1914, when he left, the status of his countrymen was highly improved.

Upon returning to India, Gandhi came under the tutelage of Gopal Gokhale, the great man of the Indian National Congress. Congress had been founded in 1885 by an Englishman with government approval, but it slowly became the voice of nationalist India. Gandhi did not immediately become active in Congress, for he spent the first few years surveying the situation. On February 4, 1916, Gandhi delivered a speech at the opening of Benares Hindu University that severely criticized the Indian community for wearing jewels when many were hungry, for allowing unsanitary conditions, for spitting in public, and for the filth in the third-class railway carriages. So distasteful were his remarks that he was shouted down and not allowed to continue. But Gandhi had launched on a lengthy campaign that was to end only in death.

Although Gandhi opposed many of the policies of the empire, he had proved his loyalty in the Boer and Zulu Wars. His regard for Great Britain was again demonstrated in 1918 when, under severe criticism, he undertook to recruit soldiers for the British Indian Army. Gandhi felt grateful for much that England had done and did not wish to take advantage when she was in trouble. However, in the fall of 1918, Gandhi had to give up his campaign for recruitment when he fell seriously ill from dysentery. It was only his wife's observation that he had not vowed to give up goat's milk that saved his life.

The passage of the Rowlatt Bill in 1919 demonstrated that the British were not going to support Home Rule. India reacted violently. Gandhi called a one-day strike. Violence broke out. The Amritsar Massacre took place on April 13, killing 379 Indians and wounding 1,137. Gandhi abruptly called off the satyagraha because he found that the people were not ready to proceed without violence. On April 18, his fasting quieted the disorders.

Between 1919 and 1931, Gandhi walked over India, preaching on cleanliness and nonviolent means of opposing Britain. He took up spinning, encouraging Indians to make their own cloth rather than buying British fabrics. In 1921, he adopted the loincloth. In 1924, he fasted for 21 days to bring peace between Hindus and Moslems. The Salt March of 1930 to break the British monopoly on salt featured a 200-mile march to the sea. At least 60,000 Indians over the country were arrested for making, buying, and selling salt. The jails would not hold all of Gandhi's followers. Gandhi and Nehru were arrested on May 5, 1930, marking Gandhi's fourth arrest since his return to India.

To retain their hold on India and to fulfill their obligations to the Indians, the British held two Round Table Conferences in London. The first occurred in November, 1930, but it failed to settle the unrest because only the Moslem leader would attend. As unrest continued, the Labour government called a second conference for the fall of 1931. Although the conservative viceroy of India had loaded the delegates with reactionaries and although many of Gandhi's followers were against participation, Congress finally agreed to send a delegation. Because of crucial issues being considered in India, Congress was reluctant to release its leaders to go to London. Therefore, in an effort to demonstrate that Congress represented all India and not just the Hindus, Congress named Gandhi as its sole representative. At least there would be one voice that could speak for all of India amid the babble of the minorities.

Gandhi arrived in London on September 12 and persisted in wearing his loincloth, supplemented with crude shawls and sandals, throughout the cold fall. After he had been presented at court, when reporters asked if he thought he had been wearing enough clothing, Gandhi replied that King George had worn enough for them both. Gandhi prided himself on the friendships he made with the poor in the slum district of London where he had chosen to live.

Gandhi attended the conference along with 13 British representatives, 19 princes, and 72 representatives of the areas known as British India. Gandhi participated freely. He went to a private dinner at the Dorchester House. When he arrived at the meeting of the Federal Structure Subcommittee carrying a flask of goat's milk and wrapped in a blanket, he created quite a stir. On Mondays, the day of the week which Gandhi had selected as a day of silence, he wrote notes to the chairman who sent back written answers. He addressed the Minorities Subcommittee several times, clarifying that Congress was against having delegates chosen by separate electorates, Hindus voting for Hindus, Moslems for Moslems, and so on. Gandhi wanted a United India.

The Plenary Session of the Round Table Conference was held on November 27 around the oval table that had served the year before, supplemented by two tables placed within the circle to accommodate the increased number of delegates. Prime Minister Ramsay MacDonald presided with Gandhi seated several chairs to his left. The session was long, lasting from 10:30 A.M. until 2:30 A.M. Fifty delegates had certified that they wished to speak (9, 145), but the London *Daily Telegraph* of December 1, 1931, reported only 33 speakers. Gandhi began his speech shortly after midnight. The *Daily Herald* of December 1 reported that the delegates were jaded and weary, but that the prime minister was determined to have all the speeches finished so that the session the following day could be devoted entirely to his own remarks.

At 11:30 A.M. the following morning, MacDonald delivered a 35-minute statement; he said that he had risen at 6:00 A.M. to draft it. Gandhi proposed a vote of thanks to the prime minister in a short, humorous impromptu speech. The prime minister's rejoinder was equally humorous. Then MacDonald sounded his gavel and the conference ended. The prime minister moved toward Gandhi and clasped him by the hand. They spoke quietly face-to-face, and then parted.

The Second Round Table Conference demonstrated the rhetorical breakdown between the Old Regime and the insurgents, a breakdown that Gandhi sensed immediately but that he found impossible to circumvent. Gandhi had said before he came to London that Congress wanted for India complete independence; he reiterated his position at the conference; but the Old Regime did not comprehend. Gandhi's speech was a last attempt to get the record straight. It exhibits the contradictions of passive resistance. On one hand the speaker says that he does not wish violence, that he seeks understanding, that he has confidence in the abilities of the Old Regime to grant reforms; on the other hand the speaker says that pressure must be maintained to achieve reform, that he is not certain how pacific this pressure can be, and that he is at a loss to know what else to do to achieve accord. If the student of revolt rhetoric hears this contradiction during stage one of a revolution, when prestigious men of words with a grievance are openly revealing the tenuousness of their position, he can be relatively certain that, unless the Old Regime moves (a) to suppress the revolt or (b) to grant substantial reforms, violence is not far away. The violence would have come much sooner in India had not World War II intervened to temper the position of the Indian nationalists.

What did the Round Table Conference accomplish? Perhaps it gave Congress time to regroup and strengthen itself. Perhaps it caused the nonviolent movement to lose momentum and therefore helped the British. For Gandhi it was a personal victory. Andrews noted that most English had considered

Gandhi as only a fanatic, but, after 1931, in a small country where ideas traveled fast, "they all unanimously respected the greatness of his soul" (*1*, 254).

Upon his return to India Gandhi was immediately jailed, whereupon he began a fast unto death to oppose separate elections for Hindus, Moslems, and untouchables. So great was Gandhi's influence that a settlement was reached after only a few days of fasting. On September 4, 1934, Gandhi withdrew from Congress and politics to devote himself to social reform. When World War II broke out, Gandhi's love for England came into conflict with his ambitions for India. But he would not bargain with the British under duress. Nevertheless the Congress's political leaders pushed for concessions. Japan's entry into the war in 1941 affected the conflict between England and the Congress, but did not curtail it altogether. In spite of pressure from the United States, Winston Churchill resisted granting India independence. In 1942, widespread violence broke out, and Gandhi was jailed until May of 1944.

From 1944 to 1947 Gandhi strove to keep India from partition. But Mohammed Ali Jinnah as leader of 100,000,000 Moslems wanted a separate state for his minority. Jinnah got his Pakistan, but not nearly as much territory as he desired. Nehru and Congress accepted partition as a way to independence. The Dominion of India was declared on August 15, 1947.

Gandhi had never agreed to partition. All through the summer of 1947 and into the winter of 1948, terrible bloodshed occurred between Hindu and Moslem. To halt the violence Gandhi began a fast to death on January 13, 1948. On January 18 a truce was declared. But only 12 days later, a young ultranationalist Hindu shot Gandhi to death. His murder brought peace to India and Pakistan and prevented a war between the two new states. But such a deed seemed a terrible price to pay for the very tranquillity that Gandhi had sought.

I Live under No Illusion

November 28, 1931
The Second Round Table Conference,
London, England

Prime Minister and Friends: Prime Minister, you will extend to me the indulgence of a physically incapable man and therefore you and this Assembly will please excuse me for my inability to stand up to address you.

The Chairman: Certainly, Mr. Gandhi.

Mr. Gandhi: Thank you. I wish that I could have done without having to speak to you but I felt that I would not have been just to you or just to my principle if I did not put in what may be the last word on behalf of the Congress. I live under no illusion. I do not think that anything that I can say this evening can possibly influence the decision of the Cabinet. Probably the decision has been already taken. Matters of liberty of practically a whole Continent can hardly be decided by mere argumentation, or even negotiation. Negotiation has its purpose and has its play, but only under certain conditions. Without those conditions, negotiations are a fruitless task. But I do not want to go into all these matters. I want as far as possible to confine myself within the four corners of the conditions that you, Prime Minister, read to this Conference at its opening meeting. I would, therefore, first of all say a few words in connection with the Reports that have been submitted to this Conference. You will find in these Reports that generally it has been stated that such and such is the opinion of a large majority, some, however, have expressed an opinion to the contrary, and so on. Parties who have dissented have not been stated. I had heard when I was in India, and I was told when I came here, that no decision or no decisions will be taken by the ordinary rule of majority, and I do not want to mention this fact here by way of complaint that the Reports have been so framed as if the proceedings were governed by the test of majority.

But it was necessary for me to mention this fact, because to most of these Reports you will find that there is a dissenting opinion, and in most of the

Gandhi's remarks first appeared in the Indian periodical, *Young India* (*16*, XIII [December 24, 1931], 407-9, 412-13). Edited versions appear in *6*, *7*, *8*, and *9*. The London *Daily Telegraph* of December 2, 1931, printed excerpts from the speech. The version offered here is largely that found in *Young India* with limited modifications taken from later versions. Reprinted by permission of the Navajivan Trust.

cases that dissent unfortunately happens to belong to me. It was not a matter of joy to have to dissent from fellow delegates. But I felt that I could not truly represent the Congress unless I notified that dissent.

There is another thing which I want to bring to the notice of this Conference, namely, what is the meaning of the dissent of the Congress? I said at one of the preliminary meetings of the Federal Structure Committee[1] that the Congress claimed to represent over eighty-five percent of the population of India, that is to say the dumb, toiling, semi-starved millions. But I went further: that the Congress claimed also, by right of service, to represent even the Princes, if they would pardon my putting forth that claim, and the landed gentry, and the educated class. I wish to repeat that claim and I wish this evening to emphasize that claim.

All the other parties at this meeting represent sectional interests. Congress alone claims to represent the whole of India and all interests. It is no communal organization; it is a determined enemy of communalism in any shape or form. Congress knows no distinction of race, color or creed; its platform is universal. It may not always have lived up to the creed. I do not know a single human organization that lives up to its creed. Congress has failed very often to my knowledge. It may have failed more often to the knowledge of its critics. But the worst critic will have to recognize, as it has been recognized, that the Indian National Congress is a daily growing organization, that its message penetrates to the remotest village of India, that on given occasions the Congress has been able to demonstrate its influence over and among these masses who inhabit its 700,000 villages.

And yet, here I see that the Congress is treated as one of the Parties. I do not mind it; I do not regard it a calamity for the Congress; but I do regard it as a calamity for the purpose of doing the work for which we have gathered together here. I wish I could convince all the British public men, the British Ministers, that the Congress is capable of delivering the goods. The Congress is the only all-India wide national organization, bereft of any communal bias: it does represent all minorities which have lodged their claim here and which, or the signatories on their behalf, claim—I hold unjustifiably—to represent forty-six percent of the population of India. The Congress, I say, claims to represent all these minorities.

What a great difference it would be today if this claim on behalf of the Congress was recognized. I feel that I have to state this claim with some degree of emphasis on behalf of peace, for the sake of achieving the purpose

---

[1] A subcommittee of the conference concerned with planning a federal legislatur⌐ for India.

which is common to all of us, to you Englishmen who sit at this Table and to us the Indian men and women who also sit at this Table. I say so for this reason: Congress is a powerful organization; Congress is an organization which has been accused of running or desiring to run a parallel Government; and in a way I have endorsed the charge. If you could understand the working of the Congress, you would welcome an organization which could run a parallel Government and show that it is possible for an organization, voluntary, without any force at its command, to run the machinery of Government even under adverse circumstances.

But no. Although you have invited the Congress, you distrust the Congress. Although you have invited the Congress, you reject its claim to represent the whole of India. Of course it is possible at this end of the world to dispute that claim, and it is not possible for me to prove this claim; but, all the same, if you find me asserting that claim, I do so because a tremendous responsibility rests upon my shoulders.

The Congress represents the spirit of rebellion. I know that the word "rebellion" must not be whispered at a Conference which has been summoned in order to arrive at an agreed solution of India's troubles through negotiation. Speaker after speaker has got up and said that India should achieve her liberty through negotiation, by argument, and that it will be the greatest glory of Great Britain if Great Britain yields to India's demands by argument. But the Congress does not hold quite that view. The Congress has an alternative which is unpleasant to you.

I heard several speakers—and let me say I have endeavored not to miss a single sitting—I have tried to follow every speaker with the utmost attention and with all the respect that I could possibly give to these speakers—saying what a dire calamity it would be if India was fired with the spirit of lawlessness, rebellion, terrorism, and so on. I do not pretend to have read history, but as a schoolboy I had to pass a paper in history also, and I read that the page of history is soiled red with the blood of those who have fought for freedom. I do not know an instance in which nations have attained their own without having to go through an incredible measure of travail. The dagger of the assassin, the poison bowl, the bullet of the rifleman, the spear and all these weapons and methods of destruction have been up to now used by, what I consider, blind lovers of liberty and freedom. And the historian has not condemned them. *I hold no brief for the terrorists.* Mr. Ghuznavi[2] brought in the terrorists and he brought in the Calcutta Corporation. I felt hurt when he mentioned an incident that took place at the Calcutta Corporation. He

---

[2] Sir Al-Halim Ghuznavi.

forgot to mention that the Mayor of that Corporation made handsome reparation for the error into which he himself was betrayed, and the error into which the Calcutta Corporation was betrayed, through the instrumentality of those members of the Corporation who were Congressmen.

I hold no brief for Congressmen who directly or indirectly would encourage terrorism. As soon as this incident was brought to the notice of the Congress, the Congress set about putting it in order. It immediately called upon the Mayor of the Calcutta Corporation to give an account of what was done and the Mayor, the gentleman that he is, immediately admitted his mistake and made all the reparation that it was then legally possible to make. I must not detain this Assembly over this incident for any length of time. He mentioned also a verse which the children of the forty schools conducted by the Calcutta Corporation are supposed to have recited. There were many other misstatements in that speech which I could dwell upon, but I have no desire to do so. It is only out of regard for the great Calcutta Corporation, and out of regard for truth, and on behalf of those who are not here tonight to put in their defense, that I mention these two glaring instances. I do not for one moment believe that this was taught in the Calcutta Corporation schools with the knowledge of the Calcutta Corporation. I do know that in those terrible days of last year several things were done for which we have regret, for which we have made reparation.

If our boys in Calcutta were taught those verses which Mr. Ghuznavi has recited, I am here to tender an apology on their behalf, but I should want it proved that the boys were taught by the schoolmasters of these schools with the knowledge and encouragement of the Corporation. Charges of this nature have been brought against Congress times without number, and times without number these charges have also been refuted, but if I have mentioned these things at this juncture, it is again to show that for the sake of liberty people have fought, people have lost their lives, people have killed and have sought death at the hands of those whom they have sought to oust.

The Congress then comes upon the scene and devises a new method not known to history, namely, that of civil disobedience, and the Congress has been following up that method. But again, I am up against a stone wall and I am told that that is a method that no Government in the world will tolerate. Well, of course, the Government may not tolerate, no Government has tolerated open rebellion. No Government may tolerate civil disobedience, but Governments have to succumb even to these forces, as the British Government has done before now, even as the great Dutch Government after eight years of trial had to yield to the logic of facts, General Smuts, a brave General, a great statesman, and a very hard taskmaster also, but he himself recoiled with horror from even the contemplation of doing to death innocent men and women who were merely fighting for the preservation of their self-respect, and things which he had vowed he would never yield in the year 1908, reinforced as he was by General Botha, he had to do in the year 1914, after having tried these civil resisters through and through. And in India, Lord Chelmsford had to do the same thing: the Governor of Bombay had to do the same thing in Borsad and Bardoli. I suggest to you, Prime Minister, it is too late today to resist this, and it is this thing which weighs me down, this choice that lies before them, the parting of the ways probably. I shall hope against hope, I shall strain every nerve to achieve an honorable settlement for my country, if I can do so without having to put the millions of my countrymen and countrywomen, and even children, through this ordeal of fire. It can be a matter of no joy and comfort to me to lead them again to a fight of that character, but, if a further ordeal of fire has to be our lot, I shall approach that with the greatest joy[3] and with the greatest consolation that I was doing what I felt to be right, the country was doing what it felt to be right, and the country will have the additional satisfaction of knowing that it was not at least taking lives, it was giving lives: it was not making the British people directly suffer, it was suffering. Professor Gilbert Murray[4] told me—I shall never forget that, I am paraphrasing his inimitable language—"Do you not consider for one moment that we Englishmen do not suffer when thousands of your countrymen suffer, that we are so heartless? " I do not think so. I do know that you will suffer; but I want you to suffer because I want to touch your hearts; and when your hearts have been touched then will come the psychological moment for negotiation. Negotiation there always will be; and if this time I have traveled all these miles in order to enter upon negotiation, I thought that your countryman, Lord Irwin, had sufficiently tried us through his ordinances, that he had sufficient evidence that thousands of men and women of India and thousands of children had suffered; and that, ordinance or no ordinance, *lathis* or no *lathis*,[5] nothing would avail to stem the tide that was onrushing and to stem the passions that were rising in the breasts of the men and women of India who were thirsting for liberty.

Whilst there is yet a little sand left in the glass, I want you to understand what this Congress stands for. My life is at your disposal. The lives of all the

[3]*Daily Telegraph*: "I would strain every nerve to secure an honourable settlement without exposing millions of India's men and women and children to the terrible ordeal of civil disobedience—but if it has to be faced, I will do it with joy."

[4](1866-1957), at this time Regius Professor of Greek at Oxford University and Chairman of the League of Nations' Union.

[5]Wooden sticks or clubs with which the passivists were often beaten.

members of the Working Committee, the All-India Congress Committee, are at your disposal. But remember that you have at your disposal the lives of all these dumb millions. I do not want to sacrifice those lives if I can possibly help it. Therefore, please remember, that I will count no sacrifice too great if, by chance, I can pull through an honorable settlement. You will find me always having the greatest spirit of compromise if I can but fire you with the spirit that is working in the Congress, namely, that India must have real liberty. Call it by any name you like; a rose will smell as sweet by any other name, but it must be the rose of liberty that I want and not the artificial product.[6] If your mind and the Congress mind, the mind of this Conference and the mind of the British people, means the same thing by the same word, then you will find the amplest room for compromise, and you will find the Congress itself always in a compromising spirit. But so long as there is not that one mind, that one definition, not one implication for the same word that you and I and we may be using, there is no compromise possible. How can there be any compromise as long as we each one of us has a different definition for the same words that we may be using? It is impossible, Prime Minister, I want to suggest to you in all humility, that it is utterly impossible then to find a meeting ground, to find a ground where you can apply the spirit of compromise. And I am very grieved to have to say up to now I have not been able to discover a common definition for the terms that we have been exchanging during all these weary weeks.

I was shown last week the Statute of Westminster[7] by a sceptic, and he said, "Have you seen the definition of Dominion? " I read the definition of "Dominion," and naturally I was not at all perplexed or shocked to see that the word "Dominion" was exhaustively defined, and it had not a general definition but a particular definition. It simply said: the word "Dominion" shall include Australia, South Africa, Canada and so on, ending with the Irish Free State. I do not think I noticed Egypt there. Then he said, "Do you see what your Dominion means? " It did not make any impression upon me. I do not mind what my Dominion means or what complete independence means. In a way I was relieved.

I said, I am now relieved from having to quarrel about the word "Do-

---

[6]*Daily Telegraph*: "I am open to a compromise providing the settlement is honorable and the liberty real. Call it by whatever name you will, but I want complete independence."

[7]The Statute of Westminster (Law Reports, Statutes 1932, vol. 22, George 5, chapter 4, pp. 13-17) was officially approved on December 11, 1931. Dominion is defined only by example, i.e., "In this Act, the expression 'Dominion' means any of the following Dominions, that is to say, the Dominion of Canada, the Commonwealth of Australia, the Dominion of New Zealand, the Union of South Africa, the Irish Free State, and Newfoundland."

minion," because I am out of it. But I want complete independence, and even so, so many Englishmen have said, "Yes, you can have complete independence, but what is the meaning of complete independence?" and again we come to a different definition. Therefore, I say, the Congress claim is registered as complete independence.

One of your great statesmen—I do not think I should give his name—was debating with me, and said, "Honestly, I did not know that you meant this by complete independence." He ought to have known but he did not know, and I shall tell you what he did not know. When I said to him, "I cannot be a partner in an Empire," he said: "Of course, that is logical." I replied: "But I want to become that. It is not as if I shall be if I am compelled to, but I want to become a partner with Great Britain. I want to become a partner with the English people; but I want to enjoy precisely the same liberty that your people enjoy, and I want to seek this partnership not merely for the benefit of India, and not merely for mutual benefit; I want to seek this partnership in order that the great weight that is crushing the world to atoms may be lifted from its shoulders."

This took place ten or twelve days ago. Strange as it may appear, I got a note from another Englishman, whom also you know, and whom also you respect. Among many things, he writes, "I believe profoundly that the peace and happiness of mankind depend on our friendship" and, as if I would not understand that, he says: "your people and mine." I must read to you what he also says: "And of all Indians you are the one that the real Englishman likes and understands."

He does not waste any words on flattery, and I do not think he has intended this last expression to flatter me. It will not flatter me in the slightest degree. There are many things in this note which, if I could share them with you, would perhaps make you understand better the significance of this expression, but let me tell you that when he writes this last sentence he does not mean me personally. I personally signify nothing, and I know I would mean nothing to any single Englishman; but I mean something to some Englishmen because I represent a cause, because I seek to represent a nation, a great organization which has made itself felt. That is the reason why he says this.

But then, if I could possibly find that working basis, Prime Minister, there is ample room for compromise. It is for friendship I crave. My business is not to throw overboard the slaveholder and tyrant. My philosophy forbids me to do so, and today the Congress has accepted that philosophy, not as a creed, as it is to me, but as a policy, because the Congress believes that is the right and the best thing for India, a nation of 350 millions, to do.

A nation of 350 million people does not need the dagger of the assassin, it does not need the poison bowl, it does not need the sword, the spear or the bullet. It needs simply a will of its own, an ability to say "no," and that nation is today learning to say "no."

But what is it that that nation does? To summarily, or at all, dismiss Englishmen? No. Its mission is today to convert Englishmen. I do not want to break the bond between England and India, but I do want to transform that bond. I want to transform that slavery into complete freedom for my country. Call it complete independence or whatever you like, I will not quarrel about that word, and even though my countrymen may dispute with me for having taken some other word, I shall be able to bear down that opposition so long as the content of the word that you may suggest to me bears the same meaning. Hence, I have times without number to urge upon your attention that the safeguards that have been suggested are completely unsatisfactory. They are not in the interests of India.

Three experts from the Federation of Commerce and Industry have, in their own way, each in his different manner, told out of their expert experiences how utterly impossible it is for any body of responsible Ministers to tackle the problem of administration when 80 percent of her resources are mortgaged irretrievably. Better than I could have shown to you, they have shown out of the amplitude of their knowledge what these financial safeguards mean for India. These mean the complete cramping of India. They have discussed at this table financial safeguards but that includes necessarily the question of Defense and the question of the Army. Yet while I say that the safeguards are unsatisfactory as they have been presented. I have not hesitated to say, and I do not hesitate to repeat that the Congress is pledged to giving safeguards, endorsing safeguards which may be demonstrated to be in the interests of India.

At one of the sittings of the Federal Structure Committee I had no hesitation in amplifying the admission and saying that those safeguards must be also of benefit to Great Britain. I do not want safeguards which are merely beneficial to India and prejudicial to the real interests of Great Britain. The fancied interests of India will have to be sacrificed. The fancied interests of Great Britain will also have to be sacrificed. The illegitimate interests of India will have to be sacrificed. The illegitimate interests of Great Britain will also have to be sacrificed. Therefore, again I repeat, if we have the same meaning for the same word, I will agree with Mr. Jayakar, with Sir Tej Bahadur Sapru and other distinguished speakers who have spoken at this Conference.

I will agree with them all that we have, after all these labors, reached a substantial measure of agreement, but my despair, my grief, is that I do not read the same words in the same light. The implications of the safeguards of Mr. Jayakar, I very much fear, are different from my implications, and the implications of Mr. Jayakar and myself are perhaps only different from the implications that Sir Samuel Hoare,[8] for instance, has in mind; I do not know. We have never really come to grips. We have never got down to brass tacks, as you put it, and I am anxious—I have been pining—to come to real grips and to get down to brass tacks all these days and all these nights, and I have felt: why are we not coming nearer and nearer together, and why are we wasting our time in eloquence, in oratory, in debating, and in scoring points? Heaven knows, I have no desire to hear my own voice. Heaven knows I have no desire to take part in any debating. I know that liberty is made of sterner stuff, and I know that the freedom of India is made of much sterner stuff. We have problems that would baffle any statesman. We have problems that other nations have not to tackle. But they do not baffle me; they cannot baffle those who have been brought up in the Indian climate. Those problems are there with us. Just as we have to tackle bubonic plague, we have to tackle the problem of malaria. We have to tackle, as you have not, the problem of snakes and scorpions, monkeys, tigers and lions. We have to tackle these problems because we have been brought up under them.

They do not baffle us. Somehow or other we have survived the ravages of these venomous reptiles and various creatures. So also shall we survive our problem and find a way out of those problems. But today you and we have come together at a Round Table and we want to find a common formula which will work. Please believe me that whilst I abate not a tittle of the claim that I have registered on behalf of the Congress, which I do not propose to repeat here, while I withdraw not one word of the speeches that I had to make at the Federal Structure Committee, I am here to compromise; I am here to consider every formula that British ingenuity can prepare, every formula that the ingenuity of such constitutionalists as Mr. Sastri, Dr. Tej Bahadur Sapru, Mr. Jayakar, Mr. Jinnah, Sir Muhammad Shafi and a host of others can weave into being.

I will not be baffled. I shall be here as long as I am required because I do not want to revive civil disobedience. I want to turn the truce that was arrived at in Delhi[9] into a permanent settlement. But for heaven's sake give me, a frail man 62 years gone, a little bit of a chance. Find a little corner for him

---

[8](1880-1959), was at this time MP from Chelsea and secretary of state for India.

[9]On March 4, 1931, Gandhi for the Congress and Lord Irwin (later Lord Halifax) for the government signed an agreement whereby the Congress ceased its boycott, peaceful picketing was permitted, and a law passed to punish the boycotters was repealed.

and the organization that he represents. You distrust that organization though you may seemingly trust me. Do not for one moment differentiate me from the organization of which I am but a drop in the ocean. I am no greater than the organization to which I belong. I am infinitely smaller than that organization; and if you find me a place, if you trust me, I invite you to trust the Congress also. Your trust in me otherwise is a broken reed. I have no authority save what I derive from the Congress. If you will work the Congress for all it is worth, then you will say goodbye to terrorism; then you will not need terrorism. Today you have to fight the school of terrorists which is there with your disciplined and organized terrorism, because you will be blind to the facts or the writing on the wall. Will you not see the writing that these terrorists are writing with their blood? Will you not see that we do not want bread made of wheat, but we want the bread of liberty; and without that liberty there are thousands today who are sworn not to give themselves peace or to give the country peace.

I urge you then to read that writing on the wall. I ask you not to try the patience of a people known to be proverbially patient. We speak of the mild Hindu, and the Musalman also by contact good or evil with the Hindu has himself become mild. And that mention of the Musalman brings me to the baffling problem of Minorities. Believe me, that problem exists here, and I repeat what I used to say in India—I have not forgotten those words—that without the problem of Minorities being solved there is no Swaraj[10] for India, there is no freedom for India. I know that, I realize it, and yet I came here in the hope "perchance" that I might be able to pull through a solution here. But I do not despair of some day or other finding a real and living solution in connection with the Minorities problem. I repeat what I have said elsewhere that so long as the wedge in the shape of foreign rule divides community from community and class from class, there will be no real living solution, there will be no living friendship between these communities. It will be after all and at best a paper solution. But immediately you withdraw that wedge, the domestic ties, the domestic affections, the knowledge of common birth—do you suppose that all these will count for nothing?

Were Hindus and Musalmans and Sikhs always at war with one another when there was no British rule, when there was no English face seen there? We have chapter and verse given to us by Hindu historians and by Musalman historians to say that we were living in comparative peace even then. And Hindus and Musalmans in the villages are not even today quarreling. In those days they were not known to quarrel at all. The late Maulana Muhammad Ali

[10] Self-rule.

often used to tell me, and he was himself a bit of an historian. He said: "If God"—"Allah" as he called God—"gives me life, I propose to write the history of Musalman rule in India; and then I will show, through documents that British people have preserved, that Aurangzeb was not so vile as he has been painted by the British historian; that the Mogul rule[11] was not so bad as it has been shown to us in British history; and so on." And so have Hindu historians written. This quarrel is not old; this quarrel is coeval with this acute shame. I dare to say, it is coeval with the British advent, and immediately this relationship, the unfortunate, artificial, unnatural relationship between Great Britain and India is transformed into a natural relationship, when it becomes, if it does become, a voluntary partnership to be given up, to be dissolved at the will of either party, when it becomes that you will find that Hindus, Musalmans, Sikhs, Europeans, Anglo-Indians, Christians, Untouchables, will all live together as one man.

I want to say one word about the Princes,[12] and I shall have done. I have not said much about the Princes, nor do I intend to say much tonight about the Princes, but I should be wronging them and I should be wronging the Congress if I did not register my claim, not with the Round Table Conference but with the Princes. It is open to the Princes to give their terms on which they will join the Federation. I have appealed to them to make the path easy for those who inhabit the other part of India, and therefore, I can only make these suggestions for their favorable consideration, for their earnest consideration. I think that if they accepted, no matter what they are, but some fundamental rights as the common property of all India, and if they accepted that position and allowed those rights to be tested by the Court, which will be again of their own creation, and if they introduced elements—only elements —of representation on behalf of their subjects, I think that they would have gone a long way to conciliate their subjects. They would have gone a long way to show to the world and to show to the whole of India that they are also fired with a democratic spirit, that they do not want to remain undiluted autocrats, but that they want to become constitutional monarchs even as King George of Great Britain is.

Sir, a note has been placed in my hands by my friend Sir Abdul Quiyum. He says: "Will you not say one word about the Frontier Province?"[13] I will,

---

[11] The Mogul rule in India dated from 1526 to around 1707. The Mogul Aurangzeb, whose reign began in 1658, used force to gain converts to Islam.

[12] The Indian States' Delegation numbered 19, including the Maharaja of Kashmir.

[13] A reference to the Northwest Frontier Province in the area of the Khyber Pass, now a part of Pakistan. The "Red Shirts," a fierce group who sought complete inde-

and it is this. Let India get what she is entitled to and what she can really take, but whatever she gets, and whenever she gets it, let the Frontier Province get complete autonomy today. That Frontier will then be a standing demonstration to the whole of India, and therefore, the whole vote of the Congress will be given in favor of the Frontier Province getting Provincial Autonomy tomorrow. Prime Minister, if you can possibly get your Cabinet to endorse the proposition that from tomorrow the Frontier Province becomes a full-fledged autonomous province, I shall then have a proper footing amongst the Frontier tribes and convene them to my assistance when those over the border cast an evil eye on India.

Last of all, my last is a pleasant task for me. This is perhaps the last time that I shall be sitting with you at negotiations. It is not that I want that. I want to sit at the same table with you in your closets and to negotiate and to plead with you and to go down on bended knees before I take the final leap and final plunge.

But, whether I have the good fortune to continue to tender my cooperation or not does not depend upon me. It largely depends upon you. But it may not even depend upon you. It depends upon so many circumstances over which neither you nor we may have any control whatsoever. Then, let me perform this pleasant task of giving my thanks to all from Their Majesties down to the poorest men in the East End where I have taken up my habitation.

In that settlement, which represents the poor people of the East End of London,[14] I have become one of them. They have accepted me as a member, and as a favored member of their family. It will be one of the richest treasures that I shall carry with me. Here, too I have found nothing but courtesy and nothing but a genuine affection from all with whom I have come in touch. I have come in touch with so many Englishmen. It has been a priceless privilege to me. They have listened to what must have often appeared to them to be unpleasant, although it was true. Although I have often been obliged to say these things to them they have never shown the slightest impatience or irritation. It is impossible for me to forget these things. No matter what befalls me, no matter what the fortunes may be of this Round Table Conference, one thing I shall certainly carry with me, that is, that from high to low I have found nothing but the utmost courtesy and the utmost affection. I consider

---

pendence for their remote, mountainous area, had been in open revolt for some time. Under regulations approved by the Round Table Conference, the province elected a council of 40 members in April of 1932 which gave them a measure of self-government.

[14] Gandhi elected to live at Miss Muriel Lester's settlement house, Kingsley Hall, in the slums of East London close to the India docks.

that it was well worth my paying this visit to England in order to find this human affection. [Applause.]

It has enhanced, it has deepened my irrepressible faith in human nature that although Englishmen and Englishwomen have been fed upon lies that I see so often disfiguring your Press, that although in Lancashire, the Lancashire people had perhaps some reason for becoming irritated against me, I found no irritation and no resentment even in the operatives. The operatives, men and women, hugged me. They treated me as one of their own. I shall never forget that.[15]

I am carrying with me thousands upon thousands of English friendships. I do not know them but I read that affection in their eyes as early in the morning I walk through your streets. All this hospitality, all this kindness will never be effaced from my memory, no matter what befalls my unhappy land. I thank you for your forbearance. [Applause.]

The Revolt Rhetoric of Gandhi

Two aspects of Gandhi's rhetoric are of particular interest. First, Gandhi's career as a radical passivist illustrates the distinctions between a rhetoric advocating *passive* lawlessness and a rhetoric advocating *active* lawlessness. Furthermore, the Indian Revolution, like its American counterpart, occurred under the tradition of free speech, so that Gandhi could publicize his calls for lawlessness, provided he was willing to accept the consequences. What effects did passivism and free speech have upon Gandhi's rhetoric of lawlessness?

First, in contrast to the secrecy that frequently surrounds lawlessness in other revolutions, Gandhi publicized and documented his violations. He often wrote personally to the viceroy, as he did in the case of the Salt March, clarifying his every move. When apprehended for his violations, he was the first to pronounce his guilt and to recommend punishment. Second, Gandhi's calls for lawlessness were always based on passive resistance to apprehension and punishment, but they often called for active resistance to the law. The making of salt was an overt act, and the inciting through rhetoric, asking Indians all over India to make salt, was an overt act. What Gandhi advocated by his passivist rhetoric was passivism toward those who would forcefully deter his actions, not passive actions on Gandhi's part. His rhetoric often featured overt advocacy of lawlessness. Third, Gandhi could be accused of

[15] Gandhi visited Manchester in Lancashire which was suffering badly from unemployment aggravated by Gandhi's policy of wearing clothes made of homespun cloth.

employing Theodore Roosevelt's philosophy of walking softly but carrying a big stick. He could always say that he himself was for passivism, but that experience had shown that passivism would not always prevail. Implied in Gandhi's rhetoric could have been the threat: If changes are not forthcoming, is the Old Regime prepared not only for my passive resistance but also for the militant resistance of others?

Gandhi knew that he was vulnerable to accusations that he was backing up his passive threats with activism. Where there was smoke, there could be fire. Gandhi's rhetoric smoked from his advocacy of passive threats and smouldered from the violence that often followed his calls for *satyagraha.* Whenever conscious efforts could exempt him from advocating active violence, Gandhi's record was clean. When in 1931 he spoke of the ordeal of fire that he might have to lead his people through, he had reference to passive resistance and he clarified his position by citing the analogy of South Africa. He concluded that a nation needs only to learn to say "no," it does not have to learn to hate. But he did make specific references to "the school of terrorists" opposed in turn by British terrorists, and he warned of the consequences that could occur if these tactics were continued. In other words, he protested that he wanted neither passive lawlessness nor active lawlessness, but he could threaten both.

Therefore the way Gandhi's rhetoric met the definition of revolution by calling for lawlessness is subject to individual interpretation. But there is no speculation as to what Gandhi wanted to achieve by his rhetoric and by his lawlessness. Nationalism was the motivating force. Religion was to be suppressed as a theme. Human rights, i.e., social and economic development, were to be achieved via nationalism. The Old Regime, as usual, procrastinated in granting independence to a colony. Perhaps without the fatigue that Britain experienced after World War II, Gandhi's rhetoric would not have achieved his nationalistic goal.

Gandhi's rhetoric pointed clearly to the focal point of dysfunction—a subjugated India. His goal was equally clear—a united, democratic India. As long as multiple dysfunction did not plague her, Great Britain was able to withstand Indian nationalism. But, when war had exhausted her economically and when social systems in England were being radically overhauled, Great Britain was forced to surrender India.

It must have been very difficult for Gandhi to see that his rhetoric demanding a united India was going to fail. His consolation was that his goal of a democratic state, comprising most of the territory that had been colonial India, could be achieved. Since Gandhi's rhetoric had made such a contribution toward a free India, it is regrettable that he did not live long enough to see that freedom function with some measure of success. Gandhi was right in arguing frequently in his rhetoric that India owed gratitude to England, for it was the precedent of a free society that England had set for India that gave India the strength to establish democracy when so many other new nations failed.

Because of loyal scribes and his own vigilance and in spite of a largely hostile press and some language barriers, Gandhi's rhetoric is in an encouraging state of preservation. But what has been preserved does not consist of a heritage of polished speeches. The Mahatma occasionally used notes, almost never a manuscript and often spoke with no assistance. He demonstrated his attitude toward notes at the Round Table Conference. During the ride to St. James' for his first speech, Gandhi told one of his fellow delegates that he had not been able to prepare his speech in advance, that he had been kept busy the night before and all that morning his mind had been a blank, but that "God will help me in collecting my thoughts at the proper time. After all we have to talk like simple men. I have no desire to look extra intelligent. Like a simple villager, all that I have to say is 'we want independence' " (15, 24). Gandhi's amanuensis, Mahadev Desai, tried faithfully to write down every word that passed over his idol's lips. Nanda said that Desai used the margins of newspapers, currency notes and even his fingernails to record Gandhi's words for posterity (11, 472). Nevertheless much was missed and Gandhi was too busy with deeds to polish up his speeches. They are, therefore, much as he spoke them.

Invention

Gandhi was certainly the respectable, prosperous man of words with a grievance—of a high caste, financially secure, foreign-educated, a lawyer, with a considerable amount to sacrifice by becoming a revolutionary. Gandhi spent most of his life freeing himself of this middle-class background and developing an ethical appeal which was close to miraculous.[16] In order to perfect his character, Gandhi cleaned out latrines with the Untouchables, abstained from food and lust, notified the government in advance of his passivist moves, nursed the lepers and maintained cheerfulness while in prison. Nanda associated Gandhi with this quotation from Professor Gilbert Murray:

[16] Gandhi of course rejected the idea that he had supernatural powers. When one follower claimed he had been cured by wearing Gandhi's picture around his neck and chanting Gandhi's name, Gandhi said: "It was God who cured you, not Gandhi, and kindly oblige me by taking that photograph off your neck" (14, 145).

Persons in power should be very careful how they deal with a man who cares nothing for sensual pleasure, nothing for riches, nothing for comfort or praise or promotion, but is simply determined to do what he believes to be right. He is a dangerous and uncomfortable enemy because his body which you can always conquer gives you so little purchase on his soul (*11*, 89).[17]

There are so many examples of the way in which Gandhi's ethos was able to motivate that it is frustrating to single out any one; but his last fast, begun on January 13, 1948, is representative. The announcement in 1947 that the British troops were to leave India and that Pakistan was to be a separate country started wave after wave of violence. Gandhi tramped from one end of India to the other, enforcing peace when nothing else would. The arrival of Hindu refugees from Pakistan put Delhi into one of its worst riots against the Moslems. In despair, Gandhi announced that he would fast unto death unless peace was restored. One man going without food not only calmed Delhi, but also quieted Pakistan.

Although Fülöp-Miller said that Gandhi detested emotional appeals (*3*, 168) and Doke proposed that Gandhi appealed particularly to the intelligence of his audience (*2*, 41), the Mahatma's speeches are full of the emotion of love and charity. Gandhi truly loved his enemies. He turned the other cheek.[18] It is difficult to inject love into a public speech without sounding artificial, patronizing, or hypocritical. But Gandhi could use it without pretense.

Gandhi, who was careful to document his sources and to be accurate in his use of evidence (*12*), said in his autobiography: "I saw that a man of truth must also be a man of care" (*4*, 16). As a child, Gandhi had been convicted of lying because he had not been able to prove his innocence. Therefore he kept careful records, for such care protected his integrity and preserved his credibility.

Arrangement

Gandhi's speeches are as difficult to outline as are those of Danton. He did not wish to appear contrived. There are few signposts, no carefully developed

---

[17]Nanda attributed the Murray quotation to the *Hibbert Journal* of 1914, but it does not appear there.

[18]While in prison in South Africa Gandhi fashioned General Smuts a pair of sandals. In 1939, many years later, Smuts sent the sandals to India as a token of his respect, saying: "I have worn these sandals for many a summer . . . even though I may feel that I am not worthy to stand in the shoes of so great a man" (*14*, 85).

introductions and conclusions, and no internal summaries. Perhaps Gandhi was too cautious in this respect. For all his love of efficiency, his, speeches are wasteful of time and words. They need tightening, and an organizational superstructure would have assisted Gandhi immeasurably in quickening the momentum of his remarks. The extent to which such premeditation would have destroyed Gandhi's image of straightforward honesty is a provocative question.

Style

Gandhi felt a great need for the phraseology of identification, beacause he was reviving almost single-handedly the application of passive resistance to modern politics. Therefore he coined some words (*satyagraha*, see *4*, 318-19) and borrowed others. But, in his Round Table address, there are only four instances in which he could be accused of resorting to the costume of words and only one of those is unequivocal. *Swaraj* for home rule appeared once, and, almost as if he had slipped, Gandhi hastened to explain the term. The only word that is repeatedly used by Gandhi that could be construed as jargon is the term "Congress," which appears 40 times. Certainly this term had a high annoyance value to those opposed to Gandhi's philosophies, but it seems problematical whether Gandhi could have avoided using it as much as he did. "Civil disobedience" (or resistance) appears only three times, as does the word "joy."[19]

Why did Gandhi use a rhetoric that purposefully avoided his costume of words, while at the same time he maintained orthodoxy of revolutionary dress, food, and ideas? The answer lies in Gandhi's acute audience analysis and demonstrates his intent to seek a solution at the Conference. He knew that the terminology of the Indian nationalist movement would annoy the other delegates, so he refrained. He could not have unobstrusively refrained from his habitual dress, for this would have made newspaper headlines everywhere. But his rhetoric could be as conciliatory as possible without its moderation calling attention to itself or, if noticed, without being considered hypocritical. Gandi knew that his speech would receive publicity at home and that its message would have to be revolutionary. But the words to express those ideas did not need to be antagonistic. Gandhi also avoided figurative language in the Round Table address, unless it appeared natural. Gandhi could be figurative, but he wished to meet Longinus's requirement that the effective figure of speech be subservient to the meaning.

[19] "Joy" could be classified as a forerunner of such terms as "flower children."

Delivery

Gandhi's delivery was as unorthodox as his invention, arrangement, and style. Fülöp-Miller said:

> His speech is passionless, quiet, and measured. For this man, who has succeeded in revolutionizing the whole of India . . . lacks the usual oratorical gesture. He hardly ever moves his arm, hardly even a finger. The modulations of his voice are even, and his way of speaking sober and simple (*3*, 168).

Doke's description is highly similar:

> Gandhi is not an impassioned speaker. His speech is calm and slow. . . . But with this quiet way, he has the gift of placing a subject in the clearest light, simply, and with great force. The tones of his voice, which are not greatly varied, bear the note of sincerity. . . . I have listened to him often, watching the faces of his audience, and while I should not call him an orator, and certainly have met with several of his countrymen whose elocution, natural and unaffected, is far superior to his, I have never met with a more convincing speaker than he. In Gujarati he naturally speaks with greater rapidity than in English, but with even less variation of voice (*2*, 41).

Gandhi's delivery on November 28, 1931, was typical. Queen Anne's drawing room in St. James' Palace was by no means as large as an auditorium, and the British encouraged a conversational delivery by constructing their round table. Therefore Gandhi could use what the London *Daily Telegraph* of December 2, 1931, referred to as his "drawling, singsong voice." The London *Daily Herald* of December 2, 1931, said: "In a hushed silence, the spokesman of Congress in quiet, unemotional tones expressed the fear that Congress and his government had come to the parting of the ways." The *Manchester Guardian* of December 1, 1931, noted that "Mr. Gandhi's speech was carefully balanced," adding that "on the whole it seems clear that Mr. Gandhi will do his best to see that the infant Constitution gets a fair chance. He is not prepared to act as fairy godmother, but neither will he assist in strangling [the] baby in its cradle." On December 2, the same newspaper reported: "Even Mr. Gandhi, though he kept the door of civil disobedience open to himself, had evidently not been untouched through appeals made to him . . ."

The British-dominated Indian press was less complimentary. The *Bengalee (Calcutta Evening News)* of December 2, 1931, predicted that the Mahatma would follow the path of cooperation, adding on December 3: "In many matters, it must be admitted that he has failed to carry the Conference with him, but even in such matters, there will be further attempts made to bridge the gulf between him and the other delegates." The overseas edition of the

Statesman of Calcutta reported on December 3, 1931: "Had Mr. Gandhi gone to London in a spirit of conciliation . . . we should today be writing a very different history of the Round Table Conference. Because he went to ask for what he knew to be impossible . . . the blame for failure rests on him."[20]

Gandhi's achievements as a speaker illustrate clearly that the leader of a revolution need not be an orator. "This shrimp as thin as a lath," Lloyd, the English magistrate, had unwillingly to confess, "carried three hundred and twenty million men with him. A nod, a word from him is a command" (*3*, 170). *Gandhiji in England*, admittedly a biased source, referred to Gandhi's speech of November 28, 1931, as "one of his greatest speeches—noble, cogent and pacificatory" (*9*, 155). Yet he delivered it seated, in a singsong voice, dressed in homespun cloth, with his pale and repulsive physical appearance. Gandhi could be the man of words so effectively that his missing teeth did not detract from the beauty of his soul.

Conclusion

The leader of a revolution cannot please everyone. But Gandhi held that he can *love* everyone. The Mahatma's words contrast sharply with those of Hancock, Danton, Lenin, and Castro. Such is the contradictory nature of the rhetoric of revolt.

Bibliography

1. Chaturvedi, Benarsidas, and M. Sykes, *Charles Freer Andrews: a Narrative.* New York: Harper & Row, Publishers, 1950.

    Andrews, a Christian missionary and confident of Gandhi, knew the intimacies of the Round Table Conference. See chapter 18.
2. Doke, Joseph K., *M. K. Gandhi: an Indian Patriot in South Africa.* London: The London Indian Chronicle, 1909.

    An account of Gandhi's early work (reissued by Ministry of Information and Broadcasting of the Government of India in 1967) by the Baptist missionary Doke.

[20] The Bombay *Times of India* chose to ignore Gandhi altogether, publishing headlines on December 1, 1931, which said: "Success of Round Table Conference, Large Measure of Agreement."

3. Fülöp-Miller, Réné, *Lenin and Gandhi*, trans. F. S. Flint and D. F. Tait. London: Putnam & Company Ltd., 1927.

Although principally a secondary source, a thoughtful account by a contemporary of Lenin and Gandhi on how their opposite philosophies both developed from "their profound feeling of responsibility for the sufferings of all the disinherited" (3, viii).

4. Gandhi, Mohandas K., *An Autobiography: the Story of My Experiments with Truth*, trans.. M. Desai. Boston: Beacon Press, 1957.

Essays written as weekly installments to Navajivan, published in Hindi and Gujarati, covering period up to 1921.

5. ——, *Collected Works*. Delhi: Publications Division, Ministry of Information and Broadcasting, 1958-.

The Indian government is attempting to put into chronological order, in both English and Hindi, all the works of Gandhi. Latest volume XXXI (1926) contains numerous speeches.

6. ——, *India's Case for Swaraj*. 2nd ed., ed. W. P. Kabadi. Bombay: Yeshanand, 1932.

Certain of the speeches, writings, interviews, etc. of Gandhi during his stay in England for the Second Round Table Conference.

7. ——, *The Nation's Voice ... a Collection of Gandhiji's Speeches in England ...*, eds. C. R. Rajagopalachar and J. C. Kumarappa, 2nd ed. Ahmadabad: Navajivan Publishing House, 1947.

Similar to 6, less complete, but more attention to Gandhi's activities in England. Includes 12 speeches Gandhi delivered in England.

8. ——, *Speeches and Writings*, 4th ed. Madras: G. A. Nateson, 1933.

Includes speeches delivered in South Africa and India, as well as all speeches delivered at Round Table Conference.

9. *Gandhiji in England and the Proceedings of the Second Round Table Conference*. Madras: B. G. Paul, 1932.

Includes lists of delegates, events on Gandhi's voyage, synopses of important statements by delegates. Only excerpts from Gandhi speeches.

10. Hawkins, Gary J., "Gandhi in Transition: 1888-1896," *Ohio Speech Journal*, III (1965), 25-28.

Gandhi's stage fright during his first efforts to speak.

11. Nanda, Bal Ram, *Mahatma Gandhi: a Biography*. London: George Allen & Unwin Ltd., 1958.

Based on primary sources by Gandhi contemporary. Well indexed, glossary of terms, selected bibliography. Chapter 35 devoted to Round Table Conference.

12. Richardson, Don, "A Note on Gandhi's Ethos," *Ohio Speech Journal*, IV (1966), 24-26.

Discusses why Gandhi felt it was not only necessary to be truthful, but that one must be able to prove truthfulness by accumulating evidence of honesty.

13. Sharma, Jagdish S., *Mahatma Gandhi: a Descriptive Bibliography*. Delhi: S. Chand, 1955.

Annotated bibliography through 1954, well indexed with comprehensive subject guide and detailed chronology of Gandhi's life. Entries 2849-88 on Round Table Conference.

14. Sheean, Vincent, *Mahatma Gandhi: a Great Life in Brief*. New York: Alfred A. Knopf, Inc., 1955.

Pages 162-68 give interesting perspective on Round Table Conference.

15. Shukla, Chandrashanker, ed., *Incidents of Gandhiji's Life*. Bombay: Vora & Co., 1949.

Essays by 54 contributors, including a description of Gandhi's visit to Birmingham during Round Table Conference, Muriel Lester's story of Gandhi's residence at her settlement house, miscellaneous comments on Gandhi's rhetoric.

16. *Young India*. Ahmadabad: Navajivan Press, 1919-1932.

Weekly in English, edited by Gandhi to promote satyagraha. Basic source on Gandhi's work over 13-year period.

Questions for Discussion

1. To what extent was Gandhi guilty of using active lawlessness to reinforce his threats of passive resistance? What evidence do you find in his Round Table address and in his autobiography that he wished to avoid this threat?

2. Qualify Gandhi's rhetoric of radical passivism as a bona fide call for lawlessness.

3. Was Gandhi justified in placing nationalism for India as his focal point of dysfunction when India was experiencing so many severe social and economic dysfunctions only partially related to her colonial status?

4. What does Gandhi mean when he belittles revolt rhetoric in his Round

Table address, saying: "Heaven knows, I have no desire to take part in any debating. I know that liberty is made of sterner stuff."

5. With the aid of the bibliography, locate three other Gandhi speeches delivered in India, and compare his use of the costume of words in these speeches with his use of the costume of words in the Round Table address.

6. Was Gandhi being inconsistent when he said that, to take up civil disobedience again would be "no joy" but that, if necessary, he would approach it "with the greatest joy"?

7. Compare how Gandhi and Martin Luther King advocated lawlessness in their rhetoric.

8. To what extent does Gandhi exemplify the prestigious man of words with a grievance who somewhat reluctantly turns to violence to change the Old Regime?

9. What use does Gandhi make of *argumentum ad misericordiam*?

10. Is the fierceness of Gandhi's attack and his uncompromising position on freedom for India compatible with the humility of his concluding remarks?

Exercises

1. Deliver a blunt speech on a topic on which you have deep personal conviction, calling for a solution but threatening *specific* passive resistance moves if your requests are not granted.

2. Practice delivering Gandhi's conclusion beginning with the line, "Last of all, my last is a pleasant task for me," until you feel the words ring true. Be prepared to deliver the conclusion to the class.

3. Deliver, without notes, a short speech in which you decidedly disagree with your target but in which you try to convince them you love and revere them highly. This is a difficult assignment, particularly if you

find it hard to love your neighbors or are reluctant to express humanitarian sentiments or have never tried loving your enemies. Remember Gandhi advocated saying it simply.

4. Deliver a speech asking for rights for a minority. Address a group that has been reluctant to recognize the organization you represent as the dominant negotiating party because of its radical views.

5. Determine to what extent Gandhi's rhetoric of revolt was redundant by going carefully through the speech three times, crossing out any portions that you think are not vital to the message. What percentage of the rhetoric are you able to eliminate?

Fidel Castro Ruz
(1927-   )

Demigod: Myth or Miss?

This short preface to establish the occasion for Castro's speech of May 1, 1960, is offered for three reasons: (1) the sources on Castro's rhetoric are of such recent origin that it is difficult, even with the best of libraries and knowledge of research techniques, to establish the nature and degree of bias of contemporary materials in several languages; (2) some of the best sources are in Spanish, for which there are infrequent and unreliable English translations and which for comprehension frequently require interpretation by a Cuban; and (3) anti-Cuban propaganda during the early part of Castro's regime and bans on shipments of materials made American libraries reluctant or unable to catalogue adequate materials on Castro.

Fidel Castro, son of a prosperous planter, married while a student at the University of Havana in 1948. The restlessness that pervaded Cuba under Batista had affected him early, for in 1947 Castro had participated in an invasion attempt on the Dominican Republic. His wife's parents, minor government officials, hoped that, after graduation from the University of Havana with a law degree, Castro would settle down, but his activism continued. In 1955, after the birth of a son, the marriage ended in divorce.

Instability in Cuban government has been traditional. Cuba, the last American territory to free itself from Spain (1898), had experienced repeated occupation by United States troops under a series of corrupt presidents. When, in 1933, a somewhat anti-American government under Grau appeared, Batista effected a coup. He subsequently permitted a Constitutional Constituent Assembly to draft the Constitution of 1940, and, under its provisions, he was elected president. When Martin defeated Batista's handpicked candidate in 1944, Batista conceded the election and emigrated. Prio became president in 1948, but was deposed by a Batista coup in 1952. The sergeant-

132

turned-colonel-turned-general continued to rule Cuba under a military dictatorship until January 1, 1959.

With such unrest, it was conceivable for a young lawyer to dream of further coups. In 1952, Castro had unsuccessfully petitioned the courts to overthrow Batista. Then, with a hard corps of young revolutionaries, on July 26, 1953, Castro led a futile attack on the fortress of Santiago.[1] He was captured and sentenced to 15 years on the Isle of Pines, during which he "reconstructed" his plea to the court, which he called "History Will Absolve Me." It was Castro's first important political pamphlet, and it called for popular elections and a return to the Constitution of 1940.

A lull in counterrevolution persuaded Batista to declare an amnesty, so that on May 15, 1955, Castro and his brother Raul were released. In July, 1955, they emigrated to Mexico to prepare for invasion. On December 2, 1956, Castro landed in Oriente Province with some 80 followers from aboard the yacht *Granma*. A peasant reported the boat and the government sent troops. The force made its way inland, but was eliminated, except for Castro and perhaps five to twelve men.

Then began the slow process of promoting an underground in the remote mountains of eastern Cuba. Contact was made with revolutionary groups in Havana, but the movement under Castro retained its individuality. In 1957, a *New York Times* reporter interviewed Castro, and his articles proved that Castro had not been killed. By the spring of 1957, Castro had only 115 men, but, since it is estimated that one guerilla can counteract 500 government troops, his force was a threat. In June, 1957, Batista's attempt at saturation bombing of the Sierra Maestra mountains failed. On July 22, 1957, Castro published his second major political pamphlet, "Manifesto of the Sierra Maestra," in the most popular Cuban magazine.

Not until March, 1958 did the United States issue an arms embargo to Cuba. In the spring of 1958, Raul Castro opened a second front in another remote area. Batista increased the army. A general strike, called for April 9, went well in Santiago, but fizzled in Havana. On May 5, 1958, Batista launched an all-out offensive against Castro, but could not prevent Raul from consolidating his second front with Fidel's forces. On May 19, 300 rocket warheads were delivered to Batista from the United States, which later explained that these were part of a shipment ordered before the embargo, an explanation hardly meaningful to the revolutionaries. On July 20, Castro signed a coalition with other revolutionary forces because, by this time, he

---

[1] This attack gave the name to Castro's cause, the *Movimiento Revolucionario 26 de Julio.*

felt strong enough not to be swallowed up. During this period Castro repeatedly broadcast over his *Radio Rebelde*, calling for the people to prepare for revolution.

By August, 1958, the rebels held the entire Sierra Maestra. The fall election that retained Batista was an obvious fraud. The rebels requested that the United States withdraw its military advisors to Batista, but Washington declined, pleading hemisphere defense. Unexpectedly, with his army intact but demoralized, and with Castro in command of only 1,500 men, Batista flew from Cuba on January 1, 1959, and Castro began his triumphant tour of the island.

The revolutionary government was faced with outstanding problems. It inherited a distrust of the United States dating from 1898 and accelerated by United States support of Batista. The political system was corrupt; the people had little experience in self-government; the one-crop economy of sugar was precarious. If the United States could have adopted a policy that would have prevented Communistic influence in Cuba, it did not.

Castro's war trials began immediately. Blanksten estimated that 557 men were executed, largely Batista police and soldiers (*1*, 118). On January 12, 1959, Senator Morse of Oregon attacked Castro in the Senate for using the firing squad, and Castro responded with criticism of the United States before the Havana Rotary Club on January 15, 1959. During this period there was no United States ambassador in Cuba. The new appointee did not arrive until February 19, 1959.

Castro put out feelers for the capital he needed. On April 15, he was in the United States, looking for assistance. On May 8 and 16, he publicly disassociated himself from communism. On May 17, 1959, Castro effectuated the Agrarian Reform Law, which was prejudicial to United States interests. The State Department retaliated with its note of June 11, stressing the need to compensate landowners while recognizing the right of Cuba to confiscate foreign holdings.

Whatever may be the reasons, financial support for Castro was not provided by the United States or by those under her influence. By December, 1959, Matos was imprisoned for treason, in part because he opposed the entrance of Communists into powerful government posts. By February, 1960, Soviet First Deputy Premier Anastas Mikoyan concluded a strategic trade pact in Havana. Perhaps Castro had been a Communist since the Sierra Maestra days. That seems doubtful. But, by early 1960, whether by choice or by necessity, Castro had allied himself with Russia.

By April 20, 1960, the House of Representatives decreed that no aid be given to Cuba unless it was in the best interests of the United States. By May

26, 1960, the United States had canceled all aid programs. At what point did the CIA start supporting subversion? It may be that it was suspicious of Castro from the start, and it may also be that the CIA's position contributed to Castro's attitude toward the United States.

In June, 1960, Castro nationalized the oil industry, while the United States canceled its Cuban sugar quota. On August 6, 1960, the electric power and telephone industries were nationalized, affecting large Cuban investments by American business. By October 19, 1960, the United States banned exports except medicine and food. By 1961, Castro had proclaimed himself a Marxist-Leninist.

The period from January 1, 1959, until January 1, 1961, was critical to the Cuban Revolution. Could a benevolent attitude by the United States during 1959 and 1960 have prevented communism from attaching itself to the human rights revolution? Draper thought "that Castro was not a Communist for all practical purposes before he took power but decided to cast his lot with the Communists sometime afterward" (11, 3 and 34-40). Mills said bluntly: "United States policies and lack of policies are very real factors in *forcing* the Government of Cuba to align itself politically with the Soviet block" (17, 179). The Eisenhower administration seemed to prefer a dictator it could control to a revolutionary it could not. What the Kennedy forces could have done, they did not. The hostility between the United States and Cuba continued under the Johnson administration. Mills concluded: "The U.S.A. is a reactionary menace to any real attempt to modify the basic realities of Latin America. Generally, whenever in Latin America people have really begun to get on the move, in the face of their movements the policies and the lack of policies of the United States have been consistently counter-revolutionary" (17, 177).

The way in which communism in Cuba was permitted to use the human rights revolution is a classical example of what Larson predicted can happen in the future. Because Castro may not have been committed to communism in advance, a content analysis of his rhetoric should be able to plot a curve showing the pattern by which communism entered his politics. The curve could show a gradual rise; or it could show upsurges followed by plateaus; or it could be highly skewed toward the year 1961.

What is the particular significance of Castro's speech of May 1, 1960, within this context? Did it mark a significant shift in Castro's position? It is difficult to select any one act or speech that marks a decided shift in Castro's position. The Agrarian Reform Law of May 17, 1959, is regarded as one turning point. Castro's first major financial transaction with the Soviet Union on August 12, 1959, when he sold 170,000 tons of sugar to Russia, was another. The strategic trade pact of February, 1960, was a major move. But even in May, 1960, a rapprochement was still possible. Overtures were made, but they were not fruitful (20, 143). The speech of May 1, 1960, was not Castro's first all-out tirade on the United States, for that had been given as early as October 26, 1959. Its significance lies in an interpretation of the rhetoric of revolution. Castro, like most revolutionaries, needed a scapegoat and the United States cast itself for the part. What a revolutionary says and what a revolutionary does may be two separate things, provided his rhetoric is not taken too seriously. Castro's speech of May 1, 1960, is an example of a war of words that developed into a war of deeds. At this point Castro had not seized American industry and the United States had not reduced its sugar quota. In spite of his rhetoric, Castro would probably have accepted serious efforts by the United States to relieve tensions. But Castro's words were taken at face value, and it was not long after May 1 that the gap had so widened that it could not be closed.

Give Me Liberty or Give Me Death!
¡ Patria o Muerte!

May 1, 1960
The Civic Plaza
Havana, Cuba

Distinguished visitors from Latin America and from all over the world who have joined us today on the platform, workers, farmers, students, members of the militia of our Fatherland, members of the learned professions, youth brigades, Cubans all:

On other occasions we have met together in great meetings, sometimes to defend our Fatherland from calumny, other times to commemorate some patriotic anniversary, other times to protest against some aggression. But never before have the people assembled together in greater number nor in a meeting so significant as today's, a day on which we observe International May Day [applause], and therefore the day of the Cuban workers as well as the day of the Cuban farmers [applause], the day of all those who produce, the day of all the humble among the people of our country. May Day not

Consulted for this translation were two Spanish versions (4 and 9) and one in English (7). Crowd reactions were taken from 9, which is a less edited version than the elaborately designed 4.

only honors those who work with their hands or with their minds, producing material goods or lending services to their country, but also in this decisive hour, May Day honors those on whose shoulders rests the defense of the nation and the defense of the revolution. [Applause.] This is also the day of the rebel soldiers [applause], of the heroic fighting men of the revolutionary army. It is furthermore the day of all the members of the Revolutionary Armed Forces and the day of the revolutionary militia because the soldiers of the Rebel Army are also farmers and workers. [Applause.] Therefore today is the day of all the revolutionaries, of all revolutionaries united, because in unity lies and will always lie the success and the strength of our revolution. [Applause.]

Today not only demonstrates that the great majority of the people support the revolution—in case there were to remain any doubt among those who are so naïve as to take pleasure in deceiving themselves or allowing themselves to be deceived—but there is something still more important: the great majority of the people is organized, because today it is an organized people who have met together. That is why we are stronger this year than we were last year [applause] because the revolution is not only in the majority, but it also has organized that majority. [Applause.] And this fact, to which all of us today have been witness, this truly impressive and unforgettable event, proves the capacity of the Cuban people. [Applause.]

Even a few months ago not a single militia unit—neither worker nor farmer—was organized. The appeal to organize the militias began in the month of October, exactly the 26th of October, as a result of that rally of protest against the aerial incursion that cost more than forty victims among our citizens.[2] Six months ago we did not have a single workers' militia. Six months ago the workers did not know how to handle arms. Six months ago the workers did not know how to march. Six months ago there was not a single company of militias upon whom to depend to defend the revolution in case of aggression. And in only six months the militias have been organized, have been disciplined and have been trained.

Our people were not, nor are they now, a militaristic people. Our people have never been nor will they ever be a militaristic people. There was no

---

[2] A reference to the leaflets dropped on October 21, 1959, but only two people were killed and those were killed by a car tearing through the streets and shooting, rather than by bombs. Castro did not announce the formation of the militia in his speech of October 26, 1959, but he did say: "Workers, students, farmers, and all the rest of you Cubans with patriotism and love for your country, if the time should come to give battle to defend our rights as Cubans . . . , these soldiers here in Havana . . . would want to have you shoulder to shoulder alongside them" (5, 19).

military tradition in our Fatherland. Cuba was not Prussia. Cuba is a country eminently peaceful and civil minded. [Applause.] In Cuba we despised marching and uniforms and arms, because for us these were always the symbols of oppression and of abuse, the symbols of privilege, the symbols of mistreatment. Arms and uniforms have been hateful to us. Nevertheless, in six months we have organized and trained more than a thousand companies of Workers' Militias, Student Militias, and Farmers' Militias! [Applause.] This formidable organization which paraded here today, built in only six months, shows what the people of Cuba are able to do. [Applause.]

Those who underestimated our people believed that we were people incapable of organizing ourselves. They believed that we were incapable of unity. Those who underestimated us believed us to be—as they believe our sister nations of Latin America also to be—a helpless nation which would submit easily. They believed we were going to be victims of disunity, of unpreparedness, of the incapacity to organize ourselves. They believed us to be incapable of defending ourselves and no doubt they even considered us to be too cowardly to defend ourselves. [Applause.]

However, what has been accomplished proves the opposite. What has been accomplished in so short a time demonstrates the extraordinary qualities of our people [applause] and shows what our people can do.

Why, however, is it that today every citizen who holds within the love of his Fatherland, each citizen who has enough sensitivity for his fellowman, and enough moral sensibility, and enough dignity to feel and to know what constitutes a sense of justice and a feeling of love for his land and his people [applause], wants today to belong to a corps of the militia, wants today to know how to handle arms, and has learned to do things that he had never done before, and to become organized to the extent that he has been organized? What is it that has made our people form militias? What is it that has made the workers, the students, the farmers, the doctors, the women as well as men, form militias and learn how to handle arms? [Applause.] What is it that has converted us into a Spartan people? What happened so that when a worker finishes his daily eight hours he goes to march three or four hours and marches at night, marches in the rain, or sacrifices his weekly day of rest to learn how to handle arms? What is it that moves him to make such a sacrifice not on one day, but on many days, and continually during many months?

To what should be attributed this fervent effort of Cubans? Simply to a reality: the reality that the Fatherland is in danger, the reality that the Fatherland is threatened. True as it is, difficult as it is, this knowledge should not discourage anybody. It is a reality that we need to defend ourselves.

[Applause.] In stating this we do not lie nor exaggerate. We have never lied to the people [applause] and above all, we will never withhold realities from the people. [Applause.]

Many things we have had to learn, many things we have all learned, all of us without exception. Today, for example, as the organized units of the people filed back and forth in endless numbers to march for seven consecutive hours, today while we have had an opportunity to see the tremendous strength of the people [applause], while we have had the opportunity to see the incomparable and invincible strength of the people, we asked: But is this people today the same as the people of yesterday? How is it possible that a people with such tremendous and extraordinary strength should have had to endure what our people have had to endure? How was it possible, with the tremendous strength of hundreds of thousands of Cuban farmers [applause], and the tremendous strength of more than a million Cuban workers [applause], and the tremendous strength of hundreds of thousands of young people like those who paraded today in the ranks of the patrols and the student militias? How was it possible? How can they be the same men and women as yesterday?

Since these citizens who paraded by here today are the same citizens that made up our people just a few years ago, how is it possible then that we should have had to suffer such extreme abuse? How is it possible that so many hundreds of thousands of families in our rural areas lived in conditions of starvation without land and were so exploited, as victims of the most heartless exploitation by foreign companies ... ["Down with them, down with them!] that lorded over our land, while those almighty who gave orders were those who in most cases not only had never planted a seed on our land but furthermore had never even seen our land? [3]

While so much courage was in the hearts of our people, how was is possible to abuse our workers so? How was so much exploitation possible? How was so much crookedness, so much theft, so much plundering of our people possible? [4] While we had so much strength, how was so much crime possible? How was it possible for a handful of men, a band of mercenaries, or a plague of petty politicians ... [cries of "Down with them, down with them! "] ...

---

[3] See *13*, 11-22 and *1*, 130. In 1956, the Department of Commerce noted: "The only foreign investments of importance are those of the United States. American participation exceeds 90 percent in the telephone and electric services, about 50 percent in public service railways, and roughly 40 percent in raw sugar production. The Cuban branches of the United States banks are entrusted with almost one-fourth of all bank deposits" (*19*, 10).

[4] See *1*, 123-25 for elimination of corruption.

to dominate our people and to direct the destiny of our people during a half century?

How was it possible for our people to have to pay a price so high that to give us a clear notion of it we would need to see united together here in a square many times bigger than this, the millions of Cubans who were left unable to read or write in our Fatherland[5] [cries of "Revolution, revolution! "] . . . the hundreds of thousands of little children who died without seeing a doctor, the ocean of suffering and anguish, of hunger and misery, of abuse and humiliation, because they were poor, or because of illiteracy, or because they were black [applause] . . . or because they were women, that the children of our land had to endure?

Ah, our people had reserves of extraordinary energy and extraordinary strength, but we did not know it, or we had not been permitted to draw that strength together, to organize it. And therefore, the priviliged and educated minorities were able to do more with the help of alien interests than our people were able to do with their tremendous reserves of strength.

That has been the great lesson of this day, because never so much as today have Cubans had the opportunity to see our own strength. [Applause.] Never so much as today could the Cuban people have an exact idea of their own strength. And the endless stream of columns, marching for seven hours, has been necessary so that our people may have a concrete idea of their own strength. [Applause.] And this great lesson should be an unforgettable lesson for us.

First, the children[6] and young people marched, opening ranks. Then the soldiers of the Rebel Army marched. [Applause.] Then the farmers' militias marched. [Applause.] Then the militias of Latin America marched [applause] with the flags of their respective countries.[7] Then the student militias marched [applause], and finally the workers' militias marched—first the women, then the men [applause], and behind or around the militias' units, the people. [Applause.] What formidable training![8] The people have been

[5] See *13*, 95-101. 1961 was proclaimed "Year for Illiteracy Education." The Ministry of Education set out to teach reading and writing to more than 1,500,000 adults. During 1961 and 1962, the schools were closed on April 17, 1961 and not reopened until February, 1962, in order that 100,000 educated students down to the age of 12 could enter Cuba's interior to teach illiterates.

[6] The *New York Times* commented on the appearance of six-year-old boys with toy guns.

[7] The London *Times* commented on "a group of Cuban women from Miami, Florida, and visiting groups from Venezuela, Mexico, and elsewhere in Latin America."

[8] The London *Times* estimated that 1,000 companies passed in review.

made conscious of their strength and the people have learned what constitutes strength. [Applause.]

The soldiers alone, the soldiers who paraded here today, constitute a force, but only a single force. The farmers alone constitute a force, but only one force. The students alone make up a force, but no more than one force. The workers alone make up a force, but a single force. The nations of Latin America represented here today constitute a force, but each one of them separately is a single force. [Applause.]

Before, the tactics of those who used to rule over our destiny consisted of dividing us and of setting one force against another.

They set the soldier against the farmer. They set the interests of the farmer against the interests of the worker. They set every faction of the people against the other factions as part of an international strategy of the big reactionary interests of the world. [Applause.] They set sister nations against each ot her and they set the various sectors of each nation against each other to serve the privileged classes. [Applause.] They set one group of the lower classes against another group of the lower classes. They took a poor farmer and made him a soldier. Then they corrupted this soldier and made him an enemy of the worker and an enemy of the farmer [applause] and weakened the people by their practice of setting one humble sector against another, and divided the people into petty political parties that brought ignorance to the nation . . . [applause and cries of "Down with them!"] . . . divided the people, the ignorant and misled people, divided them into factions supporting unscrupulous and greedy politicians. . . . [Cries of "Down with them!"] And thus they weakened the people, thus they confounded the people and thus the apparatus of the government with its rigid and reactionary institutions destroyed all hope, all possibility of progress for our society. The means to teach ideas—the movie, the majority of the press, the centers of learning, and all the administrative apparatus of the state—were at the service of this policy of oppressing and weakening the people.

That was what used to happen. And what was May Day in those days? Today the workers have not brought a single demand . . . [applause] . . . and however, and however, before, the workers used to be hardly able to walk under the weight of all the posters that they carried on their shoulders every May Day. [Applause.] The First of May was an opportunity for the workers to parade carrying posters, in the hope of satisfying those demands or some ot those demands. And so May Day used to be actually a mockery for the workers. The next year they had to return once again carrying the same posters with the same demands. [Applause.]

And when they did obtain anything, it was not offered to them graciously.

Anything they attained was granted to them only after a grueling fight, after strikes and organized movements demanding wage increases. The worker knew that he had to fight. The worker had to keep up a constant fight in order to obtain some small benefit in the economic order. He had to fight so that his most elemental rights would be respected.

Therefore, every First of May they had to come carrying their demands. What else could they do? The worker knew that what he did not do for himself nobody else would do for him. The worker knew that what he did not win by his own work nobody would win for him. Because you, worker, you, farmer, always worked for others. [Applause.] You worked for yourself and for the others too. [Applause.] You, worker, and you, farmer, and you, doctor or white-collar worker, you did your own work and the work of others. But nobody ever worked for you, laborer, nobody ever worked for you, farmer. . . . [Applause.] You gave everything, you gave your sweat, you gave your energy generously, you gave your life, you denied yourself your hours of rest, you gave to everybody, but to you nobody ever gave anything. . . . [Applause.] What you did not do for yourselves, nobody would ever do for you. You were the majority of the people, you do for yourselves, nobody would ever do for you. You were the majority of the people, you, farmers, you, workers . . . [applause], . . . you, youth, you were the majority of the people. . . . [Applause.] You who produce, you who make sacrifices, you who work, you were always faithful, and you are today and you will be tomorrow, the majority of the people. But you did not govern. You were the majority, but others governed in your stead and governed against you. [Applause.]

They invented a democracy for you—a strange, a very strange democracy, in which you, who were the majority, did not count for anything. Although you, farmer and worker, were the ones who produced the majority of the wealth and—together with the intellectual workers—produced the total of the wealth, many of those of you who produced everything did not even have the opportunity to learn to sign your name. [Applause.]

They invented a strange democracy for you—a democracy in which you, who were the majority, did not even exist politically within society. [Applause and cries of "Fidel! Fidel!"] They spoke to you of civil rights. In that situation of civil rights your child could die of hunger before the unconcerned glance of the government. Your child could be left without learning to read or write a single letter and you yourself had to go sell your work at the price that they wanted to pay you for it and whenever anybody was interested in buying it from you.

They spoke to you of rights that never existed for you. Your children could not be sure even of the right to a school. Your children could not be guaranteed even the right to a doctor. Your children did not have the guaranteed right even to a piece of bread, and you yourself did not have the guarantee even of the right to work. [Applause.]

They invented for you a democracy that meant that you, you who were the majority, did not count for anything. And thus, despite your tremendous force, despite your sacrifices, despite your work for others in our national life, despite the fact that you were the majority, you neither governed nor counted for anything. You were not taken into account. [Cries of "Down with Yankee imperialism" and "Death to Trujillo."]

And that they called democracy! In democracy the majority governs. [Applause.] In democracy the majority is taken into account. In democracy the interests of the majority are defended. In democracy man is guaranteed not just the right to think freely but the right to know how to think, the right to know how to write what he thinks, the right to know how to read what is thought by others. [Applause.] Democracy guarantees not only the right to bread and the right to work but also the right to culture and the right to be taken into account within society. Therefore this is democracy, this democracy of the Cuban Revolution. [Prolonged applause and cries of "Long live Cuba! Long live the Revolution! Long live Castro! Long live Che Guevara!" and chanting for other Cuban leaders for 20 minutes.]

This is democracy,[9] where you, farmer, are given the land that we have recovered from usurious foreign hands that used to exploit it! [Applause.]

This is democracy, where you, the sugar plantation workers, receive 80,000 *caballerias* of land in order that you should not have to live in *guardarrayas!*[10] [Applause.]

This is democracy, where you, worker, are guaranteed the right to work, so that you cannot be thrown out on the streets to go hungry! [Applause.]

This is democracy, where you, students, have the opportunity to win a university degree if you are intelligent, even though you may not be rich! [Applause.]

This is democracy, where you, whether you are the son of a worker, the son of a farmer, or the son of any other humble family, have a teacher to educate you and a school where you can be taught! [Applause.]

This is democracy, where you, old man, have your sustenance guaranteed after you can no longer depend on your own effort! [Applause.]

---

[9] Alternate translations: "Democracy is where . . ." or "It's democracy where . . ."

[10] Each *caballeria* is approximately 33 1/2 acres. The peasants had to set up their shacks on the sides of the roadbeds, because the feudal-style plantation owners were making use of all arable land.

This is democracy, where you, Cuban Negro,[11] have the right to work ... [applause and cries of "Unity, unity!"] ... without anybody being able to deprive you of that right because of stupid prejudice! [Applause.]

This is democracy, where you women acquire rights equal to those of all other citizens and have a right even to bear arms alongside the men to defend your country! [Applause.]

This is democracy, in which a government converts its fortresses into schools [applause], where the government wants to construct a house for every family so that every family can have a roof of its own over its head! [Applause.]

This is democracy, that wants each invalid to have a doctor's care!

This is democracy, that does not recruit a farmer to make a soldier out of him, corrupt him, and convert him into an enemy of the worker or into an enemy of his own farmer brother, but, instead of converting him into a defender of the privileged classes, converts the soldier into a defender of the rights of his brothers, the farmers and the workers! [Applause.]

This is democracy, which does not divide the humble people into factions by setting some against others!

This is democracy, in which a government finds the force of the people and unites it!

This is democracy, which makes a people strong| by uniting them! [Applause.]

This is democracy, which gives a gun to the farmers, gives a gun to the workers, gives a gun to the students, gives a gun to the women, gives a gun to the Negroes,[12] gives a gun to the poor, and gives a gun to any other citizen who is willing to defend a just cause! [Applause.]

This is democracy, which not only takes the rights of the majority into account, but also gives arms to this majority! And this can be done only by a government truly democratic, a government where the majority rules! [Applause.] And this, this can never be done by a pseudodemocracy. And we would like to know what would happen if a gun were given to every Negro[13] in the South of the United States, where so many times Negroes have been lynched. What an exploiting oligarchy will never be able to do, what a military caste of the kind that oppresses and plunders nations will never be able to do, what a government of minorities will never be able to do is to give a gun to every worker, to every student, to every young person, to every

[11] Alternate translation: "Cuban Black."

[12] Alternate translation: "to the Blacks."

[13] Alternate translation: "every Black."

humble citizen, to every one of those who make up the majority of the people! [Applause.]

And this, this does not mean that the rights of others are not taken into account. The rights of others count just as the rights of the majority [applause] in proportion to the extent to which the rights of the majority count, but the rights of the majority should prevail above the privileges of minorities. [Applause.]

This true democracy, this democracy to which no one can object, this sincere and honest democracy, is the democracy that has existed in our country since the first of January, 1959. [Applause.] This democracy has been expressed directly in the close union and identification of the government and the people, in this direct relationship, in this working and fighting in favor of the majority of the country and in the interests of the great majority of the country. This direct democracy we have exercised here has more purity, a thousand times more purity, than that false democracy that uses all the means of corruption and fraud to falsify the true will of the people. [Applause.]

Our democracy today has prevailed in this direct way, because we are in a revolutionary process. *Tomorrow will be as the people desire, tomorrow will be as the necessities of the people demand, as the aspirations of our people demand, as the interests of our people demand.* [Applause.] *Today there is a direct relationship between the people and the government.*

When the revolutionary process has gone far enough and the people understand that we are approaching new procedures—and the revolutionary government will always understand this just as the people understand it ... [Applause.] ... Here nobody is in public office because of ambition or pleasure. Here we are only fulfilling our duty. Here all of us are in the same position and attitude of sacrifice. Here all of us have the same willingness to work. [Applause.] Here all of us are joined in a single purpose, which is the proposition of serving a cause.

Our enemies, our slanderers, ask about elections[14] ... [prolonged cries of "Revolution, revolution"; "Why elections, why elections?"; and "We have already voted for Fidel, we have already voted for Fidel!"] ... including even

[14] In 1965, when asked about his promise of free elections in his Moncada speech, Castro told the American reporter Lockwood: "That was our program at that moment. Every revolutionary movement, in every historical epoch, proposes the greatest number of achievements possible. If you read the history of the French Revolution, you will find that the first inspirations of the revolutionaries were very limited. They even thought they would maintain the monarchy, but in the course of the revolutionary process they did away with it" (*15*, 144-45).

one Latin American chief of state, one Latin American chief of state[15] has recently declared that the Organization of American States should be made up only of those countries whose leaders are chosen by electoral processes, as if a true revolution like this one in Cuba could come into power disregarding the will of the people, as if a true revolution like this one in Cuba could come into power against the will of the people . . . [cries of "Never, never!"] . . . as if the only democratic procedure for taking over power were the electoral processes so often prostituted to falsify the will and the interests of the people and so many times used to put into office the most inept and most shrewd, rather than the most competent and the most honest. [Applause.]

As if after so many fraudulent elections, as if after so much false and treacherous politicking, as if after so much corruption, the people could be made to believe that the only democratic procedure for a people to choose their leaders were the electoral procedure. And as if this procedure were not democratic—this procedure through which a people choose their leaders not with a pencil, but with the blood and the lives of 20,000 fellow patriots[16] [applause and cries of "Fidel, Fidel!"] struggling without arms against a professional and well-trained army, trained and outfitted by a powerful foreign country, that broke their chains and, by breaking the chains that enslaved them, put an end to the abuses and crimes in our Fatherland and began a true democratic phase of progress, of liberty, and of justice. Therefore, if there is any process in which the incompetent fall behind, if there is any process in which the crooked fail, that is the revolutionary process in which virtue opens a way for itself, merit prospers, but never cunning . . . [applause] . . . never ambition, never deceit, because, in the process of revolutionary struggle, as in no other struggle, only the strong men—those with true convictions and absolute loyalty—can stay in the ranks.

And a revolutionary process does not mean only the insurrectional phase of the war, that was one phase of the rebellion, the real phase of the revolution comes later. Before that, the rebellion of our people brought about the war, and now the creative spirit of our people has brought about the revolution. [Applause.]

And for this reason we said that in Cuba a true democracy is very much at work, despite what the enemies of our revolution want to write about it and want to prove.

And at this time what is the principal job we Cubans have ahead of us?

[15] President Betancourt of Venezuela.

[16] Mentioned during his speeches and press conferences in the United States, April 15-27. See *Keesing's Contemporary Archives*, 16901A, July 11-18, 1959.

What is the answer to that question? What is it that every Cuban should know today? Why is our job now fundamental? What are the reasons why our Fatherland sees itself threatened by aggression? What has the revolution done but good to its people? What has the revolution done but offer justice? [Applause.] What has the revolution done but defend the interests of the majority of our people, of the most humble classes of our country, who constitute the vast majority [applause] and who not only make up the majority with a right of their own to count in the destinies of our Fatherland but who, furthermore, are also the part of our country that has suffered most? What has the revolution done but defend those who are not only the majority but are furthermore the exploited part of our country? [Applause.]

Where is the crime in fighting for the people? Where is the crime in wanting the farmer to have land? Where is the crime in taking land and giving land to the farmers? [Applause.] How struggling for the people, how doing what the revolution has done for the people, how the presence of this multitude here proves it, this is a multitude of flesh and bone, real men and women, men and women of the people, who came here spontaneously . . . [applause] . . . who came here paying their own expenses, who came here from different places by traveling all night long and marching for a whole day, standing on foot during an entire day, under the sun, without drinking water, without eating. [Applause.] And the presence of such a great multitude is the best proof that the revolution has fought for the people.

However, why is there so much pressure against a government that has put an end to so much injustice, a revolutionary government that has set up ten thousand schools and is converting the big fortresses[17] of the country into great educational centers . . . [applause] . . .

A revolutionary government which has put to work the soldiers who made so many sacrifices during the war and has put to work these same soldiers building schools, building roads, and building scholastic centers for the people. [Applause.]

A revolutionary government which, far different from the parasite-ridden and privileged military castes, organizes the army of workers, organizes an army of exemplary citizens, an army into which are enlisted not the worst elements of the country, as used to be the case, but the best elements of the country—those who can stand up to the real tests of a true soldier? [Applause.]

[17]There are six fortresses in the Havana area: Atarés, La Fuerza, La Punta, El Morro, El Príncipe, and La Cabaña. In the provinces, there are San Severino, El Morro in Santiago Bay, and Castillo de Jagua. Just how many of these nine have been converted is not clear.

A revolutionary government that has constructed two scholastic cities and is proposing to assist in constructing a third city; that has constructed two university cities and is proposing to assist in constructing, along with the efforts of its own students, a third university city.[18]

A revolutionary government that is building a scholastic city for twenty thousand children—the first in a series of scholastic cities, to which two hundred thousand of the most intelligent and the most talented farm children will go to study. [Applause.]

A revolutionary government that has, in its first year, built ten thousand homes for humble families.[19]

A revolutionary government that has opened to the people all the beaches where only an insignificant minority of the people used to be able to go. [Applause.]

A government that has rescued for its people the wealth that was in foreign hands.

A government that has rescued for its farmers the land that the foreign masters of our country used to exploit. [Applause.]

A government that has given employment to more than 100 thousand new citizens in a single year, to more than 100 thousand new citizens in a single year.

A government that has created a thousand cooperatives in a single year.

A government that has made landowners of all the sharecroppers, squatters, and *precaristas* who used to have to pay rent. [Applause.]

A revolutionary government that suppresses luxury in order to satisfy the most elemental necessities of the humble families.

A revolutionary government that does not sacrifice the interests of the poor to the luxury of the rich, but rather the luxury of the rich to the interests of the poor. [Applause.]

A revolutionary government that without economic resources, with a country destroyed by pillage, without borrowing a cent from anybody, without begging a solitary cent from the rich landlords who ruined our country [applause] has carried forward a creative, fruitful policy and has enjoyed extraordinary results in only sixteen months, and has enjoyed achieving great goals in only sixteen months, and which today has enjoyed raising the mone-

---

[18]These mountain "school cities" accommodate 25,000 in campus-style arrangements, with dormitories, classrooms, and sports areas and allow the students to produce enough goods to make the city economically independent.

[19]See *13*, 101-4.

tary reserves of the country to almost 150 million pesos.[20] [applause] in order to have enough resources for the industrialization of the country. And a government of a small nation which has had to carry out this gigantic work in the midst of constant needling, in the middle of constant threats, in the middle of an incessant worldwide campaign of defamation in preparation for armed aggression into our territory. [Cries of "Let them come, let them come!"]

A government that has had to work in the midst of threats, a government that has had to work in the midst of international maneuvering, a government that has had to take care of so many many needs in so brief a time, and that, in the midst of this overwhelming burden of work, has had to endure the burning of sugarcane by pirate airplanes flying out of Florida [shouting], that has been constantly harassed and heckled by diplomatic notes from a powerful country.

A government that has always seen its economic plans threatened by cuts in the sugar quota and economic reprisals.

A government that has to work while watching the endless comings and goings of Chancellory officers and the repeated setting of snares to trip up our Fatherland.

A government that, in the midst of this overwhelming work, has had to endure the most tenacious and pitiless campaign of defamation that any country of this continent has ever suffered.

A revolutionary government engrossed in the superman job of solving the problem after problem it received—that it inherited from a policy of fifteen years of foreign domination, and which, in the midst of this work, endures first the bombing of the City of Havana,[21] then the airplanes burning a million *arrobas* of our sugarcane,[22] along with the houses of our farmers, and then the explosion of a ship loaded with arms for our self-defense, an explosion that cost the lives of seventy Cuban workers.[23] [Cries of "Murderers, murderers!"]

[20]The equivalent of $150,000,000. In 1959, reserves dropped from $75,000,000 to $50,000,000, but they rose sharply again in 1960. It is difficult to substantiate or disclaim this statistic given by Castro.

[21] See Keesing's *Contemporary Archives*, A17538, July 23-30, 1960.

[22]*Ibid.* Raul Castro asserted that 20,000,000 arrobas (250,000 tons) had been burned.

[23] On March 4, 1960, the French freighter, *La Coubre*, exploded at a dock in Havana while unloading munitions from Belgium. The cause of the disaster has never been determined. Seventy-five died, and around 200 were injured.

And why does a government that, besides all these revolutionary social reforms, has put an end in our country to secular vices, such as the vice of gambling, the vice of embezzling, the crime of smuggling, the *botella*,[24] and all the other vices that our people have suffered through in secular times, why does a government that is carrying on a program so just and so definitely beneficial to the people, have to be anathematized, have to be isolated, and have to be threatened by destruction and by death?

Why does a government that has done only good for its people have to be anathematized and why do all the diplomatic big brass of a powerful nation move to destroy it and mobilize thousands of intrigues of the reactionary press and the reactionary news agencies and spread them all over the world?

Why did they not concern themselves with our people before? Why did they not concern themselves with our people while hundreds of thousands of families here were living in miserable huts? Why did they not concern themselves with our people when there was such poverty here, when the *guajiros* lived in *guardarrayas*, subsisting by planting a *yuca* plant and a *malanga* plant and a plant of *boniato*?[25] [Applause.]

Why did they not concern themselves with Cuba, with the affairs of Cuba, preoccupy themselves with the problems of Cuba when, in our country, young men were found assassinated in the streets and the police stations and the prisons were torture chambers, when the farmers were being assassinated *en masse*, when there was so much injustice and so much abuse? Why did not all this merit a line in any of those newspapers that today so attack our revolution? Why?

And today, today they call the war criminals to the American Senate to testify about the problems of Cuba. And today, when in this country nobody is tortured, when everybody knows how the rebel soldiers and the rebel policy and the rebel military conduct themselves [applause], when everybody knows that nobody is assassinated here, that nobody is tortured here, because those men who today are in charge are the same men who, during the war, respected the lives of the most ruthless enemies and cured the enemy wounded in combat.[26] [Applause.]

---

[24] Placing on government payrolls friends and relatives who did no work. In 1958, during Batista's regime, there were 3,684 *botelleros* in one single department of the government (7, 14).

[25] All three of these vegetables are tuberous. The first two are not commonly eaten in the United States, but the *boniato* is the sweet potato.

[26] See *13*, 63-64. During the rebellion, Castro broadcast to the Cuban people his humanitarian and practical reasons for caring for and releasing prisoners.

Today, when our prisons, when our billets, the small billets that today house the Rebel Army, and the police stations, are models of respect to the citizen, in which it can happen that the authorities can be abused, but never can the authorities abuse or allow anybody else to abuse a prisoner [applause]; today, when this is a truth that nobody is unaware of in our Fatherland, we read cables proceeding from Washington informing us that a group of mothers of war criminals are going to testify before an "Inter-American Peace Commission"[27] about "the torturing that the Revolutionary Government in Cuba is practicing against their families." [Shouts and whistles.] This people, this people had to undergo seven years of crime and torture; this people is aware of the irrefutable accounts of numberless acts of terror, of numberless acts of cruelty that they had to suffer in that *Quinta Estacion*[28] and in the other police stations, and in the *cuarteles*[29] and *las tropas en campaña*,[30] at the hands of Venturas, Chaviano, Ugalde Carillo and those other criminals [shouts and whistles]; this people knows better than anybody, this people knows better than anybody what it had to suffer, this people put up with and powerlessly had to put up with for seven years the cries of pain of the tortured and the screams of the mothers who lost their murdered sons, and the decimated families, and the little villages burned out and demolished and the inhabitants mutilated by the tyrannical hordes—they never had during those seven years the consolation that an "Inter-American Commission" would interest itself in their sad fate or that it would interest itself in observing the acts of horror that our Fatherland was suffering. [Applause.]

And today, today, when all the world knows our very different way of behaving, when all the world knows that we are men of a very different breed than those cowardly and contemptible men who perpetrated so many acts of barbarism; today when the torturers and the criminals of yesterday are paying the punishment that they deserved for their innumerable crimes, ah today, today an "Inter-American Commission" is going to listen to the accusations of "acts of torture" of the Revolutionary Government against the war criminals. [Shouts and whistles.]

[27]The Inter-American Peace Committee was appointed by the Organization of American States and reports to each meeting of the foreign ministers and the general conferences.

[28]This police station, located in a suburb of Havana, housed the Bureau of Investigation. The *Fidelistas* claim that tortures took place in the basement and that bodies were conveniently thrown in the river which flowed by.

[29]Small military fortresses.

[30]Military outposts.

And why? Why do they resort to these slanderous procedures? Why do they resort to these slanderous procedures? Why do they resort to these cynical procedures? Why do they resort to these shameless procedures? Simply to discredit the Cuban Revolution before the world; simply to paint us before the world as a gang of criminals and torturers; simply to discredit us; simply to plant doubt in the other sister nations of the continent; simply to prepare the conditions for aggression.

And now, the assassins of yesterday are being received in the Senate of the United States to "testify" about the affairs of Cuba! [31] [Shouts and whistles.]

But even stranger things occur, even stranger things occur and things that must bring us to the reality of the times that we have ahead. Without the least problem existing, without the least difficulty existing, one day the president of Guatemala . . . [shouts and whistles] . . . the president of Guatemala recalls his ambassador and, without the least incident having occurred, he breaks off diplomatic relations with Cuba and declares that in the Sierra Maestra—in the Sierra Maestra, the mountains that used to be the home of the soldiers who paraded here today—that troops are being prepared to invade Guatemala. It was an accusation so unfounded, it was an accusation so absurd, that it would have been beyond logical explanation by us or by anybody else if it were not that we had news that the United States Department of State was preparing an aggression against Cuba through the government of Guatemala. [Shouts and whistles.]

And, what is almost unbelievable, such a maneuver has been perpetrated very few times with such brazenness as on this occasion, because there had not arisen the least incident or pretext to justify it, even when the ambassador of that country was recalled, he left behind him notes expressing his thanks for the consideration that the Revolutionary Government had always shown him. And all of a sudden, this man who presides over the sacrificed Republic of Guatemala, this man declares that he is breaking off relations with our country and is accusing our country of preparing troops in the Sierra Maestra for aggression. Of course, absolutely no one believes him. It was a maneuver to cast Cuba in the role of the aggressor among the Organization of Latin American States, to justify an armed aggression against our Fatherland, or at least to set the stage for it.

---

[31] From May 2 to 6, 1960, a subcommittee of the Senate Judiciary Committee heard testimony from eight exiles, including two former army officers. General Francisco Tabernilla and Colonel Manuel Ugalde Carillo. The testimony is somewhat perfunctory. Both Tabernilla and Carillo fled Cuba on January 1, 1959, with Batista.

The enemies of our revolution know that they have made no progress in their efforts to organize a fifth column among us. The enemies of the revolution know that the revolution is stronger every day. They know that the revolution is more organized every day. [Applause.] They know that they will not be able to destroy the tremendous revolutionary forces and social forces that support the revolution. They know this perfectly well. They know that they cannot organize counterrevolution here, because they know that they have no place here from which to begin, nor do they have a way to begin, nor anyone with whom to begin. [Applause.]

And so they want to destroy the revolution through a maneuver of an international nature. And what a coincidence that the withdrawal of the ambassador of Guatemala in Cuba and those declarations of the president of Guatemala should have occurred exactly the same week that the 10,000 caballerias of land of the United Fruit Company passed into the hands of the *Instituto Nacional de Reforma Agraria* ... [applause] .... passed into the hands of the *Instituto Nacional de Reforma Agraria* to be delivered to the farmers! What a coincidence! What a coincidence! And what a coincidence that the maneuver should have come from no less than Guatemala, where the United Fruit Company is the all-powerful institution, should have come from Guatemala, where the United Fruit Company organized and inspired the aggression against the democratic government of that country! What a coincidence! What a coincidence that the maneuver should have come from that country where nobody can govern without the support of the United Fruit Company! What a coincidence! And what a coincidence that we ourselves, because of each just measure that we carry out in benefit of our people, we should have to be on guard against those maneuvers! And what a coincidence that, simultaneously, there should have been published a series of articles affirming that pirate ships in the Caribbean Zone were being prepared to attack any ship that should carry arms to Cuba!

In other words, on one occasion a ship bearing arms is blown up in the harbor and a few weeks later in certain newspapers which are said to be well informed regarding the affairs of the government of the United States, it is reported that pirate ships opposed to the Cuban Revolution are ready to attack ships that carry arms to our country. If we keep in mind, moreover, that in previous months we have been receiving wire releases reporting maneuvers of parachute troops and landings against guerrillas in the Caribbean Zone, when actually we were unaware that that country had any kind of problems with guerrillas in any part of the world; if here, in the very midst of our revolution and in the midst of that climate of threats, we receive notice and intelligence of the maneuvers of those troops, whose use in Cuba it seems only logical to expect, what can we think, if in the midst of all those threats and maneuvers, a ship explodes and there is talk of intercepting ships carrying arms? In other words, they want to reduce us to utter impotence, while the dangers and the threats increase.

That is the reality of our revolution. And why? What do they want to punish in our revolution? They want to punish the example, they wish to destroy the example. Why did they wish to defeat the Cuban Revolution at any cost? By any chance because we ourselves are taking anything away from them or we represent any danger to any other country, because we want to exploit any other country, because we want to make decisions about matters that are not our own? No. They want to destroy the Cuban Revolution so that the example of Cuban Revolution cannot be followed by the sister nations of Latin America. [Applause.]

What everybody knows is, what everybody knows is that they want at all costs to destroy our revolution, to sentence our revolution to death simply so that the farmers of Latin America, the workers of Latin America, the students of Latin America, the intellectuals of Latin America, and, finally, the peoples of Latin America should not follow the example of Cuba and should not someday carry out an agrarian reform and should not have a revolution in all these countries. [Applause.] They want, simply, to destroy our revolution in order to continue exploiting the other nations of Latin America.

And so they want our Cuban people to "pay the freight," our Cuban people to pay for the crimes that are being committed on other peoples; our Cuban people to pay for the exploitation of other people. In other words, they wish to destroy us because we have had the desire to liberate ourselves economically; they wish to destroy us, because we have desired to do justice; they wish to destroy us, because we want to be a sovereign people; they wish to destroy us, because we have concerned ourselves with the humble of our land, because we have cast our lot with the poor of our Fatherland, because we have remembered the *guajiro*[32] who had no land, because we have remembered the child who had no school, because we have remembered the worker who had no job, because we have remembered the family who lived in a hut, because we have remembered the sick who had no doctor, because we have remembered the student who had no books and no resources [applause], because we have remembered justice; and as if certain people in the world were obliged to live in wretchedness, in backwardness, and in exploitation; as if people were obliged to wear a yoke over their shoulders and around their

---

[32]Peasant farm laborer, sharecropper, or tenant farmer.

necks; as if certain people were obliged to be eternally resigned to misery and to frustration; as if certain people were obliged to be slaves of others; because our people have desired to break their chains, because our people have not wished to remain living in frustration, because our people wished to progress [applause]; because our men, our women, our young people, our old people want justice, want good fortune, want the noble proposition of enjoying the fruit of our labor, want to live happily and in peace in our land, which is our little bit of earth [applause]; because we had the misfortune of one day having foreign hands taking possession of our land, foreign hands taking possession of our mines, foreign hands taking possession of our natural resources and our public utilities; because we had the misfortune of having foreign hands take possession of our economy, of having foreign hands take possession of our politics and our destiny; because we had this misfortune; and because this generation of Cubans has set for itself the honorable and great task of liberating our country from these bonds, of liberating our country from this exploitation, only for this, which is just and which is a right which nobody either Cubans or any other people can argue about, which is a right which nobody dares to argue with us, for this reason, because we want to make our own decisions, because we want to live our own lives, because we want to plan our own future, and because we want to attain our own happiness, without doing any harm to any other people, because we wish to live in peace and friendship with all the other peoples of the world. [Applause.]

Why shouldn't we want friendship and peace with all the people who struggle for progress, with all the people who struggle for liberation, with all the people who struggle for their betterment? What we will never be able to approve is one nation's exploitation of another nation, or what is worse, an oligarchy exploiting another people, what we will not be able to approve is the exploitation of certain nations by oligarchies of other nations. [Applause.]

And our desire is to progress, to plan for our future, to create our own democratic institutions, to create a new Fatherland, to provide for the happiness of our people without taking anything away from any other people. Therefore, logically, we want to live in peace with other nations and in friendship with all nations, because we have absolutely no disputes with any other nation. Those who want to take something away from another nation have problems with other nations, but a nation that does not want to take anything away from any other nation can never have problems with any other nation. [Applause.]

But there is something even more important. All of us are involved in a great undertaking. The Revolutionary Government and the people are dedicated to a great work. What we want is to see this work converted someday into reality; what we want is to see this new generation grow with a distinctly new viewpoint, with an outlook very different, and with an education very different from what our generation received. We want someday to see the scholastic cities full of children. We want someday to see living and studying in those scholastic cities two hundred thousand children of farmers. We want to see the thousand new towns that we are going to build in the cooperatives in five years. We want someday to see the beautiful reality of every family living under their own roof. We want to see the day in which every Cuban has work. We want to see the day in which every sick person has his own doctor. We want to see the day in which every old person has his pension. We want to see the day in which every man and woman knows how to read and write. [Applause.] We want someday to see this Fatherland great. That is what we are fighting for.

And what man does not want to see his dreams converted one day into reality, his ideals converted into reality! And since all of us have an ardent desire for our dreams of well-being and happiness to be a reality someday for our people, we cannot ourselves be the troublemakers. Those who want to see a great work accomplished, those who are laboring hard at a great work cannot be troublemakers. The troublemakers cannot be us. The troublemakers can only be, exclusively, those who do not want us to carry out what we have set out to do. [Applause.]

The blame cannot be ours, and it is absurd that they should try to place the blame on us, when we live with all our thoughts devoted to the work that we are realizing, our thoughts on tomorrow, our thoughts on the creative work of the revolution, just as yesterday we lived with our thoughts focused on that very minute, just as yesterday we lived with our thoughts focused on the triumph of the people.

The victory of the people against tyranny took place. Then commenced the fight against hunger; then commenced the fight against misery; then commenced the fight against poverty; then commenced the fight against pain. And these battles we wish to win also and we live today with our thoughts focused on the creative work of the revolution. [Applause.] Therefore we cannot ourselves be instigators of these problems. The instigators are those who are not resigned to losing their privileges; are those who are not resigned to stop exploiting the people, are those who want to impose their unmitigated will and the illegitimate interests of the powerful potentates of the great international capitalists; are those who have not resigned themselves to live at peace with nations—in other words, those who have not resigned themselves to live in peace with nations. And that is what is happening in our country and for that we must convert ourselves into a Spartan people, because we are placed in the dilemma of resigning ourselves to and submitting ourselves to preparing ourselves to fight against any aggression. [Applause.]

And we do not ever want to be a people who, given such an alternative, are willing to bend the neck and let the yoke be placed around them again . . . [cries of "No, no!"] because we, given such an alternative, we must take the course of dignity, the course of honor, the course of the future, the only one that, in spite of all the risks, promises to us a life very different from that which the yoke promises us. And we prefer liberty with all its risks, we prefer the fight for a better future to the yoke. With the yoke we have nothing to do.

And those militias who marched by here, those farmers who marched by here, those brigades of workers who marched by here, those students who marched by here, those people who marched by here are not people under the yoke. [Applause.]

Thus, we are doing the only worthy and just thing that we can do. We are adopting the course of a people who want to be free and will be free. We are adopting the only course that the worthy men of our Fatherland at all times would have followed. We have adopted the only course that our founders taught us. We have adopted the only course that the dead demand. We have fulfilled our duty. We have been faithful to the companions who fell and we are carrying out the work of the revolution. Every scholastic center that we build bears the name of a companion fallen in battle. Every school city that we convert from a fortress bears the name of a companion we lost in battle. Every new village bears the name of a companion we lost in battle. Every cooperative bears the name of a companion lost in battle. [Applause.]

We have not attempted to preserve the memory of our fallen brothers in the cold marble of a statue. We have not placed the name of a single revolutionary hero on a park from which nobody will receive a solution to his problems. Before, while others looted the country from one extreme to the other, and betrayed the ideas and the aspirations of the founders of our Fatherland, they dedicated a statue to our *mambises*[33] in every park and they placed the name of one of our patriots on every street.

That was before. But we perpetuate the memory and the names of our martyrs in something that has meaning for all true revolutionaries. We perpetuate the memory of our martyrs by carrying out the revolutionary work that

---

[33] A *mambi* was a hero of the war for independence from Spain.

they wanted done in our country. And in this way a school where hundreds of thousands of children study is a worthy memorial to a fallen companion [applause]; a cooperative where hundreds of farm families are going to entrust their sustenance is a worthy memorial to a fallen companion; a new village is a worthy memorial to a fallen companion; a hospital that saves many lives is a worthy tribute to a fallen companion.

And thus our works bear the names of our dead. And thus every cooperative, every hospital, every school, every revolutionary project carries the name of our dead. And for this the names of those whom we lost will live eternally in the memory of our people, in the demeanor that will be assumed by a new generation of men, in the children that are going to be educated there, in the families that are going to be happy there, in the lives that are going to be saved, in the infinite benefit that these sacrifices signify to our people.

For this they sacrificed themselves, and this is what makes our nation; our revolutionary work is profoundly identified with the love which we feel for our compatriots who fell. And this is one reason more why we wish to see this work fulfilled; this is one reason more why we are willing to defend it with the last drop of our blood [applause]; . . . this is one more reason why we are obliged to follow a worthy course, because no enemy can destroy this work, nor can any enemy convert our schools back again into fortresses, nor can any enemy come back to take away from the farmers either their lands or their houses; nor can any enemy take back again the rights of our people without erasing us from the face of the earth, because before they can erase the watchword and the work, they will have to erase us. [Applause and shouts of " ¡Patria o Muerte!"]

Our murdered have not died in vain. For everywhere we travel on our land, their names present themselves constantly to our memory and to our consideration, and thus, in every one of those names goes the record of a companion who fell, either in the first clashes, in the underground fighting, in the battles in the mountains, in those first days of the fight, or in the final days. And there were so many that for every work of the revolution there is a martyr's name! And so we have the feeling that those companions remain among us, that those companions live among us, and that their names will live forever, and that the present and the future generations will know that one does not die in vain when one defends a just cause! It is worthwhile to die when for every life that is sacrificed a school is built, a cooperative comes into being, or some other good comes to our compatriots. It is worthwhile to die when death is converted into fruitful seed. What does it matter to die fulfilling a duty if the blood that is given and the life that is given up are converted into works of benefit to our fellowman, to our brothers? Sad it is to die when the life that one gives up is converted into nothing. Sad it is to die like traitors and mercenaries die, but it will never be sad to die when our death is converted into something worthwhile! [Applause.]

And this is the road and the example that we will to future generations—those generations that will be better than this one, but will never have the virtue of this one. To this generation has fallen the noble task, and to future generations who will be better than ours, thanks to the effort of our generation, they should know that this generation was pledged to the spirit of sacrifice, that this generation believed that any sacrifice was worthwhile in order to leave a better world to those who come after us.

And if we have to face any sacrifice whatsoever, we will do it happily, because that will be the greatness of this generation of Cubans, and that is what *Patria o Muerte* means[34] [an ovation and cries of " ¡Patria o Muerte!"]. that he who would take away our Fatherland must first take away our lives [applause], because we are determined to keep the Fatherland and to leave the future generations a worthy Fatherland. [Applause.] It is the expression of the determination of a people and in this brief phrase we say all, we say all that we have to say, that this is our frame of mind.

We are a humble people; we will never commit acts of aggression against anybody; no, we will never commit acts of aggression against anybody, and to those who believe that we have plans for aggression, to those who have spread it around in other countries that we are going to attack and that we are going to attack the naval base at Caimanera,[35] we tell them not to have such illusions, that yes we can give notice, give notice against a kind of Maine,[36] and that yes, we are obliged to give notice that they should be very careful with self-aggression, they should be very careful with self-aggression because they are not going to deceive anyone, for we declare here that the Revolutionary Government is not ever going to settle for an aggression of this type and that the Revolutionary Government, conscious that its detractors and those interested in destroying it, they can, in their hysteria, go so far in their hysteria as to contrive self-aggression, we can give our assurance that from us such an aggression, from us such an aggression will never come.

In other words, we are going to clarify things well— unless it is done by

[34] Roughly "Give me liberty or give me death."

[35] Guantanamo.

[36] The U.S. battleship Maine was sunk off the coast of Havana in 1898, causing the war between the United States and Spain. Castro was inferring that the United States may have blown up the Maine to provoke war with Spain, and he was warning against a similar incident at Guantanamo.

war criminals, by those who are being armed from there, unless a self-aggression is organized by mercenary elements in order to justify an armed attack against our Fatherland, it is our duty, partly because of the experience of history and partly because we know of certain perfidious methods of international politics, it is our duty to give advance notice, to give advance notice to those who are seeking any mad pretext to use armed aggression against our Fatherland, that we are not going to give them those pretexts, and that, moreover, we give notice to the world against any pretext contrived to justify an aggression against Cuba. [Applause.]

We have always said that we will never carry out an aggression against anybody, but that we are willing, at any cost, to defend our rights and our Fatherland. We have always said that nobody should expect an aggression from Cuba, but with the same firmness with which we proclaim that policy, we proclaim also that any attack against our country will have to fight to the death against the Cuban people [applause], that any attack against our country will have to face the most determined resistance that any aggressor army has ever encountered; that we know Cubans well, that we know how much dignity and how much courage there is in the heart of every Cuban [applause], that we know of the love and the passion with which the Cuban people regard their cause, and it is preferable to draw attention to this reality rather than allowing anyone to commit the mistake of ignoring it, that we know the people all too well, and that anyone who carries out an aggression against our Fatherland will be beaten! [applause] and will be beaten not only by the resistance that they are going to find in Cuba, but also by the resistance that they are going to find all over America! [applause] and by the resistance that they are going to find all over the world! [Applause.]

Because a revolution like this, that draws such formidable support from the people, that defends a cause so just and that has the solidarity of all the men of revolutionary thinking of the American continent—cannot be destroyed. And that the most reasonable, the most sane, the most intelligent thing that would be done by those who want to resign themselves to this revolution, is to resign themselves, because it is a reality [applause] and leave us in peace, leave us in peace! lest in a senseless attempt to destroy it, they lose much more than they have already lost! [Applause.]

And realities do not arise in the world through the whim of just anybody at all. Revolutions, real revolutions, do not arise through the wish of just anybody at all. Revolutions are realities that obey other realities. Revolutions are remedies—bitter, yes, but at times the only remedy applicable to evils even more bitter [applause]—and the Cuban Revolution is a reality in the world. And the Cuban Revolution is already a reality in the history of the world.

[Applause.] And the Cuban Revolution is a reality, just as the people's support of it is a reality! [applause], just as the guns that can defend it are realities! just as the men who are willing to die for it inside Cuba and outside Cuba are realities! [Applause.] And in the event that there comes aggression against our Fatherland, aggression by whatever power, under any pretext, or by any group of nations that may be ensnared by any maneuver, aggression against our Fatherland will mean war, not only against our Fatherland, but against every Cuban, in whatever part of the world he may be found [applause] and will be a struggle against the friends of Cuba and those who are willing to fight for Cuba, wherever they may be found! [Applause.]

And we express this decision to fight with a firmness equal to that with which we made it clear that our vehement desire is to see fulfilled the work that we are undertaking, that our vehement desire is to see our dreams converted into reality, and that there will never be any fighting because of our offense or provocation, because we ourselves will never be the aggressor against anybody.

To speak more clearly would be impossible. And so that nothing should be left unsaid to add just for Cubans, we must be always alert, for we do not know how many years we must be alert. That is the price that we must pay for this work. Always alert, against any aggression, whether by surprise or with advance warning! Always alert and in the same attitude of hardiness to fight wherever we find ourselves! Always alert, every soldier of the Rebel Army and every revolutionary soldier! Always alert every member of the militia, always alert every farmer, every worker, every student, every young person, every man and every woman, every old person and every child, always alert! [Applause.] Always alert in whatever circumstance; always alert in whatever condition; always the ready hardiness to resist before whatever attack, without faltering, always a firm spirit! What no one can ever crush is the spirit of the Cuban people. And no people can ever be subjugated if their spirit does not yield, if their will is not destroyed! Always alert, and ready to fight, to fight with whatever we have at hand, to fight wherever we find ourselves, but always the intention of resisting, always the intention to fight against any aggression whatsoever, always the intention to win and if not to win, to die. Always alert and willing to fight, whatever may happen, no matter what may befall us. Always alert and willing to fight, no matter who may be missing, regardless of who dies! [Applause and shouts of "¡Patria o Muerte, Patria o Muerte!"] In that way our revolution would not be destroyed because the enemy should wrest away one life, or two lives, or three lives. If a leader falls, our duty is to replace him immediately and without discussion of any sort. [Applause.] If a leader falls, immediately another will fill his place, no matter who the leader may be. And on an earlier occasion, when the circumstances were not those of today, we gave our opinion and the people made a decision. If the prime minister falls away ... [cries of "No, no!"] ... at any time (the problem is not whether or not you want this to happen, the problem is that everybody should know what he should do in every circumstance and what concerns us is that the people should know what to do in every eventuality, and that is our duty to the people) ... if the prime minister falls away [cries of "No, no!"] ... I wish to say, if the enemies of the revolution should carry out an aggression—the only realism and the only objective is to know what must be done, and to know that you immediately have a substitute for the prime minister, and you are going to say ... yes! already in that previous rally I proposed Raul for prime minister if the prime minister should fall away ... [Prolonged ovation.] If both of us should fall away, the president of the Republic will meet with the council of ministers and designate another prime minister, for now it is necessary to be prepared for all possibilities. [Applause.]

When a nation undertakes a job like the one the Cuban nation has undertaken, when a nation, small like Cuba, has powerful adversaries such as Cuba has today, all the contingencies should be foreseen, and the nation should know what it is it has to do, and what they have to do above all is to know that our nation can never be divided in the face of enemy action, and that the reaction of the people is always to close ranks. [Shouts of "Unity, unity!"]

When a nation, small like ours, takes upon its shoulders a job like the one that our people have taken, they must always know what to do. And it is of no consequence that we are small. If we conduct ourselves well, if we know what to do, we shall win, because victory always goes to those whose cause is right and to those who know how to uphold their right, know how to fight for their right. And we can be certain that if we do what we have to do, we shall be victorious, we shall be victorious. [Applause.]

So, on this First of May, what remains for us to do is reaffirm that purpose, that purpose of all of us continuing to do our duty, in our own jobs, and to ask that everybody else do the same. To express our faith in the destiny of the Fatherland, our faith in the solidarity of the sister countries of the continent, for whom we are fighting, because they will learn from our experience, will learn from the successes that we may make, and will learn even from the errors that we may make.

And so, our mistakes as well as our successes will be useful to our sister nations. We have faith in the solidarity of these sister nations and faith in the solidarity of all the nations of the world.

To the sister nations of America, may they go tell what Cuba is, may they repel the lies that are written about this generous and noble land, may they tell that these people are not here because they follow any one person, that these people are here for more profound reasons, that these people are here because in the life of the Revolutionary Government we have fulfilled our promises to the people, and the people are loyal to those who are loyal to them, and the people have faith in those who have faith in them. [Applause.]

May our sister nations know that here we have a Spartan people and of us can be said what is inscribed on the marker in the pass of Thermopylae: "Go tell the world that here lie three hundred Spartans who preferred to die rather than to surrender." [Applause.]

Thus that is what Latin America expects of us, that is what the world expects of us, and we will know how to respond to the friendship and the solidarity that we have received.

Let us swear, all of you, soldiers of the Rebel Army, members of the militia, farmers, workers, students, youth: "We raise our Cuban flags, we raise our rifles, we raise our machetes, to swear that we will keep our promise. ¡Patria o Muerte!" [Prolonged ovation by the crowd, with flags, rifles, and machetes held high.]

The Revolt Rhetoric of Castro

Castro's rhetoric of lawlessness delivered during the struggle for power in Cuba has been largely lost. His outlaw status forbade his speaking to large groups, so that there are no public speeches by Castro during stage one of the Cuban Revolution. Furthermore his earnest conversations with his small group of followers in the Sierra Maestra and his clandestine broadcasts over Radio Rebelde are seemingly lost. Castro's recorded rhetoric therefore probably dates from the second stage of the revolution, which began on January 1, 1959, when Batista surprisingly flew into exile.

Therefore Castro's rhetoric differs from Hancock's, Lenin's, and Gandhi's in that it advocates lawlessness, not against a ruling Old Regime, but against two variant types of Old Regimes: first, against the remnants of oppression that Castro intended to eradicate by force; second, against government *in absentia* from the United States. Castro had sufficient power to remove the remnants of oppression without encountering insurmountable new ones, provided the United States would remove the focal point of dysfunction between the two countries, i.e., the economic consequences of Cuba's thrust toward human rights. Castro's rhetoric of May 1, 1960, specifically pointed to the focal point of dysfunction between the United States and Cuba, a focal point that threatened the Castro regime with multiple dysfunction. It was not that the Old Regime-in-absentia did not know what adjustments to make. It was that the Old Regime-in-absentia chose not to do so.

It is easy to discern the reasons for studying the rhetoric of revolt through an analysis of Castro's rhetoric. The tendency of the Old Regime to overreact to Castro's tirades is evident. It is difficult even for the uninvolved American not to resent the boastful tone and the braggadocio of Dr. Castro. But tempests, if encouraged, do grow out of teapots and become hurricanes. What could have been a relatively minor affair became a major concern to the United States, because its overkill may have forced Castro into the hands of the Russians and certainly resulted in the attempt to establish on Cuban soil dangerous missile bases. An acute observer of revolt rhetoric should have noted that Castro was protesting too much to be expressing his true feelings. Castro's rhetoric is unique in this study, for it is the only one representing a small power under the shadow of a major power. Jealousy can make orators say the opposite of what they feel. What might have happened had Washington interpreted Castro's rhetoric as a strong desire to improve relations with the United States is an interesting but academic question. How Washington will react to the rhetoric of future Latin American revolutionaries is a very practical problem, which deserves serious consideration. What can be learned from an examination of the rhetoric of Fidel Castro that will assist in clarifying how Old Regimes should react to forthcoming Latin American revolutionaries?

Invention

Castro is a modern Alexander. He is tall, ruggedly handsome, well-educated, athletic, and has escaped death so often that he seems invincible. To women he is both father and suitor; to men he is both brother and buddy. His Spanish background, his outstanding endurance, his convoluted eloquence are in sharp contrast to his beard and slouchy uniform, his attempts to associate with the peasant, and his boyish, immature emotional reactions. He is the demigod: half god, half man. His abstinence from alcohol is in contrast to his incessant smoking; his purity from graft is in contrast to his Machiavellian politics; his affection for his old comrades is in contrast to his ruthless ability to destroy them. His divorced status makes him a Paris to all the women and an Apollo to all the men. As long as Castro continues to show strength, how can his ethos be other than high? His followers can look both up to him and down on him. It seems an ideal combination.

Castro's braggadocio is similar to Danton's. Both were big men, whereas Lenin and Gandhi were small. Castro has boasted so much that he has become discouragingly inconsistent. Draper said: "Fidel Castro . . . has said so many different things at different times that it is no longer possible to think of him in terms of anything he may have said at any one time" (12, xi). First he argued that he would have elections; then he proposed that they be postponed; then he concluded that they were unnecessary (12, 31). Why did not such inconsistent reasoning seriously damage his credibility? Undoubtedly it did, as is witnessed by the many defectors in high positions. However, it has been characteristic of Cuban leaders to promise one thing and deliver another. The Cuban people have become inured to voluble leaders. It seems too easy to say that inconsistent actions are more Latin in nature than Anglo-Saxon. Yet consistency is a virtue not required of Castro. Honesty—yes, the Robespierre brand of honesty; benevolent intent—yes, Castro's intentions must be considered selfless; humility—yes, Castro must confess to his inadequacies; expertness—yes, Castro must demonstrate that his new programs of social, economic, and political reform are working; intelligence—yes, Castro has never accurately been termed stupid. With all of these, plus his demigod characteristics, Castro has not felt the need for consistency in dealing with the Cuban people, and it does not appear to be a virtue that will be required of future Latin agitators.

Assuming then, on the basis of this discussion, that Castro's ethical appeals were high to the thousands who had assembled to hear his May Day address, what methods of argument did he use that reflect his unique rhetoric of revolt techniques?

Argumentum ad misericordiam was a form of argument of which Castro made excellent use. Early in his May Day speech he pointed to the abuses undergone by the Cuban people; in the body of his speech he asked why the reforms he proposed were being considered criminal; in the conclusion he argued that, small as it is, poor Cuba must carry the burden of revolution against great odds so that she could set the example of liberation for Latin America. The effectiveness of these arguments on his audience must have made the American foreign correspondents who were present experience some regret that the United States had so successfully cast itself in the role of the villain. Future Latin American revolutionaries will capitalize on the same argument, if given the same excuse.

Castro's argument of the threat of counterrevolution also enhanced his effectiveness. "Cuba for the Cubans" and particularly for the deprived

Cubans was a rhetoric that so exploited nationalism that it certainly was well received. Threats to this popular nationalism could be used to rally the people of Cuba. Again, the American correspondents must have regretted any excuses that the United States had provided so that Castro could argue so effectively that the Cubans should support him against the threat of Thermidor. It is impossible to know the degree to which Castro was entitled to use Thermidor as a threat in May, 1960. Castro's intelligence forces must have known of the possibility of a Bay of Pigs; Castro inherited a distrust of American policies which the CIA may have accentuated by preparations for invasion; Castro resented the welcome given to Cuban refugees in Florida. It can also be assumed that Fidel experienced the insecurity so characteristic of revolutionaries, for he had taken on enormous burdens and was about to propose fundamental changes in Cuban life. Therefore he was probably overly sensitive to the threat of counterrevolution. That his whole argument and perhaps the entire thrust of his revolution could have been counteracted by obviously benevolent gestures of the absentee Old Regime suggests the manner in which such arguments by future Latin American revolutionaries might be handled.

The argument that can best be termed "revolutionary export" is present, but, except for one or two passages, it is muted. Castro does say: "They want to destroy the Cuban Revolution so that the example of the Cuban Revolution cannot be followed by the sister nations of Latin America." But, in May, 1960, Castro was not prepared to suggest that Cuba should make overt efforts to promote revolution elsewhere. Cuba was simply to serve as an example so that other Latin American countries could profit from her mistakes and her successes. After only 16 months in office Castro did not feel strong enough to do more than insure the success of his own revolution.

Castro's use of *argumentum ad hominem* took three forms: (1) he incited the crowd to name-calling so that the onus of using personal vilification did not always rest upon him; (2) he made general references to persons, omitting names, e.g., landlords as a class are criticized and President Betancourt is alluded to but not named; (3) he did single out the president of Guatemala, probably because of the bitterness which he felt toward the United Fruit Company. The particular methods that Castro used to employ *argumentum ad hominem* can be attributed to the mass nature of his audience, which was unfamiliar with many of the individuals against whom Castro had grievances. The lesson for Old Regimes is that they should refrain from exalting questionable exiles and therefore prevent revolutionaries from making justifiable use of *argumentum ad hominem*.

Some attention needs to be given to the chain of arguments that began the speech and to the argument that, if the Old Regime had really cared about the Cuban people, it would have exhibited its sympathy before 1959. The chain of arguments proposed: (a) Cubans are not militaristic; (b) the fatherland is threatened; (c) Cubans have been greatly abused; *but* (d) because it has been threatened, a pacific people who, under abuse, could not show their strength, will be victorious against threats. This closely woven chain was so supported by the emotions of pity and pride that it must have been highly acceptable to the crowd. When Castro asked: "Why did they [the United States] not concern themselves with our people before," he raised a very provocative question, placing the United States in the following dilemma: if it was in the interest of human rights that the United States wished to intervene in Cuban affairs, she should have done so under Batista; if it was not in the interest of human rights [but rather to prevent Cuban nationalism], then the United States should let Cuba alone. In this manner, Castro attempted to underline the focal point of dysfunction between Cuba and the United States —that the difficulty was not in the area of human rights but in the area of nationalism.

The theory that Castro experienced a void in political philosophy that was filled by communism is reinforced by the manner in which Castro attempted to justify the creation of the military and quasi-military units that had just paraded by. He appeared to say that such organizations had not been his intent, but, now that they had been organized, he would need to find reasons for their existence. His distortion of the philosophy of democracy is also revealing. He reserved the right to argue for a democracy of his own definition, as if he was certain of his theories on nationalism and human rights, but not certain of the vehicle he needed to effectuate them.

As has been pointed out in discussing Castro's ethical and argumentative appeals, he can also employ emotional persuasion effectively. These two quotations from his speech essay, "History Will Absolve Me," show how effectively he can employ emotion:

> Our men were killed not in the course of a minute, an hour, or a day. Throughout a whole week the blows, the torture, and the shots continued. . . . The walls were splattered with blood. The bullets imbedded in the walls were encrusted with singed bits of skin, brains and human hair—the grisly reminders of rifle shots full in the face. The grass around the barracks was dark and sticky with human blood. . . . criminal hands . . . had written for the prisoners at the entrance of that den of death the very inscription of Hell: "Abandon all hope" (6,48).

> Throughout their torturing . . . the Army offered them a chance to save their lives by betraying their ideologic position. . . . When they indignantly rejected that proposition, the Army continued torturing them horribly. They shattered their testicles and they tore out their eyes. But no one yielded. And no complaint or

begging was heard. Even when they had been deprived of their virile organs, our boys were still a thousand times more manly than all their tormenters together. ... Frustrated by the valor of the men, they tried to break the spirit of the women. With a bleeding human eye in his hands, a sergeant ... went to the cell where our comrades Melba Hernandes and Hayde Santamaria were held. Addressing the latter ... [he] said: "This eye belonged to your brother. If you will not testify when he refused to testify we will tear out the other." She, who loved her valiant brother above all things, replied, full of dignity: "If you tore out an eye and he did not testify falsely, much less will I" (6, 51).

What are the emotions that Castro employs? Certainly he uses anger. As early as October 26, 1959, before the largest crowd organized by his regime to that time, Castro so incited the peasants brought in from the countryside to anger against the United States that cries were heard of "Paredón, Paredón!"[37] Referring to the Florida-based airplanes that were harassing Cuba, Castro said: "I do not conceive nor believe that the people of the United States could approve of such irresponsibility on the part of the authorities of their country" (3, 7). His anger therefore was typically directed at Washington and not at the American people.

Love of the fatherland, *Patria o Muerte*, was an emotion easy to exploit during the wave of nationalism that swept Cuba. Righteous indignation played a constructive role among Castro's emotional appeals. His disdain for the United Fruit Company, for the attempts to interfere in Cuba's domestic policies, for the decadent politicians under Batista were comprehensible to many both inside and outside of Cuba. Pride in the accomplishments of the revolution also pervaded Castro's oratory. It is a rare revolutionary who can deny himself this privilege, for even a Gandhi could boast of the power of Congress. But to Castro, the agrarian reforms, the crash programs in education, the abolition of segregation, the new government housing, and the creation of recreational facilities were the revolution itself. Castro had to achieve his desire for pride by pointing to economic and social accomplishments rather than by pointing to the way he had fulfilled his political promises, because, even as early as May, 1960, Castro was soft-pedaling vital aspects of the democratic process.

Future revolt rhetoric in Latin America is likely to be emotional in character. The large uneducated masses of people must be given motivational appeals to gain support for the arguments of revolution and to enable them to undergo the hardships that accompany social change. Old Regimes should not underestimate the astuteness of agitators who use emotional rhetoric before large crowds, for these same agitators may be able to be coldly logical in handling other aspects of a revolution.

[37]"To the execution wall with them!"

Arrangement

Castro's chief organizational device is repetition. Whether he plans in advance how many times he will repeat a phrase or whether he uses audience response to gauge the saturation point of repetition is difficult to determine. Probably, as with Martin Luther King's "I Have a Dream" speech, a certain amount of repetition is planned in advance, with adjustments made depending upon crowd reaction.

There is some chronological organization to Castro's May Day speech, for he began with a summary of past events and ended with what the future might hold. But the form is not evident enough to serve as a vehicle for his ideas. Castro, like Lenin, preferred to let one idea lead to another. It was enough for him to exhibit sufficient sequence, so that his audience understood why the particular point he was discussing followed the previous point and led into the subsequent idea. There was no need to impress upon his listeners a superstructure, and Castro did not even lean on phraseology to link widely separated parts of his speech. For example, there is no effort to use the theme *Patria o Muerte* to link the beginning of the address with the conclusion.

Castro's concept of organization resembles a "pageant of ideas" led out before the audience in bright adjectives, uninterrupted by pauses for scenes or acts, and joined together only by the dominating personality of the leading actor.

Style

In his May Day speech of 1960 there is little evidence of the use of the costume of words. This development is surprising. Castro could coin phrases, e.g., *Movimiento Revolucionario 26 de Julio*, and he was certainly stylist enough to create and to use phraseology of identification. Furthermore the individualistic style of clothing adopted by the *fidelismos* demonstrates that the Castro forces needed new symbols to replace old ones. Why is Castro's May Day rhetoric so free of word symbols of his revolution?

The answer probably lies in the accumulative effect of three factors. First, Fidel is an agitator who is proud of his style. Like de Gaulle, a part of his popularity is based upon his command of language. He is a vain speaker. He would hardly speak for such long hours if he were not interested in hearing himself talk. He did not wish to be banal. Repetition *ad nauseam* of trite, revolutionary phrases was not his concept of rhetoric. Banalities would have spoiled his image of himself. Therefore even the phrase *Patria o Muerte* was used sparingly, with just sufficient references to *Patria* elsewhere to prepare the audience for his conclusion without spoiling his effect. Hancock aspired to be a stylist but could not always carry it off; Danton and Gandhi suppressed their stylistic aspirations, while Lenin avoided any connotations of bourgeois style. But Castro—the lawyer, the Latin, the demigod—was vain enough to demand of himself a style free of banality, but also a style highly classical in its flavor.

Second, during the earlier period, just after he had come to power, Castro did not know where his identification would eventually lie. He was in the process of rejecting democracy, but he had not yet adopted communism. Therefore he was in a political limbo that minimized his capacities for identification. Castro had to satisfy himself with references to a "Spartan people" and to talking about his *trabajadores cubanos, campesinos cubanos, obreras, compatriotas,* and *el pueblo cubano.*

A third reason why there is so little use of the costume of words in Castro's May Day address of 1960 is that, unlike the American, French, and Indian revolutions, the first stage of the Cuban Revolution, which should have featured men of words with a grievance, was severely curtailed by censorship. A similar set of restrictions curbed the rhetoric of the Russian Revolution, but some 27 years of exiled writing and speaking, plus the adoption of Marxist terminology, had furnished a backlog of terms for Lenin. This was not so for Castro.

One of the interesting stylistic aspects of the May Day speech is Castro's purposeful avoidance of the words *United States.* Recent research tends to show that association with ideas develops favorable attitudes toward those ideas[38] and Castro was probably aware that he could have intensified aversion to the United States by name-calling that featured a particular costume of words aimed at the Old Regime-in-absentia. His failure to do so could be given several interpretations. First, it could be said that, in May, 1960, Castro was not beyond reconciliation with Washington. Second, he may not have wished to offend needlessly the many foreign dignitaries and press representa-

---

[38] See Robert Zajone, "Brainwash: Familiarity Breeds Comfort," *Psychology Today* (February, 1970), pp. 33-35 and 60-62.

tives who were present, some of whom were in sympathy with United States policy or who would have found it tactless to sponsor an overt attack on Washington.

Castro's Spanish is highly figurative. The most prominent device is repetition. Anaphora is common. In the May 1, 1960, speech, Castro began fifteen grouped sentences with the phrase "democracia es ésta en que tú . . ." A more subtle form of "internal" repetition to develop rhythm is noted below:

> Los soldados *solos*, *los* soldados desfilando, *solos* por aquí hoy, **constituyen una fuerza**, pero una sola fuerza; *los* campesinos *solos*, **constituyen una fuerza**, pero no más que una fuerza, *los* estudiantes *solos*, **constituyen una fuerza**, pero no más que una fuerza; *los* trabajadores *solos*, **constituyen una fuerza**, pero una sola fuerza; los pueblos de America Latina representados aquí hoy, **constituyen una fuerza**, pero cada uno de ellos por separados una sola fuerza . . .

Los, an article, and the adjective *solos* begin five thought patterns which, with irregular numbers of words separating them, form a "syncopated" anaphora, i.e., the words that introduce each phrase are interrupted, in four instances by a single noun and in the fifth by a modified noun. The effect is an attractive, offbeat repetition. Was Castro's avoidance of a sixth repetition of *los . . . solos* accidental or purposeful? Did he sense that a sixth *los . . . solos* would have detracted from the five that he had already established? Did he consciously play "the numbers game," keeping his anaphora gracefully to an uneven number of five? Or was the whole thing just accidental?

Constituyen una fuerza ends five thoughts, forming an epistrophe without variation, and this epistrophe is followed by a syncopated epistrophe of five, revolving around the prepositional phrase, *pero una sola fuerza*. The thoughts are thus begun with the same wording and ended with a doubling of the same wording, without the sequences becoming mechanical.

The configurations of the Cuban music of which Castro is so proud and the rhythm of Castro's oratory compare favorably. Undoubtedly Castro leans on this rhythm to assist him with his extemporaneous delivery, but the crutch has become a cross to the crusader, and he holds it high. It is his trademark in rhetoric.[39] Note how clearly the following chiasmus is put with the juxtapositioning of the two underlined phrases:

> Un gobierno revolucionaria que no sacrifica los interes del pobre al *lujo del rico*, sino el *lujo del rico* a los interes del pobre.

[39] With the exception of some limited historical references, there is in the May Day speech little use of the figures of comparison, i.e., metaphor, simile, analogy, parable, and so on, and there are almost no figures of exaggeration, i.e., hyperbole, litotes, personification, apostrophe, etc.

Castro can combine chiasmus with parallel structure:

> I remember that I said that the revolution was a fight to death between the interests of the people and the interests of the antipeople, between the revolutionists and the counterrevolutionists. And if the revolution does not annihilate the counterrevolution, the counterrevolution will surely annihilate the revolution (*3*, 27).

Perhaps Castro felt that his peasant audiences would not understand the figures of comparison and exaggeration, but, with their feeling for rhythm, would respond to the figures of composition. Or perhaps Castro had only developed skill in using one type of figure of speech.

Delivery

A discussion of Castro's delivery in general will be followed by the particular characteristics of his presentation on May 1, 1960.

It is difficult to categorize Castro's delivery. Draper called it "stream of consciousness oratory" (*11*, 60), for there are certain Joyce-like and Faulkner-like properties present. Matthews said that Castro's oratorical style is unique and unmistakable, "hypnotic in its repetitive rhythm and rounded out with fine phrases" (*16*, 167-68). If indeed Castro is hypnotic, he achieves that feat by a blend of powerful vocal strength and powerful bodily reinforcement. The pictures of Castro speaking show him constantly posturing, hand thrust out, head to one side, body askew. There is no mention of a rich and powerful voice or of a carefully executed gesture, for these are not characteristic of Castro, but there are repeated references to his personal magnetism. Lockwood, who spent long hours with Castro in private conversation, stressed the great energy and powers of concentration which Castro focuses upon his listener. Lockwood found that the carefully constructed sentences flowed out "in cadence" and that each word had "the ring of absolute conviction, the product of a mind never in doubt" (*15*, 78). Despite his desire to remain impartial, Lockwood was impressed with Castro and the effectiveness of Fidel's delivery:

> What is even more compelling than Castro's mind is his manner, the way he uses his voice and his body, especially his eyes, to reduce the listener to surrender. If he is effective in a public speech, where the listener is at a relatively safe "aesthetic distance," in private conversation, focusing the full force of his personality upon you at close quarters for hours at a time, he is formidable (*15*, 78).

What makes a study of Castro's oratory particularly enticing is that his speeches last such a long time (*16*, 167). It is easy for American newspaper men to become bored during such long speeches, particularly if their knowledge of Spanish is limited. For example, the *Washington Post* of May 2, 1960, reported that thousands had started to leave the square where Castro was speaking until a large roar from the crowd brought them back. With such masses of people, there are always many circulating around the edge, so that it could be that it was this fringe group that surged forward when the crowd sent up a roar. Castro's oratory was not meant for American reporters, but for his Cuban followers. Matthews reported that, despite the difficulty of Castro's long speeches in the United States, "it so happened that Cubans listened to Fidel from beginning to end, and anyone taking the trouble to read the text of his speeches would find that they are effective, clearly reasoned, interesting and well organized" (*16*, 167). Matthews found that Castro's rhetoric was delivered with all his "natural oratorical gifts, his fervor and passion, his vivid gestures and all the paraphernalia of his extraordinary personality" (*16*, 167).[40]

The details of what transpired on May 1, 1960, will further clarify Castro's delivery techniques. May Day is of American extraction, stemming from the Chicago riots at the turn of the century, but it has become an event of significance in the Socialist world. The government of Cuba planned a parade which the *Washington Post* said lasted five hours, followed by a speech which the Havana *Post* of May 3, 1960, said began at 5:00 P.M. and ended at 8:43 P.M., a little over three and one-half hours. The Civic Plaza in Havana is an enormous esplanade, roughly the size of six football fields, surrounded by the concave Palace of Justice, which lies behind the new statue of Marti; the National Agrarian Reform Institute; the *Instituto Nacional de Ahorro y Vivenda;*[41] the National Library; the Ministry of Communication; the Finance Bureau, and the National Theatre.[42] The buildings are modern, large, and widely spaced so that parts of the crowd could stand between the buildings and on their grounds. Fidel Castro Ruz and other government leaders reviewed the parade, standing before the huge, white, obelisk-like statue of the Cuban revolutionary leader Marti. An enormous Cuban flag served as a backdrop to the reviewing stand. The *Diario las Americas* of May 3, 1960, esti-

---

[40] Castro's delivery over television is also impressive. From the first days after taking control, Castro has spent much time using this medium to explain the position of his government. In the early period of the revolution, Mills evaluated Castro's television strategy as follows: "He explains and he educates, and after he speaks, almost every doubt has gone away. Never before has such a force of public opinion prevailed for so long and so intimately with power. . . . So long as Fidel is there," Mills reported, "the Cuban people feel that they are going to be 'all right' " (*17*,123).

[41] Literally the National Institute of Saving and Housing.

[42] The square adjoins the highway leading to the Cuban airport and is located on the outskirts of Havana. The buildings were begun under Prio and completed under Batista. An older statue of Marti stands in the area near the National Capital.

mated that 125,000 to 150,000 persons filed by, while the *New York Times* of May 2, 1960, spoke of 10,000 troops; 60,000 workers, peasants, and students; and several thousand children. "In an atmosphere where patriotic and revolutionary fervor blended with the good-natured gaiety of a country fair," said the *Times*, "unit after unit of soldiers, policemen, sailors and uniformed civilians filed past the reviewing stand on the stone steps of the huge white statue of José Marti . . ." At one point, said the *Miami Herald* of May 2, 1960, Castro put on one of the *campesino* straw hats, but he took it off before he began speaking. There were numbers of foreign dignitaries on the reviewing stand, including representatives from Bolivia, Chile, Ecuador, Colombia, El Salvador, the United States,[43] Great Britain, Haiti, Mexico, Nicaragua, Panama, Peru, Paraguay, Puerto Rico, the Dominican Republic, Uraguay, Venezuela, East Germany, Yugoslavia, Red China, and Mali. The procession varied in composition from smartly dressed troops in white helmets and white leggings to workers in berets, dark shirts, and sloppy khaki trousers.[44]

Estimates of the crowd vary from 250,000 to 1,500,000. Certainly Castro looked out over a sea of faces. There were many large Cuban flags in the crowd and placards bearing Castro's picture. Umbrellas over some protected them from the sun, while others wore berets, straw hats, and turbans. The London *Times* of May 2, 1960, reported that "balloons, white pigeons, and helicopters were overhead as the military parade came to an end and Dr. Castro began to speak." The frequent interruptions from the audience were noted in one of the government versions of the speech (9), but the comment of the *New York Times* that the crowd chanted "Cuba, yes; Yankee, No" for 13 minutes was not reported in the government release of the text. The *Miami Herald* reported: "At one point, the whipped-up demonstrators began chanting with machine-gun rapidity: 'Fidel! Fidel! Fidel! Fidel! ' " The chant continued for almost ten minutes, while Castro sought to quiet the screaming, applauding crowd, and then began clapping his hands in response to the cheers in the manner reminiscent of the Communist practice." Evidently one of the largest ovations occurred when Fidel brought up elections. The *Washington Post* said that "a roar of approval went up at the reference to criticism" and that "the crowd took up another chant, 'We have voted for Fidel,'

---

[43] In a letter to the author dated February 13, 1970, Philip Bonsal, the United States Ambassador to Cuba in 1960, stated that he was not present at the parade or at the speech, but said: "I expect I witnessed a good bit of both on television." The "representative" from the United States may have been Waldo Frank, author and journalist.

[44] *Noticias de Hoy*, XXII, No. 101 (May 2, 1960), 1-4 provides the most detailed description of the festivities of May 1, 1960

and kept it up for five minutes." The *Miami Herald* said that the crowd chanted "We have already voted for Fidel," followed by "but by the blood of the people."

The occasion did not call for a highly reasoned discourse, and Castro understood that plainly. Audience participation was necessary, if people were to stand for three and a half hours on a warm evening. The man of words, Fidel Castro, was equal to the occasion.

Conclusion

Whether Castro goes down in history as a statesman or as a demagogue remains to be decided. But, if Latin America is to experience a series of human rights revolutions, Castro's rhetoric may set the pattern for other revolutionaries who will find in his speaking a successful method of maintaining contact with the people.

Bibliography

1. Blanksten, George I., "Fidel Castro and Latin America," in *The Revolution in World Politics,* ed. M. A. Kaplan. New York: John Wiley & Sons, Inc., 1962.

   Professor Blanksten of Northwestern University wrote such an impartial essay that the editor felt obliged to defend Blanksten's position. Excellent footnote references.

2. Burks, David D., *Cuba under Castro.* New York: Foreign Policy Association, 1964.

   This 61-page pamphlet with discussion questions and references of the F.P.A. headline series, written by a University of Michigan historian, is the best short objective account of the revolution available.

3. Castro, Fidel, *Always Determined. Always Ready to Face Sacrifice!* Havana: Confederation de Trabajadores de Cuba, 1961, 32 pp.

   Speech (translated into English) at memorial for patriots who fell during the March 13, 1957, attack on the Presidential Palace; delivered March 13, 1961; noted for its similarity to the May Day address. If card catalogue does not list this item, consult your pamphlet collection.

4. ——, *Cuba: 1ro. de Mayo de 1960: Discurso del Doctor Fidel Castro Ruz, Primer Ministro del Gobierno Revolucionario.* Havana: Departmento

de Relaciones Publicas, Ministerio de Relaciones Exteriores, 1960, 57 pp.

Spanish edition available at the University of Florida, includes photographs of May Day celebration.

5. ——, *Fidel Castro Speaks with the People of Cuba.* Havana: Confederation de Trabajadores de Cuba, 1959, 32 pp.

Castro's first all-out attack on the United States. Available at Duke University.

6. ——, *History Will Absolve Me.* New York: Fair Play for Cuba Committee, 1961, 79 pp.

The 1961 edition of reconstituted speech, published by Lyle Stuart.

7. ——, *Labor Day Address about the Destiny of Cuba.* Havana: Confederation de Trabajadores de Cuba, 1960, 23 pp.

English translation of May 1, 1960, speech, available at Duke University, is a routine job with a few explanatory footnotes.

8. ——, *Patria o Muerte! Discurso Pronunciado por el Primer Ministro del Gobierno Revolucionario, Dr. Fidel Castro, al Despedir ante Pueblo, en la Tarde del 5 de Marzo de 1960* . . . Havana: Instituto Nacional de Reforma Agraria, 1960, 24 pp.

Although this speech bears the same Spanish title as the May 1, 1960, address, it was delivered earlier. Available at the University of Florida.

9. —— *Patria o Muerte. Discurso Pronunciado por el Doctor Fidel Castro Ruz, Primer Ministro del Gobierno Revolucionario, el Dia Primero de Mayo, en la Plaza Cívica, en Conmemoración del Dia Internacional del Trabajo.* Havana: Confederation de Trabajadores de Cuba, 1960, 39 pp.

Spanish edition available at the Library of Congress, important for its frequent notation of audience response.

10. Casuso, Teresa, *Cuba and Castro*, trans. E. Grossberg. New York: Random House, Inc., 1961.

Casuso asked to be relieved as Ambassador Extraordinary and Plenipotentiary of Cuba and Delegate to the U.N. in October, 1960, because she opposed the Communistic trend. See her statement about Fidel's not being a Communist in 1959 (160) and her description of Castro's rhetoric (178).

11. Draper, Theodore, *Castroism: Theory and Practice.* New York: Frederick A. Praeger, Inc., 1965.

Draper enlarged a paper he wrote in 1964 for the Hoover Institution on War, Revolution, and Peace. More sympathetic than unsympathetic.

12. ———, *Castro's Revolution: Myths and Realities.* New York: Frederick A. Praeger, Inc., 1962.

Three essays, the first two originally published in *Encounter* and as special supplements to *The New Leader*, and the third in pamphlet form by *Encounter.* Draper's exchange of letters with Matthews in appendix clarifies strengths and weaknesses of both men.

13. Huberman, Leo and P. M. Sweezy, *Cuba: Anatomy of a Revolution.* New York: Monthly Review Press, 1960.

A sympathetic account by two journalists who visited Cuba for three weeks in March, 1960. Note valuable epilogue following a second three-week visit in fall of 1960.

14. Illan, José M., *Cuba: Facts and Figures of an Economy in Ruins,* trans. G. A. Wehby. Miami, Fla.: 1964, n.p.

A hostile account of Cuban economy by former Cuban undersecretary of finance from January, 1959 to March, 1960.

15. Lockwood, Lee, *Castro's Cuba, Cuba's Fidel.* New York: The Macmillan Company, 1967.

Lockwood, journalist who visited Cuba in summer of 1964 spending long hours in Castro's official party, presents largely sympathetic comments. Text material much more valuable than colorful pictures.

16. Matthews, Herbert L., *The Cuban Story.* New York: George Braziller, Inc., 1961.

Matthews, veteran reporter for the *New York Times*, secured sensational interview with Castro in February, 1957, has continued personal contacts. Tries to be objective, but does not always succeed.

17. Mills, Charles Wright, *Listen, Yankee.* New York: McGraw-Hill Book Company, 1960.

Mills, a Columbia University professor, after a visit to Cuba, concluded that much published about Cuba in the United States is far removed from reality.

18. Taber, Robert, *M-26: Biography of a Revolution.* New York: Lyle Stuart, 1961.

Pro-Castro treatise by a radio-television reporter affiliated with C.B.S. on days preceding January 1, 1959.

19. U.S. Department of Commerce, *Investment in Cuba.* Washington, D.C. U.S. Government Printing Office, 1956.

A government release describing investment possibilities in Cuba.

20. Williams, William Appleman, *The United States, Cuba, and Castro.* New York: Monthly Review Press, 1965.

Williams, who calls himself "an American radical" and is a professor of history at the University of Wisconsin, offers a sympathetic and penetrating analysis.

Questions for Discussion

.

1. Interview a former citizen of Cuba concerning his personal reactions to the rhetoric of *fidelismo*. It may be that, if your interviewee is hostile toward Castro, this hostility will be increased if you exhibit favorable reactions to Castro.

2. Read two other speeches by Castro delivered between January 1, 1959, and January 1, 1961. Consult your card catalogue and then your pamphlet collection. Be prepared to discuss similarities and differences between these two speeches and the May Day address, with particular reference to the themes of revolutionary export, *argumentum ad misericordiam*, Thermidor, and *argumentum ad hominem*.

3. Now that public address systems have been perfected, the rhetoric of agitation is able to make use of one of its natural habitats, the great outdoors. What differences might Castro have made in his May Day speech had it been given indoors? Would the periods of audience response have been more or less difficult to control?

4. Examine the May Day speech in Spanish to determine if there are systematic differences in the way Castro uses *pais* and *Patria*. Was the ratio between the two purposeful or accidental?

5. What proportion of the May Day address is devoted to arguments that arouse pity, i.e., *argumentum ad misericordiam*?

6. Read George Blanksten's "Fidel Castro and Latin America" (*1*).What is your reaction to his delineation of the role of the Old Regime in Cuban politics? Do you agree with his conclusion on page 133 that the role of communism in Cuba "is motivated more by rejection of the United States than it is by acceptance of the Soviet system?"

7. What are the sub-arguments in Castro's rhetoric that support the theme of Cuba for the Cubans, i.e., nationalism?

8. If you wished to use the May Day address to point out the necessity of controlling overreaction to revolt rhetoric, what particular passages

would you single out that may not mean what they appear to mean and what possible interpretations would you make of these passages?

9. Why do you think Castro chose to talk so long? What rhetoric techniques did he use that permitted him to speak for extended periods without a manuscript? Where in the May Day speech do you think the interest of the audience would have been at its lowest? at its highest? If you were going to cut the speech, how would you proceed?

10. Consult photographs of Castro, particularly those taken while he speaks, and discuss the image you think Castro is trying to depict. This chapter suggested the demigod. Others might be the Christ-like figure, the movie-star idol à la John Wayne, or an over-six-foot-tall Lenin. See Lockwood, pp. 36, 37, 38, and 39; also *13* for photographs. Also consult the index to the *New York Times*.

Exercises

1. Deliver a short, one-theme speech in which you feature an anaphora using at least ten repetitions of the same phrase at the beginning of ten consecutive thought patterns. See how many words you can include in the repetitive phrase without appearing mechanical.

2. See if you have understood the difference between the revolt rhetoric of Castro and Gandhi by composing a four-to-six-minute speech in which you role-play a Cuban objecting to United States policy as Gandhi would have done.

3. Examine two speeches by Castro that were delivered after 1961 to investigate whether the costume of words one would expect to accompany communism has entered into Castro's rhetoric.

4. Examine the May Day speech and produce a model that shows the interrelationships of the themes of nationalism and human rights. Consider using black cutouts to represent the more dominant theme and white cutouts to represent the recessive theme, and mount the cutouts on red paper to make them stand out. Do not be afraid of showing ingenuity in your model.

5. Choose a particular passage of the speech and insert *argumentum ad hominem* in the passage in at least five places Mention President Kennedy and his Secretary of State Dean Rusk by name, plus three others. Be prepared to read your revised passage to the class and discuss what effect you think the insertions would have had on the crowd on May Day, 1960.

Index